THE ORIGINS OF BRITISH SOCIAL POLICY

THE ORIGINS OF
BRITISH SOCIAL POLICY

EDITED BY PAT THANE

CROOM HELM LONDON

ROWMAN AND LITTLEFIELD TOTOWA N.J.

© 1978 Croom Helm
Croom Helm Ltd, 2-10 St John's Road, London SW11
ISBN 0-85664-331-9

British Library Cataloguing in Publication Data

The origins of British social policy.
   1. Great Britain – Social policy
   I. Thane, Pat
   361.6'2'0941   HN386

ISBN 0-85664-331-9

Reprinted 1981

First published in the United States 1978 by
Rowman and Littlefield
81 Adams Drive,
Totowa, New Jersey

Library of Congress Cataloging in Publication Data

Main entry under title:

The Origins of British social policy.

   Includes bibliographical references and index.
   1. Great Britain – Social policy – History –
Addresses, essays, lectures. I. Thane, Pat.
HN 382.073 1978   309.1'41'08   77-29132
ISBN 0-8476-6052-4

Printed in Great Britain by Biddles Ltd, Guildford, Surrey

CONTENTS

CONTENTS

PREFACE

The essays in this volume were presented to a conference on the history of British social policy, 1870–1945, held at the University of Manchester in September 1976. The conference was financed by the Social Science Research Council.

INTRODUCTION

Pat Thane

It is tempting to suggest that the history of social policy has been left too long in the hands of those whose primary interest is the study of the social policy and administration of their own day. Almost inevitably this has led to a kind of Whiggism, to looking at history as a process of evolution towards the relatively advanced condition of the present; to looking at it through 'the wrong end of the telescope', taking insufficient account of the difficulty of understanding past events in the very different context of their time.

That wise man, Richard Titmuss, did not make such an error. In 1955 he summed up the state of work in this subject, which has changed only a little since:

> Some students of social policy see the development of 'The Welfare State' in historical perspective as part of a broad, ascending road of social betterment provided for the working classes since the nineteenth century and achieving its goal in our time. This interpretation of change as a process of unilinear progression in collective benevolence for these classes led to the belief that in the year 1948 'The Welfare State' was established.[1]

After pointing out that equity between citizens had not been achieved by 1955, that indeed the great bundle of activities which were popularly believed to comprise a 'Welfare State' had created new inequalities, he concluded:

> *that* today, is the real challenge to social policy and to those who, mistakenly, still look to the past for a solution.[2]

The past he referred to was the mistaken one he had described. The aim of this collection of essays is to describe and interpret aspects of the history of social policy as something far more complex than a 'broad, ascending road of social betterment', but as a past out of which the continuing inequalities after 1948 seem unsurprising, since the policies we examine were less dedicated to removing them than the conventional picture assumes.

This picture has been of a break, slight from the 1870s, but sharp after 1905, from the bad old days of the repressive New Poor Law, which assumed individual responsibility for poverty, to greater understanding of, and provision for, the many whose poverty was at last recognised as involuntary.[3] As John Brown points out, analysis of this presumed change has relied heavily upon T.H. Marshall's conception of progress in the twentieth century to a greater concern with social rights, from a belief in the permanence and rightness of class inequalities to a widespread belief in equal citizenship.

Of course, the idea of progress is not entirely irrelevant to the discussion of social policy changes. Anne Crowther shows that there were real improvements in workhouses between 1890 and 1929. Pat Ryan shows that the unemployed received some relief in the 1920s, as in the nineteenth century they did not, except, sometimes, from the Poor Law. The aged poor received pensions for the first time in 1908; family allowances were introduced in 1945. But with improved provisions for the poor went stricter distinctions between the morally 'deserving' and 'undeserving', worthy of the original intentions behind the New Poor Law.

Faith in the reality of such a distinction remained, despite real difficulties in implementation. How were 'deserving' and 'undeserving' to be distinguished? The question was discussed by, among others, the Select Committee on Old Age Pensions of 1899:

> *Sir Courteney Boyle.* What amount of undeservingness would disentitle a man to a pension?
>
> *Robert Knight (Secretary of the Boiler Makers and Iron and Steel Shipbuilders Trade Union).* If it had been found that he had had opportunity to better his condition and he had not done so, if he spent his money on intoxicating drinks, I for one would condemn him very strongly for it.
>
> *Boyle.* If a man had two pints of beer on a Saturday night?
>
> *Knight.* Oh well, if you come to ask me questions of this kind I am not in a position to answer.
>
> *Boyle.* I am not trying to convict you of not having thought the thing out, but we are obliged to think the thing out ourselves . . . supposing we put forward a scheme which disentitled a man to a pension because he had spent his money on intoxicating drinks, the amount would come up at once — how much would disentitle a man?
>
> *Knight.* I should hardly think that, because it would be a question,

I do not think anyone would be able to answer.

Boyle. I am afraid someone will have to answer . . . take a man who had been convicted of drunkenness ten years ago 15 times, and had taken the blue ribbon 3 or 4 times afterwards . . . and had broken the pledge?

Knight. I could not answer . . . (in his experience as a Guardian) we say that in all cases the deserving poor are sufficiently well known to the whole of the authorities in the place to mark them out.

Which Boyle, from his experience as a Poor Law Inspector, had good reason to dispute.

Treble also notes the willingness of local people in Glasgow still, in the 1900s, to label the involuntarily unemployed 'undeserving'. Progress in understanding the causes of poverty, away from the assumption that a high proportion of it was due to moral failing, was slow indeed. There is little sign of a revolutionary[4] change in ideas before 1914 and little by 1945.

As McCord points out, the 'undeserving', the drunken and feckless existed. But it was still asked all too rarely to what extent their failings were the *result* of intolerable conditions, whether the failings of a few should be generalised to quite so many of the poor, or whether the poor should be punished for their failings so much more severely than deviants of other classes. A feckless 'residuum' existed, but it was smaller than was popularly believed before 1914, and for long after.

The idea of progress in social policy must also be modified in other respects. Although unemployment relief outside the Poor Law was extended from 1911, Ryan and Macnicol demonstrate that legislation was administered in order, to paraphrase Barbara Wootton's comment, that the 'working classes' would not 'belie their name'. The intention after 1927 to apply the 'genuinely seeking work' principle in districts, like the Welsh mining valleys, where there was no work to be sought, could have had no other purpose, certainly not equity between classes or 'greater concern with social rights'.[5] The aged poor got their pensions in 1908, but on conditions as clearly designed to distinguish 'undeserving' from the most conspicuously 'deserving' as the Poor Law itself. Macnicol demonstrates the persistence of the 'less eligibility' principle of the Poor Law in the family allowance legislation of 1945.

Although legislation provided new and real benefits, there was a significant gap between the legislation and the reality of a world in which many could not be self-helping or live respectably when there

were jobs too few and wages too low. The emphasis of policy on encouraging work and self-help was not bad in itself, but inappropriate
for many at whom it was directed.

Not all of the restrictive conditions embodied in social legislation
were put into effect. The 1927 Unemployment Insurance Act was not
quite as fully and immediately implemented as the Blanesburgh
Committee would have liked. Some of the intended disqualifications
from old age pensions were not implemented or were quickly repealed.
Yet the intention behind legislation is as important as the implementation. Intentions so restrictive were likely to be reflected in ungenerous
administration, as in the case of unemployment benefits they clearly
were. The aged, who could not be expected to work, and hence were
past self-help, aroused more sympathy, earlier than the unemployed,
workhouse inmates or poor families. The Pensions Act was less harshly
administered than other legislation. All of this points to the need for
more precise analysis of the formative period of modern social welfare
in Britain between the 1870s and 1945. The essays in this book add to
work of this kind in the past few years by Harris, Hay and Stedman
Jones.[6]

The emphasis of much work on new departures in policy in this
period has led to neglect of the later years of the Poor Law, despite
the fact that it was the major source of relief to the poor until 1914,
and in a more limited way (and with a change of name in 1929) until
1948. Crowther, McCord and Ryan examine different aspects of this
period of Poor Law history. They emphasise the variations in local policy
possible for Boards of Guardians until 1929. McCord notes the neglected
subject of the influence of ratepayers upon local policy. Ryan, in a
detailed study of deviant Poplar, gives a vivid account of the pressures
upon the Poplar Guardians, and of official government policy towards
out-relief.

Anne Crowther's study of the workhouse between 1890 and 1929
emphasises the long survival of the determination of Poor Law policy
to encourage respectability and self-help. She also raises, with some
relevance to current problems, the question of the pauper's own
response to relief.

The question was asked from the 1890s — but not answered — as to
whether the obvious widespread dislike of the Poor Law was due to
fear of the 'stigma' or 'taint' of pauperism, due to a feeling of being
singled out and labelled as a social failure, or to rational dislike of harsh
administration and unpleasant workhouse conditions. Crowther suggests
that dislike of the workhouse could be due to rational fear of total

institutionalisation rather than to fear of 'stigma'. She points to the
major problem that the use of this term, which is frequently employed
in studies of social policy, may disguise a variety of rational feelings.
There were stronger objections by recipients to policies which were
harshly administered, such as unemployment relief, than to benefits
such as pensions which were given selectively to the very poor, but
were generously administered. Many pensioners criticised the adequacy
of the pension, but there is no sign that they felt 'stigmatised'. Nevertheless, if paupers did not feel 'stigmatised' it was not due to the intentions
of Poor Law policy, whose aim all too often was that the pauper should
feel a social outcast.

It is not, of course, surprising that, after seventy years in which the
only official provision for the poor had been the restrictive Poor Law,
that the Liberal social legislation of 1906-14 should have embodied so
many principles only marginally different, at best, from those of the
Poor Law. The climate of ideas does not change so fast. Nor was
experience so different when the heavy, unprecedented, costly load of
unemployment fell on a staggering economy after 1920.

As McCord points out, ministers, such as Joseph Chamberlain, and
civil servants, such as those who made the National Health Insurance
Act of 1911,[7] were not all malign monsters. Many of them understood
the problems of poverty with which they dealt. Some initiated
legislation, as Lloyd George initiated health insurance, others were
persuaded by pressure groups, as was Asquith to introduce pensions,
and as with Eleanor Rathbone's pressure for family allowances.

Good intentions, however, were restrained by counter pressures
such as the refusal of the Treasury to pay for large measures. This may
have been due, as McCord suggests, to the real insufficiency of government revenue. Such judgements are more difficult for the twentieth
than for the nineteenth century.

In 1914 government expenditure on the 'welfare' items described in
this book totalled £20.5m, out of a total expenditure of £192.3m.
Local government expenditure was £19.6m out of a total of £148.3m.[8]
Yet it remains difficult to estimate whether more could have been
afforded. Certainly a Treasury still dominated by Gladstonian principles
was unwilling to expand government expenditure in new directions. But
such a judgement is doubly difficult for a society in which there
remained widespread hostility to 'welfare' expenditure, whether or not
government revenue was sufficient for such departures.

Advances in social policy were constrained by influential public
opinion which, powerfully in 1914 and still in the 1920s and 1930s,

believed in the virtues of self-help and work for all, and still did not
recognise its inappropriateness for many in need. It is, however,
arguable and was strongly argued at the time, that work was the best
way to social betterment for the poor since a stronger economy and
regular wages would solve many of their problems. But in the absence
of opportunities to do so for many individuals before the 1939-45 war,
the policies described in this book contributed relatively little either to
the lessening of poverty or to greater equity or cohesion between
classes. All provided minimally only for those in need, with the exception of family allowances which did little for those who most needed
them. Such action could preserve rather than diminish social differences.

Also important were the local pressures on attempts at reform by
local government. As McCord describes, ratepayers were often hostile
to increased rates or to the prospect of aid to the 'undeserving'. Although,
from Ryan's account, Poplar ratepayers pressed for more generous relief
to the poor, local attitudes varied in this as in other respects. Social
legislation was characterised by a multiplicity of aims, not just to relieve
poverty but to maximise economic growth, as Macnicol documents well
for the 1930s, to maintain social stability and to inculcate such norms
as respectability and family cohesion into those supposedly rejecting
them. Powerful pressure groups, such as those of the employers, as Hay
describes, stress their own policy aims. This variety of pressures and aims
behind social legislation, documented by all of the papers, is the major
weakness of the 'broad path of betterment' school of the history of
social policy.

The sheer immensity of social problems before 1939 must, however,
be remembered. What could have been done, at what cost, for the near
30 per cent Booth found in poverty in London in the 1880s, or for the 2.7
million registered unemployed in 1932? Jobs could not have been found
without, or probably even with, a dramatic change in the organisation
of the economy at any point in this period. Probably more *could* have
been spent on pensions or family allowances. But to have provided
more adequately for the unemployed, for example, would surely have
been more costly than the economy could initially have afforded. Higher
social expenditure might have solved some social problems by increasing demand and job opportunities. But Alfred Marshall's suggestion
to this effect in 1895[9] was ignored, and Keynes' more sophisticated
formulation rejected until the Second World War.

Limitations on expenditure and the structure of the economy do not,
however, account for many of the principles behind legislation.
Historians and sociologists have attempted to characterise the attempts

of legislation to inculcate norms of work, sobriety and family responsibility as attempts to achieve 'social control', to put an end to class
divisions by bringing about shared norms. Hay defends the use of the
concept, in a limited fashion, to describe the clear normative aim of
many aspects of policy. But, as he suggests in his conclusion and as has
already been pointed out, the attempt to control was only one element
in social legislation. The employers of whom he writes, for example,
had other aims. The attitudes of Alfred Mond and W.H. Lever to
pensions were a mixture of philanthropy and self-interest.

The conception of social policy legislation as one means of establishing hegemony over the mass of the population has something to be
said for it. As my own paper points out, some working-class groups
saw it in this light.

It is often suggested, on the other hand, that social welfare was a
victory for working-class demands and values, and without their
pressure would not have come about.[10] Many working-class groups did
demand social reforms, as the only means of improving the lot of the
poorest and of increasing security for the whole working class. It is
certainly arguable that the growth of working-class political and
industrial organisation, from the 1880s, contributed much to the
growing awareness of the problem of continuing poverty, and that
politicians believed that their demands for improved conditions had to
be met in some fashion. To this extent working-class pressure was
important throughout the period. But the legislation was in all cases
more limited than the demands of working-class groups and, as Hay's
essay, among others, points out, was also designed to satisfy other
interests.

The weakness of working-class pressure for welfare more beneficial
to the poor is nicely illustrated by Pat Ryan's study of Poplar, where
the Labour Guardians'attempts to operate the Poor Law in the interests of
the local working class, as they interpreted them, led to government
attempts to restrain their actions and later to suppress them altogether.

The pressure of organised working-class groups had some effect in
putting welfare issues on to the political agenda, though it is difficult
to assess their relative importance compared with that of politicians
like Chamberlain or Lloyd George, reformers like Booth and Rathbone,
and employers' organisations. And, as McCord points out, and as it
would be foolish not to expect, many working people opposed social
welfare because of the cost of rates or belief in self-help and dislike of
the 'residuum'.

The impact of war upon social policy is not much referred to in this volume although the papers span the period of the First World War. It has been extensively, and often inconclusively, discussed elsewhere.[11] The weakness of much discussion of the relationship between war and social policy is the failure to set the discussion in the context of the pre-war situation and to analyse to what extent policy was indeed the product solely of the war, or to what extent the war actually retarded legislation. For example, the First World War was followed by important housing legislation, but such action had been promised by Asquith's government had the war not intervened. The Boer War almost certainly retarded pension legislation by nine years, although it did contribute to the concern for the health of children, which resulted in the school meals and school medical inspection legislation of 1906.

The Second World War did influence the extensive social legislation of 1945-8[12] and important changes in other countries affected by the war. Such measures as a national health service, however, were widely discussed, even by doctors, in the 1930s, although the war experience almost certainly speeded up its implementation.

The First and Second World Wars were beneficial to those Britons who were not killed in bringing about full employment, higher family incomes and hence better diet and health, although the education of children suffered between 1914 and 1918 as teachers went to war, houses were neither built nor repaired and hospitals were requisitioned for soldiers. But the improved social conditions were not the result of social policy. Indeed the real improvements since the Second World War have been due more to a long period of full employment and higher wages than to the 'Welfare State'.

An element, though by no means the only one, in policies following the First and Second World Wars was to retrieve the losses in health care, housing and education during the war. In general, too much writing on the relationship between war and social policy has been based on the mistaken assumption that the experience of real improvements after 1945 can be generalised to other wars. Precarious generalisations have been built on slender evidence.

Also, of course, many periods of implementation of new social policies have not been associated with war. The periods between 1906 and 1914, and during Neville Chamberlain's reign as Minister of Health between 1925 and 1929, when the age for old age pensions was reduced to 65, widows' pensions introduced and the Poor Law formally abolished, are periods of this kind.

The international change in attitudes to social welfare from the 1880s should also be taken into account. Many countries with highly

capitalised, developed economies, either industrial or agricultural
(Germany, Denmark, France, Australia and New Zealand among others)
experienced from the 1880s active discussion of measures such as old
age pensions and unemployment provision. This should warn us against
assuming that the changes discussed in this volume were peculiar to
Britain. It also provides us with the possibility of explaining some international changes. From the 1880s, interest in welfare measures emerged
in countries with developed economies (including the USA during the
heyday of the progressive movement), with the resources of finance and
bureaucracy to provide welfare, and with labour movements and sometimes employers[13] demanding change. Similarly the experience of
depression in the 1920s and 1930s led to experiments in many countries,
to some degree, with economic planning in the 1930s and 1940s. In both
cases differences in local experience led to different forms of state
welfare and of economic planning emerging in the different societies.

In Britain decisive influences upon policy were the long tradition of
laissez faire, of individual freedom from state control, which delayed
comprehensive social policies, and the size of her social problems, the
legacy to the sons and grandsons of the first industrial nation which
their emigré cousins in Australia and New Zealand escaped.

These essays analyse specific areas of policy and of pressures upon
policy. They suggest something about how certain social problems came
to be identified, and of the reasons why the various areas of legislation
took the form they did. They suggest a little about how ideas were transmitted from individuals, through pressure groups to civil servants and
ministers, although this subject requires much further study. They
provide something of an antidote to the 'broad path of social betterment' approach to the history of social policy.

They also omit large areas of social policy, such as health and
housing; say little about the implementation of legislation, its effects
upon recipients and their feelings about it. They largely neglect, as
most historians of social policy do, the especial problems of poor
women. Women however were a majority of the population, were less
able to help themselves when unmarried or widowed due to low wages
and employment opportunities, and were if married, less likely to
receive benefit when unemployed than men, and could rarely be
members of self-help organisations such as friendly societies and trade
unions.[14]

Very many aspects of the history of social policy remain to be
explored, but this volume suggests that the present highly imperfect
'Welfare State' had its origins in the imperfections of the past.

Notes

1. R.M. Titmuss, *Essays on 'The Welfare State'* (1958), p. 34.
2. Ibid, p. 55.
3. B.B. Gilbert, *The Evolution of National Insurance in Great Britain*, (1966), pp. 9, 14.
4. B.B. Gilbert, op. cit., p. 10.
5. Alan Deacon in A. Briggs and J. Saville (eds.), *Essays in Labour History*, Vol. 3, (1977).
6. J.R. Harris, *Unemployment and Politics*, and *William Beveridge*, (1977); G. Stedman Jones, *Outcast London* (1971); J.R. Hay, *The Origins of the Liberal Welfare Reforms* (1975).
7. Sir H.N. Bunbury (ed.), *Lloyd George's Ambulance Wagon, Being the Memoir of W.J. Braithwaite*, 1911-12, (1957).
8. B.R. Mitchell and Phyllis Dean, *Abstract of British Historical Statistics* (1962), pp. 400, 417.
9. *Report of the Royal Commission on Old Age Pensions*, 1895. Minutes of Evidence.
10. V. George and P. Wilding, *Ideology and Social Welfare*, p. 19; D. Thompson, *New Reasoner*, Vol. 1, No. 4, 1957.
11. A. Marwick, *Britain in the Century of Total War* and other works on this subject by this author.
12. R.M. Titmuss, *Problems of Social Policy* (1975).
13. J. Weinstein, *The Corporate Ideal in the Liberal State 1900-14* (Boston, 1968); Alan Deacon, op. cit.
14. Pat Thane, 'Women and "Welfare" in Victorian and Edwardian Britain', *History Workshop*, forthcoming, 1978.

RATEPAYERS AND SOCIAL POLICY

Norman McCord

In this short and tentative essay I want to draw attention to one factor
affecting the evolution of social policy which has in my view been
unduly neglected, not only in connection with the 1870–1914 period
but for earlier and later periods also. The development of a public
system of welfare benefits includes an inherently redistributive element,
in that it necessarily involves taking money from some sectors of
society in the form of rates and taxes in order to finance help for those
in certain other sectors of society. Although there has been a good deal
of work done on the actual plight of the poor and on the evolution of
general concepts of social policy, there has been as far as I know
relatively little work undertaken with a view to understanding those
who paid the rates and taxes which were applied to public schemes of
social amelioration.

This is not perhaps so very surprising, when one considers the back-
grounds and the interests of most people engaged in research into the
history of social policy and social administration, for we are very far
from being a typical or representative group. We tend to be interested
to an unusual degree in matters of politics and ideology, in the activities
of pressure groups and the elaboration of theories of society. Such
relatively pedestrian and mundane affairs as the beliefs and attitudes of
taxpayers and ratepayers have proved less attractive, but that does not
mean that they have been less influential or even less typical. Indeed a
strong case could be made for arguing that a failure to pay more attention
to the groups who in the Britain of 1870–1914 paid the rates and taxes
has been a serious bar to our understanding of that society. The minority
who were in serious need of public assistance were relatively impotent
during that period, while those who paid rates and taxes were in a
variety of ways in a position to exercise effective influence in the
framing and administration of social policy within a profoundly unequal
society. Indeed it is highly probable that a study of the taxpayer and
the ratepayer will tell us more about the evolution of social policy than
a study of the poor.

The attitudes of taxpayers and ratepayers were neither simple nor
uniform, and all that is intended here is to draw attention to one or
two aspects of ratepayers' behaviour which have cropped up prominently

in some recent work on the social history of north-east England. It is
certainly worth our while to consider the ratepayers of the 1870—1914
period very carefully, for during that period a high proportion of the
public money expended for social purposes was drawn from the local
rates, and expended by local authorities subject to direct influence
from a ratepaying electorate. Moreover, we are dealing with a period in
which the local integration and inward-looking character of most communities remained strong in comparison with our own contemporary
situation, even if these characteristics were somewhat eroded in comparison with earlier periods.

At the same time, the local oligarchies which controlled the
machinery of local government almost everywhere were also significant
groups in constituency politics in parliamentary terms, so that their
views and their attitudes were genuinely influential. From time to time
enthusiastic social reformers were to be found engaged in scathing
criticism of ministers and senior civil servants who were reluctant to
accept the solutions to social problems proffered by various pressure
groups. It was not always, however, that those in office were simply
obstructionist or selfish; it could often happen that a minister or a
senior civil servant was in reality better informed as to the attitudes of
the dominant minorities within a thoroughly unequal society than a
social reformer might be.

It would be wildly unrealistic to expect local studies of social administration in the 1870—1914 period to reveal bodies of town councillors
or Poor Law Guardians absorbed in fundamental debate about the nature
of society and the basic tenets on which the national social policy
should be based. For the most part elected local authorities were
absorbed in very different matters of a more mundane nature, as they
had been before and were to continue to be subsequently. For an
elected local authority in the 1870—1914 period to be much involved
in agonising reappraisal of its own *raison d'être* was rare indeed. Where
strong feelings between differing groups of elected representatives were
to be encountered, they came much more commonly about questions
such as the control of official patronage or whether the workhouse
inmates should be allowed beer at Christmas.

Local authorities still tended to act as jealous defenders of local
autonomy against any attempted encroachment by central authority;
central government departments commonly found it impossible to
enforce any great uniformity of practice or principle on councils or
Boards of Guardians. For example, when the public assistance
committee of Northumberland County Council took over the functions

of the old Poor Law authorities in 1930 they felt it something of an achievement to be able to standardise relief payments in that one county within two years. Local authorities were substantially controlled by ratepayers, and if the social policy of the 1870–1914 period is to be understood, we have to understand the ratepayers as well as any other groups which we may consider relevant.

Ratepayers were very far from being a socially homogeneous group. Everyone who occupied rated property had some kind of personal interest in the level of local taxation, and this included those who lived in rented property, whether their concern with the rates was direct or indirect. Some ratepayers were, of course, very rich, whether as individuals or as some form of corporate body. Many ratepayers of the 1870–1914 period were, however, very far from rich. One feature of those years, for instance, was a continuing increase in the number of workers who were direct ratepayers by virtue of owning house property. At the 1907 conference of the Building Societies Association, held in Newcastle, one of the speakers told the meeting that[1]

> Those who are connected with Building Societies know perfectly well that working men have, in thousands of cases in Newcastle upon Tyne, purchased their houses – not only purchased their house to live in, but . . . were in a short time able to buy other houses, and have gone on until when old age came upon them they had a very good annuity.

There may be some hyperbole here, but it is highly unlikely that such a claim was merely fabricated, and there is other evidence for the emergence of property-owning groups in clearly working-class contexts in this period. In areas where the co-operative movement was strong, many societies embarked upon ambitious programmes of either building houses for members to buy, or making mortgage funds available, or both. At Wallsend the local society began building in 1868, and the hundreds of houses they built still for the most part survive in, for instance, Mutual Street, Equitable Street, Provident Terrace and Rochdale Terrace. The Crook co-operative society, overwhelmingly composed of miners and their families, advanced nearly £35,000 in mortgages between 1895 and 1910.[2] At Bishop Auckland the society, again largely a miners' society, arranged 1,400 mortgages between 1895 and 1910.[3] Because a miner or a shipyard worker bought a house to live in, he did not in any meaningful sense cease to be a worker, but he did acquire a more direct interest in the scale of the rates and the way in which they were spent. Of course only a minority of workers entered the category of house-owners, but in many cases they were workers who were influential within their own society. They included men like John Raine, who worked 42 years in the Durham pits. He was a devoted trade unionist, and served as county delegate from the Black Boy pit for 12 years. He was president of the local co-operative society from 1886 to 1903. He retired from work in 1884 to live on the proceeds of his 'industry, steady habits and thrift'.[4] Sources like the celebration histories of local co-operative societies contain many stories of the more thrifty and successful workers who contrived to become small-scale property-owners, usually without ceasing to be essentially members of working communities. Groups like office-holders in trade unions and co-operative societies were prominent in this category, so that their significance did not depend solely upon their numbers. What is sufficiently plain is that it is not possible to distinguish rate-payers and workers as if they were separate groups during the 1870–1914 period.

A very high proportion of welfare expenditure came from the local rates and the level of the local rates was a matter which directly concerned people at many different social levels. The structure of the rating system was such as to exhibit conflicting claims, especially in periods of stress. Rates were levied at a uniform rather than a graduated level and although there could be a good deal of flexibility in practice there was no formalised system of rebates for small ratepayers such as we have recently acquired. Causes which pushed up calls on local relief funds often reduced at the same time the ability of many ratepayers to meet additional rate demands. At a time of prolonged depression, for example, the need for greater relief expenditure would coincide with serious financial difficulties for some groups of ratepayers – small shopkeepers, for example. During a prolonged Tyneside strike in 1886 the Mayor of Newcastle, the industrialist Benjamin Browne, appealed to the Newcastle Guardians to revert to large-scale outdoor relief to the able-bodied. The Guardians unanimously rejected this plea because[5]

> a considerable proportion of the rates are drawn from a class very little removed from pauperism, who had a hard struggle to pay the demands made upon them by the Overseers, and that any con-siderable increase in their burdens would have the effect of causing them to become paupers.

A study of many Boards of Guardians during the 1920s will show them facing two conflicting pressures, both of them representing a genuine case. On the one hand the vociferous champions of the un-employed urged the expenditure of more generous sums in relief, on the other hand representatives of a variety of organisations which included ratepayers argued that any substantial increase in rate demands would break the precarious financial viability of many ratepayers, who were also hard hit by economic depression.

It was not only in hard times, however, that the level of rates and their application was a matter of immediate concern to ratepayers drawn from a very wide range of society. Even in normal times the level of rates and the way in which they were spent for social purposes was a matter of keen local knowledge, interest and concern. In the period 1870–1914 it remained true to a great extent that the beneficiaries of social spending – as for example those who received some form of Poor Law relief – were personally known to very many of the ratepayers who actually footed the bill for these purposes. A situation in which much of the money was raised from local ratepayers for the benefit of local people in need could on occasion lead to greater generosity on the part of local administration – indeed it can be demonstrated that this often happened – but local knowledge of those seeking help was not by any means a universal recipe for greater sympathy.

A major and neglected factor in the evolution of social policy in twentieth-century Britain has been the presence of very many people who have combined generous enthusiasms with a limited perception of reality. It was not so easy for many ratepayers of the later nineteenth and early twentieth centuries to remain unaware of the fact that the aged do not always grow old gracefully or that the sick and the weak are not always pleasantly pathetic. Local knowledge could often bring home some of the real practical problems of social work in an un-mistakably clear way. Consider, for instance, a few events at the Houghton-le-Spring Union workhouse at the turn of the century.[6] In 1890 Elizabeth Bell received 14 days in prison for disorderly conduct, and in the same year two other female inmates were also before the magistrates

the one for tearing and destroying the bed-clothing, and the other for disorderly and refractory conduct in the Workhouse.

In 1891 Sarah Graham was before the magistrates for 'very cruel treatment' of an infant inmate. In 1893 John Hall was in trouble for returning to the workhouse drunk, while on one Saturday night in 1894 Joseph Tweedy and John Newton returned to the workhouse drunk and bearing a bottle of laudanum. In 1902 William Gribbin was given seven days' imprisonment for drunkenness; after his escapade he

> on presenting himself for admission to the Workhouse in a drunken condition, had owing to his violent conduct, been taken before a Justice and committeed to prison for a further period of fourteen days.

In 1905 the door of the relieving officer's office was kicked in by a vagrant annoyed at being refused a ticket of admission to the casual ward for a second night.

Incidents of this kind were usually prominently reported in the local press, and they provided some kind of foundation for such attitudes among ratepayers as that expressed by Alderman Richardson in opposing a proposal to build council houses in Newcastle in 1891.[7]

> There was a residuum of the population incapable of helping them-selves. The residuum was the result, to a large extent, of hereditary causes, but mainly the result of a life of debauchery, sin and often crime . . . If it was right and incumbent upon them to provide shelter for these people, it was equally incumbent upon them to provide food and raiment for them. Therefore the Corporation might begin to erect bakehouses and clothing establishments tomorrow. By that means they would get themselves upon an inclined plane, which would land them in the vortex of pure municipal socialism.

I think it is important to remember that such sentiments would be echoed not only by richer ratepayers, but by very many respectable workers and their families, who were likely to know more about the less prepossessing aspects of social need than many of their present-day successors who inhabit a less localised context. It is reasonable to assume that at local level attitudes towards social policy in the 1870–1914 period were determined more by personal knowledge of those categories who required help — and perhaps in especial degree the less attractive elements among them — than by any widespread popular addiction to general theories of politics or society.

A related aspect of concern to the ratepayer at various social levels was the abuse of public funds by the scrounger and the parasite, again something likely to be more notorious and appreciated in a more coherent localised community. Certainly welfare fiddling is not a modern invention, but was a frequent occurrence under both the Old and the New Poor Laws. We have already seen how during the engineers' strike of 1886 the Newcastle Guardians refused to reintroduce large-scale outdoor relief because of the effects this would have on the rates and therefore the poorer ratepayers. In their reply, however, they also made another point[8]

> Out-door relief has for many years been, for good reasons, kept down to the lowest point. Relieving officers have found imposture so rife among the applicants that they have wisely done all in their power to put an end to a system so fruitful of evil.

There may be exaggeration here, but it is very unlikely that this was a tale without any factual foundation.

In the much more strongly locally-integrated communities of 1870–1914 it was much easier for ratepayers to be aware of any cases in which their money was extracted by scroungers or parasites. It seems probable, for instance, that many ratepayers would have applauded the action of the Houghton Guardians in 1895 in deliberately and indignantly arranging publication in local newspapers of the case of Ann Clark of Dubmire village, who had just applied for relief for herself and her children. Recently widowed, she had received a £10 friendly society benefit, and had then spent £10 14s on her husband's funeral, including a £2 10s coffin, £1 on cab expenses and £5 on funeral clothing, and had then applied for poor relief. The Guardians, and no doubt many rate-payers in this mining area, would not be happy at seeing such conspicuous extravagance speedily followed by a demand on the poor rates. In 1910 the same Board of Guardians discovered that when Robert Richardson had successfully applied for relief he had concealed the fact that he held a savings bank account holding £249 — a sum much larger than many ratepayers could ever accumulate; he was forced to disgorge the £65 9s 6d he had been paid from poor law funds.

Similar cases, usually well publicised in the local press, could readily be multiplied, and played a significant role in determining public attitudes, and especially ratepayers' attitudes, to questions of social policy. It seems likely that direct personal knowledge of cases of this kind would exist more commonly among those who had to foot the bill in the 1870–1914 period, when the bulk of the money came from rates levied within a locally-orientated community, than in a later situation

in which most social expenditure is administered relatively anony-
mously and the bulk of the money is extracted in a more amorphous
form by general national taxation.

In terms of the scale of the various kinds of abuse, and the total
amounts involved, these cases may appear merely trivial, but their
effect on public opinion outweighed their number. This applies in the
context of both of these perennial problems affecting plans for
social amelioration – on the one hand the fact that those in need of
help will often include elements with personality or behavioural traits
which are far from popular or prepossessing, and on the other hand
the tendency for the provision of benefits to attract parasites. Again
the point is important that resentment at the expenditure of ratepayers'
money on the drunken, the vicious, or the scrounger, was by no means
confined to the wealthier sectors of society. The present tendency for
'abuses of the welfare state' to be noticeably more prominent in newspapers which workers and their families voluntarily choose to buy and
read is not a new circumstance, and the resentment of the 'respectable'
workers against the undeserving has a long tradition. Certainly the
suspicion and hostility towards higher expenditure for social purposes
which these circumstances have created cannot be analysed as simply
a class phenomenon.

It would be tempting to continue these themes into the post-1914
context, when they continued to be important in determining public
attitudes to social policy; the temptation must be resisted, but perhaps
one inter-war glimpse may be allowed. It comes from the recollections,
published in 1938, of an amiable, intelligent and perceptive man of
left-wing leanings, who had found himself a few years earlier one of the
many unemployed in County Durham: he described life in a lodging-
house for the unemployed.[9]

> The lodging was rough, the bedding sparse, and the food consisted
> mainly of thick slices of bread and margarine, with milkless tea,
> fried blackpudding and onions and a little cheese. The talk at meal-
> times was mostly about football or sport and hardly ever about
> politics or women – the main subject of interest to all was 'fiddling',
> i.e. the various means by which they could supplement their relief
> without reporting to the authorities.

An entirely comprehensible viewpoint, but one unlikely to commend
itself to many ratepayers in a local government area in which rates
were running at 8s 6½d in the pound for relief purposes alone, as against

a national average of 2s 8½d.

Another related element affecting the attitudes of ratepayers towards the spending of public money for social purposes was the extent to which the administration of public services appeared efficient and honest. There was, in the Britain of 1870–1914, as in earlier and later periods, a widespread distrust of local and central government as reliable and disinterested instruments. Here too, as in the case of the unprepossessing or parasitical applicants for help, it was not so much the general level of competence and honesty which counted, for a few well-publicised cases of ineptitude or default could have a disproportionate effect on public opinion, especially on the opinion of those whose money was involved. In the Britain of 1870–1914 examples of incompetence or dishonesty were probably less common than they had been earlier, but the record was certainly very far from unblemished as far as the agencies of both central and local government were concerned.

A few examples will readily illustrate this point.[10] In 1876 the Local Government Board in London angrily accused the Hexham Rural Sanitary Authority of incompetence, and threatened that unless administrative efficiency was sharply tightened up, steps would be taken to dissolve that local authority. A few years later the chairman of the Hexham Rural Sanitary Authority was writing to the Local Government Board, complaining bitterly about the ineptitude of that central department, and especially about the prolonged failure to deal with the RSA by-laws; it transpired that the by-laws had been lost in the LGB office. Another local incident points the same way in 1879. Plans for the extension of the Houghton-le-Spring Union workhouse and for an extension of the local Wesleyan school were sent by their respective sponsors to different sections of the LGB central establishment at the same time. Both were confirmed with the result that the workhouse's new wards for infectious diseases were sited next to the school extension, which was a conjunction hardly likely to imbue local ratepayers with a high opinion of the efficiency of the agents of either central or local authority.

An incident from the history of the South Shields Poor Law Union may serve to illustrate how a number of aspects of the relationship between ratepayers and social administration could come together. During a serious depression in the mid-1880s organised pressure from ratepayers, many of whom were themselves under severe pressure from the depression, forced the Guardians to adopt a programme of expenditure cuts. One specific demand was for the reduction of official salaries, and among other reductions the guardians reduced the stipend of their part-time clerk from £200 to £125; when this officer retired a few years later it was discovered that he had done something to restore the cut informally by repeatedly dipping his hands into union funds.

Even where actual dishonesty did not take place there could be aspects of official administration which made ratepayers suspicious of the uses to which their money might be put. In order to attract staff of reasonable quality for responsible posts it would be necessary for local authorities to offer salaries appreciably higher than the incomes of many ratepayers; this in practice proved a major factor in cheeseparing in local government salaries and often inhibited the recruitment of officers of adequate calibre. The radical *Newcastle Chronicle* noted on 3 November 1877 that at Tynemouth the municipal elections had been conducted with exceptional vehemence, on account of the public hostility aroused by the council's decision to increase the salary of the borough surveyor. Local councillors who had voted for the increase were summarily ejected by the ratepaying electorate. This was far from an isolated incident in the local politics of the 1870–1914 period.

Moreover, circumstances often suggested the existence of nepotism or the fiddling of patronage, even when no obvious impropriety was involved. At Gateshead, in the hotly contested election in 1836 of the borough's first town clerk, Thomas Swinburne was defeated by the Mayor's casting vote. Family pride was vindicated by the election of this Swinburne's son as town clerk in 1856. He died in office in 1893, and was succeeded by his son William, who had become assistant town clerk in 1891. William Swinburne remained in office till he resigned in October 1929 a few months before his death.[11] Many parallels to such hereditary service and office-holding could be found; even when good service was given suspicion of nepotism was inevitable.

A disinclination to part with one's money has been neither uncommon nor unnatural, nor is it necessarily unreasonable or discreditable. A ratepayer of the period 1870–1914 did not have to be wicked in order to be deeply suspicious of schemes to increase the burden on him for public purposes. In most cases the evidence at his disposal would suggest to him that some at least of the money he paid was likely to be spent on individuals and purposes of which he disapproved, and he was not likely to have an uncritical faith in the efficiency or probity of official agencies. Such attitudes were not confined to either the reactionary or the rich. One thread of inconsistency which runs through much of British radicalism in the nineteenth century was far from dead — the simultaneous support for the provision of social amelioration and the maintenance of rigid economy in public expenditure — while we have seen that ratepayers were drawn from a wide spectrum of society, including many workers who were by no means always committed to doctrines of higher spending and higher rates for public purposes.

If concentration here has largely been on ratepayers and local taxation much the same attitudes can be detected as widely held about parliamentary legislation and central government spending; this is scarcely surprising, for there was obviously a very considerable overlap between ratepayers, taxpayers and parliamentary electors in the Britain of 1870–1914.

One example — far from unique — may be cited to point the parallel. In 1876 the Crook and Neighbourhood Co-operative Corn Mill, Flour and Provision Society Ltd, essentially a miners' society, met to celebrate the opening of a new store. (In 1874 they had cancelled their annual tea party in favour of a trip to Sunderland, 'if possible when the Channel Fleet are in'.) The keynote speech at the 1876 store opening was delivered by a visiting radical speaker from Newcastle. Here is the main point he made, amidst loud applause:[12]

> When, in a country like this, they raise for the government yearly the sum of £70,000,000, and they had the confounded impudence to tell them it is not enough, was it not time the people stood upon their independence, and told the government that if they could not conduct the business of the nation in a better manner than to be compelled to spend £75,000,000 a year, it was time that they went away, and that somebody else took their places?

Even long after 1914, British electoral history, with an increasingly democratic electorate, does not show any very great popularity for parties dedicated to programmes of increased public spending. In 1935 the self-proclaimed national government could win 53.7 per cent of the popular vote; Labour won its great 1945 victory with 47.8 per cent. We know that in 1935 Ellen Wilkinson was returned for Jarrow, 'the town that was murdered'; what is less often mentioned is that in that very unaristocratic and very unbourgeois constituency the Conservative candidate in 1935 obtained 46.9 per cent of the popular vote.

When miners at Crook applauded demands for cuts in public spending, and nearly half of Jarrow's electors were prepared to vote Conservative, and when ratepayers were affected by the attitudes and considerations already discussed, it will be apparent that the framing of more extensive social policies faced serious practical difficulties in a context in which those in need possessed little authority while those who had to pay taxes and rates possessed much. It will be apparent too that these matters cannot be comprehended in simple romantic terms of the rich against the poor, or in terms of crude class conflict theories.

To understand how it was that despite these important adverse circumstances considerable progress was made in the development of more enlightened social policies is a large question beyond the compass of this short note, but there were in fact two crucial factors which in practice were capable of outweighing the obstacles to increased social spending. The first factor was the presence at various social levels of devoted and hard-working groups of social reformers, though nowhere were those involved in such activities anything like a majority. It may be reasonably conjectured that, in a profoundly unequal society, the most effective of these groups were to be found in the dominant minority sectors of society which were capable of exercising effective influence in parliament and government.

Moreover, a major element in the evolution of social policy in the 1870–1914 period was the continuing importance of unofficial philanthropy in the establishment of welfare provision. As in the earlier nineteenth century advances in welfare provision were more commonly the work of unofficial pace-setters than of official agencies. While again no social class enjoyed a monopoly of this kind of activity, it will be sufficiently obvious that those who possessed the necessary resources and leisure played the more important role in establishing and financing charitable enterprises. Examples of this kind of work could easily be multiplied, but the pioneering of special facilities for tuberculosis sufferers is just one of many fields in which unofficial philanthropy led the way for subsequent official action.

The intimate connection between philanthropic innovation and subsequent official agency is by now well appreciated. In the Britain of 1870–1914 there was no necessary contradiction between a distrust of official expansion and a willingness to subscribe to unofficial charitable agencies, which were for the most part themselves essentially local manifestations of local concern. It is significant that, while many workers were suspicious of higher rates and taxes for social purposes, the period after 1870 saw a marked change in the financing of many local philanthropic agencies – hospitals and clinics, for example – which often came to depend less on major donations, subscriptions and legacies and more on multiple small regular subscriptions from groups of workers anxious to obtain full access to the facilities concerned and to improve their quality.

The second crucial factor was the continued growth in wealth. This was a factor of fundamental importance in trying to understand the development of more enlightened social policies. It is not enough to have improved welfare techniques and noisy pressure groups; it is essential that the means to pay for social amelioration should be obtainable without placing on taxpayers and ratepayers demands which they will strenuously resist — especially in a context in which ratepayers and taxpayers tend to be influential, and recipients of welfare payments relatively impotent. Here are some figures for the increase in rateable value of a number of towns in north-east England during the period with which we are concerned.

	1870	1907
Sunderland	£258,000	£706,000
Gateshead	£134,000	£427,000
South Shields	£125,000	£421,000
West Hartlepool	£67,000	£262,000

While it would be foolish to suppose that increased resources were the sole cause of extended improvement in social conditions, it seems in practice to have been one major prerequisite. This can be illustrated by the example of the local authority at Wallsend.[13] After a considerable struggle local reformers succeeded in 1866 in procuring the creation of a local board. This was for some time, however, a Pyrrhic victory, for the subsequent elections were won convincingly by candidates opposed to public spending. The new authority's expenditure in 1867—8 was as follows — scavenging £2 14s, rent of boardroom and cleaning it £6 9s 4d, sundries 13s 7d; in addition a tiny loan was raised to build a very short length of sewer, and that was all. Later in 1868 the growing district of Carrville persuaded the board to provide nine street lamps at an estimated cost of £24 p.a.; in Wallsend local politics this counted as a significant victory for progress. In September the board voted six to two against a proposal to pave and drain one of the main streets; in December they similarly rejected out of hand a plan to light the short but important stretch of street connecting the railway station and the high street, the chairman remarking

> that such as were compelled to be in the place after dark might provide themselves, as their fathers had to do, with lanterns.

Rateable value at Wallsend rose from under £30,000 in the later 1860s to nearly £80,000 in 1891, and was to rise much higher in the early twentieth century. The increased resources were matched by an increasing willingness on the part of the local authority to sanction expenditure for social improvement. The board still refused to pave the high street in 1872, but appointed a medical officer of health in 1874, and raised the stipend of this part-time post to £50 in 1877. In 1882 they added a surveyor at £52 and in 1883 an inspector of nuisances at £40. By 1891 the board was capable of nerving itself to spend £6,500 on a local hospital. It would be difficult to understand these changes without an appreciation of the increased resources involved in the striking growth in rateable values brought by economic development.

The rateable value of Newcastle rose from roughly £150,000 in 1850 to £2,500,000 in 1927. By 1911 the town employed well over 500 men in its cleansing department, with the city covered by a carefully worked-out network of districts. In 1873 the 'sanitary committee' of Newcastle Council was in fact only a sub-committee, but by the early twentieth century it was a principal standing committee, including many leading council members, and with a system of eight standing sub-committees to administer its ever-growing resources. In 1882 Newcastle's Medical Officer of Health had a staff of a chief and four assistant inspectors of nuisances, a chief and an assistant inspector of provisions, and two clerks. By 1907 this had grown to a chief inspector, assistant chief inspector and nineteen assistant inspectors of nuisances, a chief inspector and two assistant inspectors of provisions, a superintendent of midwives, six health visitors, and six clerks, not counting the considerable staffs now employed in the city's own hospitals. Of course, increased resources did not tell the whole story of such growth by any means, but a vital part of this kind of story was the fact that vastly increased rateable value enabled public authorities to expand their activities without raising rates to a figure which the ratepayers would find intolerable.

We must therefore try to understand the development of social policy not simply in the history of ideas and of politics, but also in the light of the increased wealth generated by the growth of industry and commerce, which provided the means to finance extended programmes of social reform. No doubt the shape taken by that economic growth is repugnant to many of our own contemporaries, but that has little or nothing to do with understanding the Britain of 1870–1914. Professor Hobsbawm has told us, with admirable common sense, that 'it is absurd to assume that socialism was a practical possibility in the Britain of Peel and Gladstone';[14] the assumption would be little less absurd for the

Britain of Salisbury and Asquith. The continued increase in national wealth was an indispensable prerequisite for the elaboration of more enlightened social policies. It is difficult to see how, in the absence of this crucial factor, the acquiescence of a taxpaying and ratepaying electorate could have been won, in a society in which hostility to official interference and to the extension of government spending was still very far from dead.

Notes

1. 'Report of Proceedings at Annual Meeting', Building Societies Association, 1906, p. 73.
2. Edward Lloyd, 'History of the Crook and Neighbourhood Co-operative ... Society |Ltd', (Pelaw, 1916), p. 232.
3. T. Readshaw, 'History of the Bishop Auckland ... Co-operative Society Ltd', (Manchester, 1910), p. 215.
4. Ibid., pp. 280–1.
5. Volume of press cuttings on 'Newcastle Relief Funds, 1885–6', in Newcastle Central Library.
6. R.G. Barker, 'Houghton-le-Spring Poor Law Union' (M.Litt. thesis, Newcastle University, 1974), pp. 170–1, 227.
7. I owe this quotation, from Newcastle Council Proceedings 1890–1, pp. 430–1, to Mr John Noddings.
8. As note 5.
9. J. Common, 'Seven Shifts' (1938), pp. 125–6.
10. I owe the references to the Hexham cases to Miss Gloria Cadman's current work on the Hexham Poor Law Union. For the Houghton example, Barker, op. cit., p. 163. For South Shields, P. Mawson, 'Poor Law Administration in South Shields, 1830–1930' (M.A. thesis, Newcastle University, 1971), p. 128.
11. J. Oxberry, 'The Swinburnes of Gateshead, A Century of Public Services', Newcastle, n.d. but c.1929.
12. Lloyd, op. cit., p. 141.
13. W. Richardson, 'History of the Parish of Wallsend' (Newcastle, 1923), pp. 367 et seq.
14. *New Statesman*, 29 December 1972.

THE LATER YEARS OF THE WORKHOUSE 1890–1929

M.A. Crowther

The New Poor Law instituted a workhouse system which has been
almost universally execrated, but whereas its beginnings are well
documented, its end is still something of a mystery.[1] The later years of
the workhouse lacked the vigorous publicity of the 1830s and 1840s:
its scandals no longer involved paupers fighting over rotting bones or
masters flogging female inmates. Instead there was minor peculation or
petty tyranny. Paupers did not die from lack of medical attention, but
there were complaints of insufficient food and lack of comfort. The
workhouse in 1900 was criticised less for its cruelty than for its
dreariness, its regimented squalor, its failure to deal appropriately with
different types of inmate. Meat dinners, blankets, heating, pianos, books,
pictures and even doctors, nurses, spectacles and false teeth, all
proliferated in workhouses during this period, but are not the ingredients
of dramatic history; and such improvements as occurred are usually
described as inadequate.

One reason for this neglect of workhouse history is that historians
have concentrated on the 'break-up' of the Poor Law. It is reasonable
to follow the Webbs' argument that schemes for unemployment
insurance, pensions, and child welfare were removing successive groups
from the need for Poor Law relief. After 1918 attention shifts to the
battle between the Ministry of Health and the few unions who were
refusing to impose strict conditions on outdoor paupers. Historians tend
to rejoice more over a stray sheep like Poplar than over the ninety and
nine who remain in the fold. This small group of rebellious unions
did have considerable impact on social policy by strengthening
Chamberlain's resolve to take power away from Guardians and hand it to
the county councils as more 'efficient' (or docile) bodies.

Yet radical views over the question of outdoor relief did not
necessarily imply a generous approach to the workhouses as well: on
the contrary, dislike of the workhouse system could lead to considerable
meanness in the treatment of indoor paupers.[2] Conversely, a strict
administration of outdoor relief was not necessarily accompanied by
parsimony towards the workhouse inmates: Manchester, which operated
tough policies towards the able-bodied and casual poor, developed an
expensive and impressive series of specialised institutions for the indoor

poor. When in 1926 the Ministry of Health replaced three of the insubordinate Labour-controlled Boards of Guardians, they sent in their own nominated Guardians who produced reports hostile to the displaced Boards. The reports castigated the Labour Guardians for their outdoor relief policies, but found nothing remarkable in the workhouse management.[3]

There is need for some reassessment of the role of the workhouses in the development of the Welfare State. In 1911 George Lansbury published a pamphlet entitled *Smash Up the|Workhouse!* – a sentiment echoed by many other critics, but the problems of the workhouse did not end with local government reorganisation in 1929, or even after 1945. The word 'pauper' disappeared; the people themselves did not. The Local Government Act of 1929 was intended to phase out the general mixed workhouse and place the inmates in specialised institutions under county control, but the Act was not innovatory either in its principles or its effects. It merely sanctioned a system of specialised institutions which had been slowly developing for several decades, and tried to speed up this process. But the county councils did not suddenly produce a new policy of institutional care. County councillors were often former Guardians; the workhouse master became the hospital steward, the nurses and other staff continued as before, and the old buildings were usually retained. The workhouses between 1890 and 1929 were not declining, but were laying the foundations for the present system of locally controlled institutions. Both need and social convention determine who shall enter these institutions; no system of outdoor care has managed to replace them.

The chief institutions maintained by the Guardians were the general mixed workhouses and the separate infirmaries, which were administered by a different staff from the workhouse, though commonly built close to it. By 1914 there were also a variety of other institutions, the most common type being homes for children. Large urban unions still ran the great 'barrack' schools which had been favoured in the early years of the New Poor Law, but smaller unions were encouraged either to foster children with local families or to build 'scattered' or 'cottage' homes. Before the war a few urban unions had experimented with 'test' workhouses for able-bodied men.[4] From the 1890s there were some new homes for the aged poor, though they housed less than a thousand people by 1908.[5] Unions might also have separate wards for infectious patients and for vagrants, or even a convalescent home in a coastal resort, while Manchester experimented with a colony for epileptics. On the whole, the smaller the union, the less likely it was to have special provision for any class of pauper, except perhaps the children.

The term 'workhouse' will obviously not cover all these institutions. Technically it should apply only to the mixed institutions where work was nominally imposed to deter the able-bodied applicant, but since all the indoor poor passed through the workhouse doors to the receiving ward for medical examination and classification, the general workhouse remained the hub of institutional relief. Only the sick could be admitted directly to the infirmaries, when these were separate from the workhouse. From 1913 the Local Government Board actually gave up the name 'workhouse' in favour of 'Poor Law Institution'. As very little work was now done by workhouse inmates, most of whom were elderly, ill, or children, the change of name did reflect a real change in the institutions, but this did not stop the old name from being commonly used, even in the private memoranda of government departments.

The importance of institutional relief is shown in its heavy cost to the poor rates. It is, however, difficult to separate indoor from outdoor relief expenditure because of the notorious confusion of Poor Law statistics. The building accounts, for example, do not show what was spent on the institutions, as opposed to administrative buildings, dispensaries for the outdoor poor, and so on. The expenditure recorded for outdoor relief sometimes included paupers boarded in the institutions of other unions. The Guardians also paid towards the keep of paupers in institutions outside their own control; pauper lunatics committed to county asylums were a fairly heavy charge on the poor rate (an average of 16 per cent of total expenditure from 1900 to 1914, rising to 18 per cent during the war). Similarly, many Guardians placed young blind or deaf paupers in charitable institutions.

In 1913 the Local Government Board calculated that since 1900 it had cost four times as much to maintain each indoor pauper as one on outdoor relief.[6] In these years the proportion of relief spent on the outdoor poor was falling slowly from a peak of 25.8 per cent in 1896 to 22.5 per cent in 1910. Then the advent of old age pensions caused a rapid drop to 16.4 per cent in 1912. Yet there were always rather more than twice as many outdoor paupers as indoor ones, until pensions and the war caused the ratio to drop to around 1.5 to one. Even if generous estimates are made for the salaries of relieving officers and other expenses not included in the outdoor relief accounts, it is likely that the bulk of Poor Law expenditure, perhaps up to 70 per cent, went on the various Poor Law institutions, not counting the sums paid to the county asylums.

In 1920 the new Ministry of Health gave a more detailed account of relief costs. In 1918–19, when the effects of war were still apparent, the institutions took up 77 per cent of all relief expenditure, reflecting the drop in outdoor relief which had accompanied high employment rates. The Ministry also tried to distinguish between the cost of the general workhouses and other types of Poor Law institution. Even after decades of growing specialisation, the workhouses took up a considerable proportion:[7]

Paupers in:	% of all expenditure on indoor relief (£13.6m)	% distribution of inmates in the various institutions on 1 January 1920 (270,569 inmates)
Lunatic asylums	25.4	30.4
Homes for children	11.8	11.4
Metropolitan Asylums Board homes for the feeble-minded	3.4	2.9
58 separate infirmaries	13.9	8.6
Institutions of non-Poor Law bodies	3.0	5.0
Other institutions, mainly workhouses	42.5	41.7

It cost far less to maintain an inmate in a general workhouse than in a specialised institution; the average weekly cost of a workhouse inmate was 20s 3½d a week, as opposed to 30s 4½d for an infirmary patient.[8]

Before the war, institutional relief absorbed the greater part of the poor rates. It may not have been the most important factor in social politics, but it probably dominated much of the day-to-day running of the Poor Law unions. The national figures also masked enormous variations in local practice. London, in particular, spent a much higher proportion of its resources on indoor relief, for the Common Poor Fund allowed the cost to be spread over the whole Metropolitan area. Local expenditure on indoor relief was affected by many pressures: the amount and nature of pauperism in the area, the relationship between the Guardians and their electors, the zeal and efficiency of officials, and local attitudes towards the workhouse. Hence Lambeth, a very large parish with severe underemployment had developed from the late nineteenth century a reputation for harshness towards the outdoor poor: in 1891–2 it spent only about 15 per cent of its large annual budget on them. The rest went on administration and indoor relief, including 17 per cent to its officers' salaries and pensions. The outdoor relief expenditure dropped steadily until the war, reaching a mere 7.5 per cent in 1911–12. Unemployment forced more expenditure on outdoor relief after the war, but even in 1928 it was only 18 per cent.[9] Compare this with Basford (Notts.), a partly industrial union with a long history of unemployment in the textile trades and a tradition of favouring outdoor relief. Here, in 1898, 44 per cent of the budget went on the outdoor poor: high employment during the war almost halved this, but by 1929 it was up to 48.5 per cent.[10]

The most substantial account of the last years of the workhouse is still the final volume of the Webbs' *Poor Law History*, published in 1929. It is also in this volume that the Webbs became least objective, for it covered ground over which they had been battling for the previous twenty years. In many ways it was an extension of the Minority Report of the Poor Law Commission of 1905, though modified to suit the decade of mass unemployment in which it was written. It contains a lengthy account of the workings of the Commission, and uses illustrations from Beatrice Webb's personal diaries. As in so much of the Webbs' work, including the Minority Report, the reader tends to be swayed more by the powerful generalisations than by the mass of detailed description. In fact both the *Poor Law History* and the Minority Report contain accounts of all kinds of institutions, both well and badly run, but the general picture is one of meanness, stagnation and inefficiency. The Minority Report condemned the indiscriminate herding of the 'deserving' and the 'undeserving' in the workhouses in language which deliberately reflected that of the 1832 Poor Law Commission.[11] The same argument appears in both: that workhouses were simultaneously too comfortless and deterrent for the respectable helpless poor, and too attractive to the able-bodied loafer.

The *Poor Law History* and the Minority Report both pointed to the same solution as the 1832 Commissioners: separate institutions for the different categories of inmate. Of course the Minority Commissioners departed radically from the original principles of the New Poor Law in many respects, but nevertheless, the vision of a series of specialised institutions differed only in scope, not in principle, from the plan laid out in the report of 1834. The question is whether, in their desire for a better future, the Minority did not unnecessarily denigrate the existing institutions.

The Majority Report did not differ much from the Minority over the future of indoor relief, but although the Majority were critical of some of the promiscuous and badly managed workhouses they had seen, they also emphasised the great diversity of existing institutions:[12]

There is, perhaps, no point in Poor Law administration upon which it is more difficult and dangerous to generalise than the work-house itself. We have visited many of these institutions, and find them different from each other as light from darkness. So much depends upon the amount of interest taken by the Guardians, upon the temperament of the master and matron, upon the policy of the Board, and upon the nature of the district and of the building itself, that no one description will apply to all, although|all alike may conform to the minutest details of the Local Government Board Regulations.

Whereas the Minority would have handed the institutions over to a series of special authorities for each kind of social problem, the Majority were prepared to leave them under one Poor Law type of agency.

All Commissioners, therefore, were agreed that the general mixed workhouse must go. Indeed, who could be found to defend it except some of the more backward guardians? Other bodies were offering the same ideas on separate institutions: in 1908 the Royal Commission on the Care and Control of the Feeble-Minded recommended special accommodation and treatment for this group outside the Poor Law. In 1906 a departmental committee on vagrancy suggested compulsory labour colonies for vagrants; and labour colonies not merely for vagrants but the unemployed as well were favoured by a surprising array of disparate people, including all the Poor Law Commissioners, the Charity Organisation Society, the Salvation Army, and Labour-dominated Guardians like Poplar. They disagreed over who should run the colonies and whether they should be punitive or remedial. It would seem that the general mixed workhouse was about to sink under the weight of opprobrium.

The demand for separate institutions must be considered as one indication of growing respect for professional treatment. The specialisation envisaged in 1834 had been a simple one, the main groups being defined as the able-bodied men and women, the old, and the children. Hospitals and lunatic asylums existed, of course, but mainly in the large centres of population, and were by no means (and with good reason) accepted as the best means of treatment. On the whole, people with money would pay to keep themselves and their families out of institutions, except perhaps for the few exclusive establishments which charged high fees. By the end of the nineteenth century this had changed. The great voluntary hospitals continued to treat a wide variety of ailments, but were far more careful in separating them. Specialisation was growing in physical and to a lesser extent in psychological medicine.[13] Medical knowledge was still severely limited but surgery was safer, nursing more professional, wards cleaner and nutrition better understood; and all this made the possibility of a cure far greater in an institution than in the homes of the poor.

Contemporary surveys of poverty demonstrated that most working-class budgets could not have stretched far enough to provide the standards of comfort and nursing which were available in the workhouse. To a hard-pressed family faced with supporting a helpless person, institutional treatment must have seemed more acceptable than in the recent past. This is demonstrated by the growing popularity of Poor Law infirmaries amongst those who were not technically destitute, and the increased willingness of the poor to place their feeble-minded relatives in Poor Law institutions and to pay part of the cost.[14] The institution was not necessarily attractive; but it was less deterrent than before.

Many reformers believed that a good institution was better than a bad home. They wanted not only to devise systems for better and more specialised institutions, but to have power to detain certain people in them for their 'own good'. The feeble-minded poor were the most obvious case, and particularly feeble-minded women with illegitimate children. The Royal Commission on the Feeble-Minded urged the government to consider some kind of detention, and the Mental Deficiency Act of 1913 allowed Guardians to apply for such cases to be placed in county institutions for their own safety. In any case, Guardians sometimes used unorthodox methods to detain them in workhouses. The master could refuse them leave to go outside the workhouse, but could not prevent them from discharging themselves: in Newcastle the Medical Officer evaded this by 'remanding' them for observation and threatening to certify them if they applied to leave.[15]

Other schemes for institutional detention abounded before 1914. The Poor Law Commissioners wanted labour colonies run by the state for the 'in and out' class of able-bodied paupers, and for 'unfit' parents who refused to support their children. The Guardians already had considerable powers of detention. Since the 1880s they had been able to detain vagrants for two nights (three at weekends) in order to extract work from them, and they could also refuse to let the 'ins and outs' discharge themselves for up to a week; but the Commissioners envisaged even longer periods of compulsory detention, to deter able-bodied loafers from seeking relief.

Here the Majority and the Minority parted company: both believed in labour colonies, but the Majority, in the traditional manner, were interested only in people who tried to live off the rates. They recommended a system (euphemistically described as 'continuous care and treatment') into which a JP could commit not only the idle unemployed, but people who indulged in 'vice or pernicious habits'. This would include mothers of more than one illegitimate child, and drunkards and gamblers.[16] Presumably if people were drunken, diseased, squalid, unhealthy or unemployed without bothering the relief agencies, no notice would be taken of them.

The Minority would have gone much further: they recommended coercion for people who lived in an unhealthy manner, with compulsory removal of their children, and this was to apply even to those destitute people who refused to ask for relief.[17] To be fair, the Minority expected that under their schemes of labour exchanges and public health, the only able-bodied unemployed would be an 'irreducible minimum' whose detention society could tolerate.

The Royal Commission, however, was fundamentally united, not only in the idea of punitive detention for the able-bodied loafer, but in a scheme for providing places of safety where everyone who was a danger to himself or others could be sent. The local authority should deal not merely with people who applied for relief, but should actively seek out those who needed help, and force them to accept it. Hence they desired compulsory removal of old people who could not look after themselves, of children whose parents were 'unsuitable', and the feeble-minded; also sick people who were infectious, malingering, or living in insanitary conditions.[18] The Majority somewhat tentatively recommended that powers might be given to the local authority to refuse to release from institutions certain sick paupers, including those with venereal disease or tuberculosis, elderly people who were infirm, and the children of 'ins and outs' if they were suffering from ophthalmia.[19]

The Commissioners did not entirely separate the medical from the purely social problems; hence both the chronic sick and the morally 'unfit' were to be compelled to enter institutions. In the case of venereal diseases, of course, the medical and moral problems were combined: the institutions were intended to solve both. Institutions would be curative, protective, educational, reformatory or penal, according to type. They seemed to provide the answer to all the intractable problems which social reform would not solve. New methods of social administration might wipe out unemployment, prevent sickness, give pensions and child welfare services, but there would always be the problem of the helpless, the 'degenerate', the 'unfit', the 'work-shy', the 'Weary

Willies and Tired Tims'. The Commissioners wished to hunt each group
into its appropriate receptacle; the Majority somewhat diffidently, the
Minority with considerable ruthlessness.[20]

It is clear that both factions of the Poor Law Commission had the
moral as well as the material welfare of society at heart. They did not
hesitate to expose the failings of the pauper class, and their separate
institutions were intended to provide classification which allowed the
'respectable' to be removed from the company of the depraved, and
the children to be free of contamination from adult paupers. The
following quotations will serve to illustrate the similar assumptions in
the two reports:[21]

> Of those who are in the workhouse there is ... a certain class –
> not as yet very large – to whom it has most unfortunately become
> attractive, the class of able-bodied loafers.
>
> It is one of the most disquieting features of the last few years that
> this 'offer of the House' is being increasingly accepted, sometimes
> sullenly, by respectable men unable to find any alternative, but,
> more frequently, with cynical alacrity, by a certain type of 'work-shy'
> of 'unemployable' who finds the gamble of picking up a living with-
> out persistent toil going against him.

It is important to consider these prejudices, which are as central to
the 1905 Commission as they were to the Commission of 1832. If the
Commissioners' attacks on the general mixed workhouse, and on Poor
Law institutions generally, were based as much on moral as on material
considerations, then the failure of the Guardians to meet the set
standards is more understandable. Some Guardians, in taking their
decisions, found that efficiency and conventional morality did not
always coincide. Who was to decide what constituted moral unfitness?
In small unions the Guardians might know most of the paupers personally,
or the Relieving Officer would be knowledgeable about people's past
lives. In a large union such information was harder to acquire, and a
pauper's behaviour once in the workhouse determined his treatment.
The Local Government Board had in fact been trying to encourage
unions to separate the deserving and the undeserving indoor paupers for
some years, but had run against practical problems.

The policy towards the aged poor in workhouses provides a good
example of the problems encountered by the enthusiastic moral classifier,
for these were an important group in the workhouses. No regular census
of the various age groups of inmates was carried out before 1913, but

the Royal Commission found that on 31 March 1906, people over 60 made up 46.5 per cent of all persons relieved.[22] Of these, nearly half were in the workhouses. Charles Booth's work had shown how the likelihood of becoming a pauper increased with age; thus in 1890, of every thousand people aged from 65 to 70, 68 were workhouse paupers, and 125 were on outdoor relief. Amongst people over 70 the likelihood of pauperism was even greater.[23] First Booth and then the Royal Commission on the Aged Poor argued that one of the greatest hardships for this group was the compulsory herding of the respectable with the depraved in the workhouses.

The Local Government Board in the late 1890s was impressed by the strength of public feeling and political pressure to 'dispauperise' the elderly. They therefore recommended outdoor relief wherever this was suitable – though the Minority Report claimed that few boards of Guardians allowed enough for old people to live on comfortably. The Board also tried to make indoor relief less unattractive for the aged poor; from 1895 they allowed much greater freedom and a better diet in the workhouses, and urged the Guardians to give preferential treatment, including tobacco and snuff rations, to the deserving. Some Guardians did try to provide separate accommodation, in a special block of the workhouse buildings, a home, or even a row of small cottages. In 1900 St Olave's (Southwark) opened a new institution on a 34-acre property, to hold 812 aged inmates in comfort. It was described as 'a home of rest for those worn-out sons of the State who through no fault of their own have come to poverty in their old age and are in need and necessity'.[24] Lambeth had two workhouses, one for the deserving aged and infirm, the other for younger paupers and the less deserving aged. The public provided gifts, concert parties and jaunts for the aged poor, and these usually went only to the deserving. But only populous unions had such specialised accommodation.

Other unions did make some effort to discriminate in favour of the deserving aged, and this usually involved adding to the already large powers of the workhouse master. It was he who classified the old paupers according to character and decided who should have the tobacco and snuff ration. Reports from the inspectors between 1895 and 1898 show the immense difficulties which this provoked. The 'indulgences' varied according to the decisions of the Guardians: at Newport in 1895 the aged had half a day out every week, and a whole day each month; in Swansea they had to be content with only one day a month. Cardiff not only allowed a day's leave weekly, but divided the aged into three classes, each clothed according to character: class I had ordinary clothes, class II wore tweed, and class III corduroy. Coventry had also instituted a 'merit' class, but the conditions for entrance were very stringent: at least ten years' previous residence in the union, and never having been on poor relief before. As a result, only nine men out of 120 and five women out of 174 were judged meritorious, and could have separate dayrooms, extra liberty and permission not to wear workhouse uniform.[25]

The inspectors noted the problem of moral classification: should a pauper be judged virtuous on his past or his present conduct? Some favoured investigation of the pauper's past by the Guardians and relieving officer; most argued that any quiet and well-behaved old pauper should be admitted into the ranks of the deserving, but warned that this might encourage sycophancy towards the workhouse master. In the eyes of most masters, a virtuous pauper was simply one who was clean, did not swear, and did what he was told. In Bath the deserving old women were placed in the 'Blue Ward', had their own garden yard and tea kettles, and could dine apart from the others. This caused so much jealousy among the elderly inmates that two old women actually refused to be promoted; there were also great quarrels when the master tried to get the less deserving inmates to clean the Blue Ward. The master and matron felt that the whole system merely added to their troubles – a dangerous proceeding with officers who were usually overworked. The old men were also classified, and the guardians were found to be trying to bribe an old man to enter the workhouse by offering him 'Class I'. J.S. Davy, later Chief Inspector, made the most reasonable comment:[26]

> no human tribunal – not even one composed of popularly elected Guardians of the poor and of officers whose appointments have been sanctioned by the Local Government Board – is justified either by knowledge or moral authority in pronouncing judgment on the character of their fellow creatures.

If the Guardians and inspectors were confused about the precise purpose of indoor relief, it was because the old and relatively simple idea that indoor relief should be merely deterrent was breaking down, and no clear alternative was seen. Specialised institutions were felt to be the answer, but on what principle should they be classified? Only in the case of children and the sick did segregation seem straightforward, but even here there were problems. The large children's homes mixed long-term resident children with the children of the 'ins and outs', but transient children might have an undesirable influence on the others.

Because they might carry not only bad habits, but disease, the 'in and out' children were often left in the workhouse, or spent most of their time in the probationary ward without education. In the case of the sick, doctors rather than Poor Law administrators claimed authority: the Bath Guardians had attempted to carry their moral classification into the sick wards, but this failed because the sick had to be dieted according to their needs rather than their characters.

Hence throughout the period the Guardians might well be found 'offering the house' for a variety of reasons. Such an offer was still used by strict boards to deter able-bodied applicants, but for other classes the Guardians were not always sure whether they were offering the house as a deterrent or as a necessary place of safety. There is evidence in local records that Guardians tried to use the same workhouse in both ways: they might withdraw outdoor relief from old people who were becoming filthy or neglected, or use the threat of the workhouse to compel a family on outdoor relief to clean up its home. Lambeth regularly offered the workhouse to families whose homes were dirty, or where the circumstances were felt to be improper, as in the case of a woman sharing her room with an adolescent son.[27] The problem was, as the Minority Commissioners pointed out, that these well-intentioned pressures had no force, and if an applicant decided to scrape along without any help, no one could prevent him. Furthermore, the Commissioners had themselves conducted surveys which indicated that people who refused indoor relief suffered hardship, and were hardly in a position to improve their habits. The Local Government Board increased the confusion by recommending in 1914 that widows with children on outdoor relief should be classified according to character: the 'weak' mothers might be forced into good behaviour by threat of the workhouse; if this failed, they would be 'better off' inside it, with their children taken into the workhouse schools.[28]

It has been shown that the arguments used against the workhouse were twofold: that it did not care for the helpless efficiently, and that it was too attractive to the idle unemployed. In 1895 one of the inspectors reflected on the comparative comfort of the workhouse, with its warmth, nutritious food, entertainments, and readily granted leave, and he concluded:[29]

There are no importunate Creditors, no pecuniary troubles. The consequence of all this is — as I believe — that a certain number of younger men ... lazy men, shiftless men who have not succeeded in life ... *do* slip into the Workhouse with the intention of staying there if they can.

It is worth trying to discover how much substance there was in these comments, for in fact the whole question was still bedevilled by that curious convention of the Poor Law which until 1891 attempted to define as able-bodied anyone who received temporary medical relief either for himself or his family. The inspectors had shown in 1880 that 'able-bodied' was interpreted by many unions to include the halt, the lame and the partially blind – anyone who was not confined to bed.[30]

After 1891 more effort was made to distinguish those 'ordinarily in health', but\the categories remained suspect. The Majority Report made a curious distinction between the 'able-bodied in health' and the 'able-bodied sick', and reported that there were 9,944 of the former class in the workhouses at the end of March 1906. The Minority agreed, and quoted their investigator, Dr T.C. Parsons, who had said that there were in every workhouse 'a number of men in every way as well developed physically as the average of the general population'.[31] Yet an examination of Parsons' evidence shows that very large numbers of these men, while technically able-bodied, were labouring under handicaps which made them very difficult to employ. A quarter of the able-bodied men were over 55 years of age. Furthermore, Parsons found amongst the able-bodied defects such as deafness, lack of height (men under five feet were at a disadvantage as casual labourers), hernias, slight feeble-mindedness, chronic bronchitis, and nervous disorders. He examined 423 able-bodied men in English workhouses and found only one-third of them capable of a full day's work.[32] Even in the able-bodied test work-house in Manchester, only 36 out of 80 men were fit enough for heavy labour. Though there were no doubt 'a number' capable of ordinary work, the tendency in official reports was always to be imprecise about what that number was.

War and then depression changed this, but the truly able-bodied never came back to the workhouses. In 1915 the Local Government Board stated that the only healthy paupers in the workhouses were people suffering from premature senility, or 'in a greater or less degree inefficient'.[33] As the number of inmates had dropped by less than 2,000 since 1913, one may conclude that the able-bodied loafers had fled to join the war effort, but that their numbers had been greatly exaggerated. From this time there was little talk of labour colonies. After the war the numbers of workhouse inmates began to climb slowly again, but did not reach their 1913 level during the 1920s, unlike the out-relief figures, which by 1927 were almost three times the level of 1913.

Few unions appear to have tried to use the workhouse as a deterrent for the able-bodied unemployed: this had not worked in the 1840s and it was not likely to be acceptable in the 1920s, in spite of the plaints of the Ministry of Health. From 1922 almost every annual report argued that relief levels could be brought down if only proper principles were applied, but even Lambeth, one of the strictest boards, said that its hands were tied; it was not possible to offer the workhouse to unemployed men who had previously been receiving unemployment insurance.[34] The last serious attempt to 'offer the house' to able-bodied men came in the long coal strike of 1926. Twenty-seven unions withdrew outdoor relief from strikers, but there was no great movement into the workhouses. Strikers and their families managed to get by with trade union help and co-op credit, often at the cost of their health.[35]

In considering the charge that workhouses provided inefficient care because of their mixed nature, two groups may be noticed particularly: the feeble-minded and the sick. All critics of the workhouse attacked the policy of mixing the feeble-minded with the old people, or using them as nurses for the infants. In 1908 the Royal Commission on the Feeble-Minded urged their removal to special institutions, but these recommendations applied mainly to the 'improveable' cases and to the young. The Commissioners were prepared to leave the chronic and senile cases and the older 'unimproveables' to be nursed in the workhouses. A Board of Control rather than the Poor Law authority should be responsible for them, but suitable Poor Law buildings might be used.[36]

The Mental Deficiency Act should have achieved some of these ends, but its effects were hindered by the war, and during the 1920s there was no strong attempt to remove the feeble-minded from the workhouses. This was less the fault of the Guardians than of the Board of Control and the county councils, who failed to use their power to build special institutions. In 1925 the Board of Control was negotiating with an unwilling Ministry of Health to move cases back into Poor Law buildings because of shortage of space in the asylums.[37] Financial stringency in public expenditure did not permit the kind of changes envisaged in 1908, and in the end it was lack of money rather than the question of who was responsible for the feeble-minded which determined their treatment.

Before the war imbeciles probably made up 12 to 20 per cent of workhouse inmates, and there is no evidence that this changed in the 1920s. It was reported in 1925 that 'anyone who has visited ... the Cardiff Workhouse, will find that ... it is a glorified mental hospital, without the equipment and without the medical care that a mental hospital should have'.[38] There was as little justification for placing the mentally handicapped in the large county asylums as there was for placing them in the workhouses: neither type of institution was equipped to treat them. Guardians were also tempted to keep some of the less serious cases in the workhouses to act as labour in those days when able-bodied paupers were decreasing. Was this inhumane, or did it give these people a closer approach to normal life than the county asylums would have done? The Commission of 1908 heard of several cases where imbeciles were apparently happy at being given useful work and regarded the workhouse as home, but the practice was rightly regarded as inferior to individual treatment. The workhouse officers were not trained to care for such cases.

The game of shuttlecock between workhouses and county asylums continued until 1929, when the Local Government Act, by reclassifying Poor Law institutions, did provide some special buildings for the handicapped, but there was no rapid action even then. Many of the old Poor Law buildings still remain as geriatric or mental asylums, and the provision for this group under the Welfare State has hardly been so impressive that the practice of the 1920s can be condemned out of hand. The Guardians were no more parsimonious than any other section of local government: county councils, like the Poor Law unions, varied in their generosity.

Many of the same comments may be made of sick paupers. The Poor Law Commissioners roundly attacked the Guardians' hospital provisions. Dr John McVail's report on the infirmaries found enormous variations, from tiny rural workhouse wards with only one nurse, to the large urban infirmaries; but even in the latter, the provision was always inferior to the voluntary hospitals. The infirmary at Kingston-on-Hull, with 335 beds, had no resident doctor. Even Guardians who were generous with equipment were likely to be niggardly with staff, and there was little incentive for a good officer to stay in a Poor Law hospital where the pay and conditions were unattractive. The voluntary hospitals had one nurse for every two or three beds; in the Poor Law infirmaries each nurse had from seven to 22 beds.[39] Infirmaries could be used for the training of nurses, but not for medical students, which also discouraged the medical profession.

The Local Government Board made some reforms in 1913 by handing authority over the sick wards from the untrained workhouse master to the medical staff. After the war the large infirmaries were opened for medical students, and Guardians were encouraged to employ specialists and use the services of consultants. The pay of both doctors and nurses rose rapidly, though it still lagged behind the voluntary hospitals. At a time when guardians were spending little on new buildings, they had to provide new hostels for nurses in order to attract staff, competition for their services being very great.

By the 1920s the problems of the Poor Law infirmaries were no longer entirely the fault of the Guardians; a study of a large infirmary like Lambeth shows that by this time the Guardians usually accepted the directives of the medical staff without question. It was the policy of the voluntary hospitals themselves which contributed to the problem. They often refused to take chronic, elderly, and hopeless cases, leaving the Poor Law institutions with patients who required much nursing but had little hope of a cure. The Poor Law infirmaries still had to take most of the venereal cases until after the war, as voluntary hospitals refused to accept them, and even the specialised Lock hospitals often would not admit the same person twice. Sick children were still placed in workhouse wards with adults, but in Lambeth it was the medical staff who objected to the children being sent away to a special hospital, on the grounds that their own work would then be less interesting.[40]

The treatment of tubercular patients posed similar problems to those of the mentally handicapped. The county councils had power to provide sanatoria, but were often dilatory. Guardians complained that because the waiting list for council sanatoria was so long, even insured patients had to enter Poor Law hospitals. In South Shields, for example, the Guardians had the entire responsibility for the care of tuberculosis; they were the residual authority and could not refuse to take cases which should have been in the charge of other bodies.[41] Without strong government pressure and financial aid, neither of which was forthcoming in the 1920s, the workhouse remained a common receptacle.

The Ministry of Health must take much of the blame for this rudderless drifting towards the specialised institutions which everyone in theory desired. The last year of the Local Government Board had been fairly active. John Burns, hoping to forestall the break-up of the Poor Law, had attempted to hasten institutional improvements, and by 1913 the Board had developed a policy which would have involved compulsory removal of children from workhouses, more medical staff with greater authority, and more money spent on the Poor Law institutions.[42] Many of the Guardians were also alarmed, and were prepared to begin reforms lest their authority be removed. This activity might have continued had it not been for the war and the depression.

The Ministry of Health was even less willing than its predecessor to sanction expenditure, except of the most necessary kind. In 1924 it noted with satisfaction that the average weekly cost per inmate had fallen by 19 per cent since 1921–2.[43] This no doubt reflected falling prices, but also reduction in new buildings. The Ministry discouraged building plans, and Guardians in the depressed areas found that in any case they were having to borrow not, as in the past, for land and construction, but to pay their outdoor relief bill.[44] At a time when the rates were failing to meet the cost of outdoor relief, institutional expenditure was bound to suffer. The whole series of Ministry of Health reports for the 1920s urged economy in institutional relief, on grounds well known to the Royal Commission of 1832 – that if some guardians were managing to keep the cost down, then the rest must be too extravagant.

Chamberlain's act of 1929 attempted to rationalise workhouses into specialised institutions without too much extra expenditure, though the block grant was a major incentive for counties to spend. But change was slow; the counties were no more eager than the Guardians to build new hospitals, asylums, vagrant hostels or geriatric homes, and it was only by shuffling the inmates between existing institutions that further specialisation was achieved. Removing the financial power from small local units to larger ones, and even to the government, did not solve the question of cost, though it probably ensured more equality of treatment than could be obtained amongst Poor Law unions of greatly varying size and wealth. Government parsimony rather than local parsimony became the chief impediment.

One further charge needs to be considered: the view expressed by so many Poor Law critics, that the institutions could not fulfil their proper function under the Poor Law because people refused to enter them, fearing the 'workhouse taint'. The evidence for this conflicts: generally speaking, the more specialised a union's institutions were, the less the 'stigma' was felt; hence there was much less reluctance to enter the separate infirmaries than the sick wards of the mixed workhouse. Few of the northern industrial unions had ever used their workhouses as a test for the able-bodied; they tended to be semi-almshouses for the aged and sick, and local feeling attached little blame to entering them.

It is possible that as the living standards of the working class improved, workhouses may have been more resented because they were no longer the inevitable lot of so many of the poor.[45] Oral tradition provides a wide variety of impressions from 'they were queueing up to get in' (of Newcastle workhouse), to a violent antipathy which extends even to the buildings in their present use (of Lambeth).[46] Ultimately it depended on the Guardians for they could make the workhouse appear shameful in a variety of petty ways. Few Guardians in the twentieth century made the aged poor wear a uniform outside the workhouse, but Poor Law clothes could easily be recognised if the Guardians insisted on buying to contract. They still did not wish to provide more than the ordinary poor could have obtained, and so one finds Poplar as well as Lambeth providing peg legs instead of the more aesthetic but expensive artificial limbs.

Yet even if we assume that the 'stigma' of the workhouses was so great that many people accepted privation rather than enter them, could not the same be said of many modern institutions? All institutional life involves a certain loss of freedom, subjection to a regime, obedience to professional staff.[47] In the case of short-term patients this may be borne without complaint. For the long-term patient, the helpless and the hopeless for whom the Poor Law provided, even a modern, expensive, specialised institution has its terrors. Old people did not care for the workhouse; contemporary experience suggests that they do not care for 'rest homes' except as a last resort. How many prefer to suffer in their own homes rather than enter an institution? The stigma has gone: the problems of institutional life remain. Nor did institutional scandals suddenly die with the Welfare State, for the people whose charge it is to care for the most helpless members of society continue to be placed under considerable strain, and abuses still occur, especially in hospitals where staff are overworked, or where the institution has become too remote from the outside world.

This has not been an attempt to resurrect the reputation of the general mixed workhouse, nor to save the Guardians, the Local Government Board or the Ministry of Health from justifiable criticism. But it should be remembered that the critics of the workhouse all offered as a solution a more specialised system of institutions. These could not be cheap to run, and would always be at the mercy of an authority with financial difficulties. In recent years both financial and social considerations have led some local authorities to favour large subsidies for families to enable them to care for their helpless members without placing them in institutions, and many schemes have been devised for by-passing residential institutions altogether. Books like Goffman's *Asylums*, which have long been required reading for students training in social work, reflect the distrust of some contemporary social thinkers for 'total institutions'. The workhouse was an early model of modern residential institutions. Although it will always be popularly associated with the Victorian period, it was a twentieth-century institution as well, and not all of the problems associated with it have disappeared.

Notes

1. This essay deals with the workhouse system in England and Wales, and all statistics refer only to these areas; differences in the Scottish system make generalisation difficult.
2. This seems to have applied particularly in Wales, where there was a long tradition of hostility to the workhouse system. Outdoor relief was given where possible, and infirmaries were often inadequate. See T.D. Jones, 'Poor Law and Public Health administration in the area of Merthyr Tydfil Union 1834–1894', M.A. thesis, Wales 1961, pp. 390, 407. Also *8th Annual Report of the Ministry of Health*, Parl. Papers 1927 (2938) ix, p. 888.
3. E.g. *Ministry of Health. Chester-le-Street Union . . .* PP 1927 (2818) xi, p. 1128.
4. S. and B. Webb, *English Local Government*, Vol. 9: *English Poor Law History*, Part II, pp. 375–95.
5. HMSO, *Report of the Royal Commission on the Poor Laws and Relief of Distress*, 1909. Minority Report pt. I, p. 22.
6. *43rd Report L.G.B.* PP 1914 (7444) xxxviii, p. 104. This does not include the cost of maintenance in the county asylums.
7. *1st Report M.O.H.* PP 1920 (932) xvii, p. 302. The expenditure percentages do not include the casual poor, and the inmate precentages do, but their number at this time was so low (around 2,000) that they do not affect the conclusion.
8. This figure is for England and Wales excluding London, where infirmaries were more expensive and elaborate. The weekly cost of a workhouse inmate in London was 18s 5½d, and of an infirmary patient 37s 6¼d.
9. GLC County Hall, La Bg 14.
10. Notts. archives, PUB/3.
11. *Minority Report*, p. 10.
12. *Majority Report* i, p. 174.
13. For a general history see B. Abel-Smith, *The Hospitals 1800–1948* (1964).
14. S. and B. Webb, *Poor Law Policy* (1910), pp. 122, 216,ff. *Report of the Royal Commission on the Care and Control of the Feeble Minded* PP 1908 (4202) xxxix, p. 219. But they noted that the shame of pauperism and loss of the franchise prevented many families from seeking institutional treatment for their feeble-minded members, p. 204.
15. *R.C. on Feeble-Minded*, PP 1908 (4202) xxxix, p. 221.
16. *Majority Report* ii, pp. 240–1.
17. *Minority Report* ii, p. 715.
18. *Majority Report* ii, p. 239, *Minority Report* i, p. 231.
19. *Majority Report* i, p. 243.
20. For a critique of the Minority Report for over-classification, see U. Cormack, 'The Royal Commission on the Poor Laws 1905–9 and the Welfare State', in A.V.S. Lochhead (ed.), *A Reader in Social Administration* (1968), pp. 93 ff.
21. They are respectively from *Majority Report* i, p. 185; *Minority Report* ii, p. 465.
22. *Majority Report* i, p. 59.
23. C. Booth, *The Aged Poor in England and Wales: Condition* (1894), p. 42.
24. *Lancet*, 21 July 1900, p. 204: the words are those of the chairman of the

guardians.

25. PRO MH 32/93. F.T. Bircham, 19 September 1895. T.H. Murray Browne, 24 September 1895.
26. Ibid. J.S. Davy, 5 October 1895.
27. County Hall, La Bg 64/1, 21 October 1896, p. 611.
28. *44th Report L.G.B.* PP 1916 (8195) xii, p. 608 ff.
29. PRO MH 32/93, H.B. Kennedy, 21 September 1895.
30. Lengthy reports on the subject appear in PRO MH 32/93, 1878, 1880.
31. *Majority Report* i, p. 66. *Minority Report* ii, p. 466.
32. *R.C. on the Poor Laws*, appendix vol. xxiv. PP 1910 (5076) lii, p. 53.
33. *44th Report L.G.B.* PP 1916 (8195) xii, p. 557.
34. County Hall, La Bg 94/1, 17 April 1926, p. 201.
35. P. Ryan, 'The Poor Law in 1926', in M. Morris, *The General Strike* (1976), p. 375.
36. *R.C. on the Feeble Minded* PP 1908 (4202) xxxix, p. 239.
37. PRO MH 57/23.
38. Ibid., *The Provision of Mental Hospital Accommodation, Report . . .* (1925), p. 25.
39. *R.C. on the Poor Laws* PP 1909 (4573) xlii, p. 49.
40. County Hall, La Bg 94/1 17 March 1926, p. 194 ff.
41. P. Mawson, 'Poor Law Administration in South Shields 1830–1930', MA thesis Newcastle (1971), p. 101.
42. See the Poor Law Institutions Order 1913.
43. *5th Report M.O.H.* P.P. 1924 (2218) ix, p. 860.
44. B.J. Elliot, 'The Last Five Years of the Sheffield Guardians', *Trans. Hunterian Arch. Soc.* x, pt 2, p. 135.
45. Mawson op. cit. p. 136. N. McCord, 'The Implementation of the 1834 Poor Law Amendment Act on Tyneside', *International Review of Social History* xiv, 1 (1969) p. 107.
46. My evidence from oral sources is admittedly scanty; it is much easier to obtain reminiscenses from people who visited the workhouse or who worked in it, than it is to find those who will admit to having been inmates, even as children. I hope to conduct more of this kind of inquiry.
47. See E. Goffman, *Asylums: Essays on the Social Situation of Mental Patients and Other Inmates* (Pelican 1968) for sociological discussion of this subject, especially 'On the Characteristics of Total Institutions'.

'POPLARISM' 1894–1930

P.A. Ryan

Introduction

'Poplarism' has had a bad press from historians. In essence a method of assisting the unemployed and the underprivileged through the unlikely machinery of the Poor Law, it was widely stigmatised in the 1920s by both the press and politicians, whose criticisms created the bogey of 'red' Guardians demoralising the poor and squandering the rates. The most valuable study available – that of the Webbs in the last volume of their Poor Law history – is a contemporary account, dominated by the authors' own moral assumptions about the inherent evil of unconditional outdoor relief or 'doles'.[1] More surprisingly, recent historians have restated the stories of the 1920s uncritically using language which prejudices the case and leaves little room for objective assessment.[2]

This paper will examine the development of radical policies by the Poplar Guardians from the late nineteenth century until the abolition of the Boards in 1930. It will argue that Poplarism represented a deliberate attempt to use the existing institutions of local government, as represented by the Boards of Guardians, to protect and maintain working-class living standards in the periods of crisis, 1903–6 and 1908–9, and in the continuous depression of the 1920s. Poplar was not a typical Poor Law union, but it has been chosen because of its notoriety, and because it provides one of the best documented examples of local administration being used for admittedly political ends by organised labour, first as a minority group and, after 1919, as the controlling party.

Poplar's radicalism as regards welfare was not confined to the treatment of unemployment, but as this was increasingly the major issue in social policy in the period, this paper will concentrate on this aspect. It is hoped to clarify the relationship between local politics and the emergence of government policy, particularly in the 1920s when successive governments were under pressure to create some sort of national policy on unemployment, to analyse the role of organised pressure groups in local politics, and to identify the forces making for change.

Poplar – The Background

The policies cannot be understood without some knowledge of the social context in which they developed. 'Poplar' describes both the Poplar Union (made up of the three civil parishes of Bow, Bromley St Leonards and All Saints, Poplar) and the Poplar Metropolitan Borough established in 1899 under the London Government Act. The boundaries, most unusually, coincide. The parliamentary constituency of Poplar comprised Poplar parish and the southern part of Bromley parish; the other 'Poplar' constituency was Bow and Bromley which covered the parish of Bow and the northern part of Bromley.[3]

At the end of the nineteenth century this was an overwhelmingly working-class area, and though not quite the poorest East End union, by all available social indicators it ranked amongst the most deprived.[4] By the end of the nineteenth century it was probably getting poorer as the middle classes and better-off artisans moved out to suburban Essex.[5] The crux of Poplar's social problem was the very large proportion of unskilled and casual labour among the workforce, dependent on the docks, transport and haulage, railways and manufacturing industries such as clothing, food, jam-making, matches, etc. Even engineering, Poplar's most skilled, best paid industry was prone to irregularity.[6] It has been estimated that about 29.9 per cent of the male workforce was unskilled in 1901, and 25.3 per cent semi-skilled.[7]

Labour Politics

The emergence of labour politics must be seen against this background. Up to 1914 two figures were dominant, Will Crooks and George Lansbury. After the war Crooks (who died in 1921) was less important and the Lansbury family was identified with Poplarism in the public eye. This is misleading in some ways, as the Poplar Labour movement consisted of many dedicated local socialists who were responsible for the continuous programme of education and organisation which gave the post-war Labour Party its impressive grass-roots strength.[8]

Both parliamentary constituencies were represented by Liberal and Conservative MPs until 1910, when Lansbury was elected for Bow in the December election.[9] However, in local politics Poplar, since the 1890s, had been, together with Woolwich and West Ham, one of the most successful areas in London for the new Labour movement. A Poplar Labour Electoral Committee was founded in December 1891 by a meeting of delegates from 'labour, temperance and advanced societies' with the aim of seeking independent labour representation on local bodies. By 1895 it had succeeded in getting Crooks on to the LCC, and could list its representatives on the Board of Guardians, the Poplar and Bromley Vestries, and the Tower Hamlets School Board.[10]

The Labour League (as it became) was Lib-Lab in character and occasionally came into conflict with the other major labour organisation in Poplar, the Marxist Bow and Bromley Social Democratic Federation. This had been founded by Lansbury and a group of ex-Liberals in 1892, and quickly established itself as a vehicle for the militant left, with strong backing in the Gas Workers Union. The SDF had a consistent policy of attempting to capture local government. In Poplar Lansbury and two others quickly became Guardians. Ultimately, Lansbury and his supporters broke with the SDF, after which they formed an ILP branch which affiliated to the Trades and Labour Representation League founded in 1904.[11]

This rather mixed labour group never obtained an absolute majority on the Board of Guardians before 1914, its membership ranging from 7 to 10 out of 24. On many policy issues, however, it was able to gain the support of organised pressure groups of the unemployed, and was able to dominate the Board until 1910, when there was a marked reaction against 'advanced' policies.

The labour group was opposed in the 1890s by a mixture of Independents, Conservatives and Liberals, and from 1905 by an extremely militant ratepayers association, the Municipal Alliance, formed by an amalgamation of Conservatives and Liberals — though non-aligned Liberals remained outside it — in response to the financial demands of higher rates resulting from socialist policies. A similar situation existed on the Poplar Borough Council whose labour membership overlapped with that of the Guardians.

The activity of labour groups in local government represented a coherent policy. The SDF and ILP argued that local government could be used in the interests of the working class, though both recognised the limitations of 'palliative' social policies under capitalism.[12] As regards the Poor Law, the SDF argued that although its basic objective 'was to keep the working people in the labour market', local control made it a potentially more democratic instrument than, for instance, the County Councils with their provision for co-opted members.[13] On these grounds the party opposed the recommendations of both the Majority and Minority Reports of the Royal Commission on the Poor Laws for the abolition of the Guardians. A leading member, Harry Quelch, expressed this view in its extreme form in a public debate with Lansbury. He claimed that 'so far from the Poor Law being bankrupt, if it had been administered in the interests of the workers, in it lay the possibilities of social revolution'.[14] This attitude was the direct forerunner of that of the Communist Party in the 1920s.

The period in which Poplarism first flourished, therefore, was one in which socialists of different types were formulating ideas about the Poor Law. These, if carried to their logical conclusions, would have stood the law on its head, by exploiting to the full the legal provisions of the statutes and relief regulations, and by subjecting Boards of Guardians to popular control. These policies were to come to fruition in the drastically changed circumstances of the 1920s.

In practice the policies of the Labour Guardians in Poplar were initially very similar to those of advanced Radicals and Progressives. They embraced a wide spectrum of advanced, but fairly non-political, reform covering matters such as workhouse administration, better treatment for the old and an expansion of facilities for children. These could be criticised as 'extravagant' by aggrieved ratepayers but were not normally regarded as subverting the basic principles of the Poor Law. The Local Government Board Inspector for London spoke favourably of Poplar in his annual reports and it was not until the emergence of 'indiscriminate' out-relief policies for the unemployed that the wrath of the Poor Law Department was aroused.[15]

The ideas of the labour group as regards social policy and unemployment were not always consistent, as they evolved gradually in response to a series of problems, but certain recurrent points can be distinguished. Both the SDF and ILP argued, with varying degrees of emphasis, that unemployment was a structural feature of a capitalist economy, aggravated in Poplar by the preponderance of casual labour. Ultimately, they believed, the solution lay in the social ownership and control of the economy, but more immediately they urged a range of policies – the eight-hour day, a national department of public works, programmes of reafforestation etc. – to help eliminate the problem.[16] Such policies were concerned more with the provision of work than with questions of out-relief or doles to the unemployed themselves.

This emphasis appears again in the discussions of the Poor Law. Above all, the Poplar Guardians demanded rate equalisation throughout London – a demand which was supported by many non-socialists – together with the organisation of London into one union for the treatment of the unemployed. This London union was to be empowered, with government financial aid, to establish farms, workshops and labour colonies which would not only provide training facilities for the genuinely unemployed, but also regulate and detain the 'loafer' and 'habitual pauper'.[17] It is this evidence of strongly entrenched ideas about the 'residuum', 'the loafer' and the 'malingerer', and the clear distinction drawn between this group and the respectable unemployed that is perhaps most striking to the modern reader.[18]

Both Crooks and Lansbury – and SDF writers such as Quelch – argued that they were against giving relief to the unemployed without any conditions, but in the absence of available work, saw it as an unavoidable evil. Quelch perhaps expressed the position most clearly:

> I do not consider that an able-bodied person is entitled to relief at all, but I do say that an able-bodied person is entitled to the opportunity of self-maintenance. That is our position. An able-bodied pauper appears to us to be an anachronism in a rational, civilised society.[19]

Logically therefore, when work was provided, the man who refused it was liable to be detained and controlled by society, though it would seem that Lansbury and Crooks were prepared to see compulsory detention as essential for the reform of capitalist society rather than as necessary or desirable in a socialist society.[20]

Poplar Unemployment Policies

Poplar was faced with three crises of unemployment in the period 1894–1914, the first in the winters of 1893–4 and 1894–5, the second in the depression of 1902–5 and the third in 1908. They illustrate the gradual evolution by local authorities of policies to tackle unemployment, moving away from the traditional methods (public works, stoneyards, etc.) to a more sophisticated approach, which involved nevertheless a heavy reliance on the Poor Law and led to intervention by the Local Government Board (LGB).

In all three periods the Board of Guardians was at least in part responding to popular pressure. In the later crises they were attempting to draw attention to what seemed to them to be the unfair burden of local responsibility.

Poplar Policy in the 1890s

In the 1890s Poplar met the recurrence of its unemployment problem with traditional methods. Crooks described to the Davy Enquiry of 1906 the Guardians' co-operation with philanthropy in the winter of 1892–3. A distress committee, set up by the Rector of Poplar, raised £5,000 to deal with the distress arising from unemployment. Crooks pithily described how his influence had changed this committee, from one dominated by clergy and social workers, to a workmanlike body:

'Well', I said, 'you will never do anything with gentlemen like these:
what you have got to do is get hold of the trade union secretaries,
or the secretary of a temperance society, or the secretary of a
friendly society, and ask him to come and help you, and he will be
able to discriminate between the waster and the deserving man.'[21]

The Guardians themselves do not seem to have taken special measures.
The labour group was not elected until April 1893 and in the summer
of 1893 the Bow and Bromley SDF and the Gasworkers Union attempted
to persuade the Guardians to call a conference on unemployment.
Lansbury, acting in conjunction with the SDF, raised the question of
labour colonies for the first time.[22] He tried unsuccessfully to exert
pressure on the Guardians by introducing deputations of the unemployed
demanding to be set to work. This was because the Rector's Distress
Committee had accepted an offer by A.S. Hills of the Thames
Shipbuilding Company to provide £1,000 for relief works if the District
Board did likewise.[23] Crooks claimed that he persuaded the Board to
accept. Hence a Labour Bureau was established at which the men
registered whilst the Rectory Committee investigated all applicants.
About 600 men were given three days'work, such as road-paving and
stone-breaking, but the total cost was over £15,000, about double
what the work would normally have cost. Hills himself later expressed
disillusionment with this method of relief.[24]

Lansbury clearly had not enough influence to wean the Guardians
away from orthodoxy in 1893–4, but was enabled to do so by severe
weather in February 1895. This led to deputations of the unemployed
approaching the Guardians again. On 15 February 1895, at an
emergency meeting summoned by Lansbury and his two SDF colleagues
after liaison with the unemployed groups, the Guardians voted
unanimously to open a stoneyard.[25] Lansbury and the SDF group
were clearly the dominating force. Crooks disliked the stoneyard, which
he argued was both demoralising for respectable workers and prohibited
discrimination between them and others. On 5 March he moved a
successful motion for its closure, only the SDF group of three opposing.
The reaction to the closure was violent; 150 men entered the workhouse
demanding relief.[26]

This conflict between Crooks and Lansbury was less concerned with
stoneyards as such — both disliked them — than over the nature of their
response to popular pressure and the extent of distress. Lansbury —
Chairman of the Board from January to April 1895 — explained in a
letter:

You will have heard that our representations to the Board of Works were of no avail and as a consequence the Guardians are opening a stoneyard. I am sorry but people must be fed, it is aweful (sic) all one has to see and hear. I feel desperate sometimes, and it is always an effort to be moderate.[27]

The pattern which emerges, of unemployed demonstrations, contact between the Lansbury group and the unemployed and the pressurising of Guardians, was one which was to become familiar in the future.

1903

The experience of the stoneyard was not repeated. The Poplar Guardians seem to have accepted the repeated objections to their use in the Local Government Board's Annual Reports. The unemployment question did not appear in an acute form again until 1903; such criticism as was directed against the Guardians by ratepayers, among others, was concerned with questions such as out-relief to the aged, widows, etc. and lenient administration of the casual wards.[28]

By 1903–6 the two leading Labour Guardians in Poplar, Lansbury and Crooks, were public figures. Crooks became MP for Woolwich in 1903, first Labour Mayor of Poplar in 1901–2, and had held the position of Chairman of the Poplar Board of Guardians since 1897. Lansbury was well-known in Labour and Progressive circles as a writer on social policy, and, in 1905, was appointed a member of the Royal Commission on the Poor Laws.

Poor Law administration in Poplar in 1903–6 should be seen in the context of the prolonged agitation about unemployment carried out by the SDF, ILP and the Labour Committee for the Unemployed.[29] Poplar played a leading role in this agitation, both through public statements by Lansbury and Crooks, and through the organisation of demonstrations such as the deputation of women and unemployed, led by Mr and Mrs Crooks, Lansbury and Harry Quelch, which approached Balfour on the inadequacies of the Unemployed Workmen Act on 6 November 1905.[30] The Unemployed Workmen Act could be regarded as partially fulfilling Poplar's demands since 1894, as Sidney Buxton admitted in a private letter to Lansbury.[31] However, Poplar's demand for rates equalisation was not achieved in 1905. J.S. Davy argued in his Report of 1906 that in 1903–6 a high rate of pauperism was deliberately fostered in Poplar as a strategem

to produce a situation which would compel the government to interfere, so as to bring about an equalisation of the rates within the metropolitan area, and legislation with regard to unemployment in accordance with the political views of the leaders.

This is a plausible argument, though there is no direct evidence to support it, as there is, for instance, for the events of 1921. It must be said that Davy also played down other evidence relating to the treatment of unemployment in Poplar, not simply by the Guardians, but as part of the concerted policy involving the Borough Council and the Distress Committee. This resulted in the decasualisation of work provided as relief by the Council, which won the praise of such orthodox commentators as the Rev J.C. Pringle and Mr Cyril Jackson.[32]

Such a policy, however, by curtailing the number of men on relief projects, was bound to increase pressure on the Guardians by the unemployed. Although Poor Law orthodoxy could still assert that outrelief should not have been given to the able-bodied, the situation clearly placed tremendous strains on the entire system. In the context of Poor Law administration as a whole, Poplar is the most extreme example of a tendency which the Local Government Board noted in several unions following the Local Government Act of 1894, namely for Guardians to be elected on liberal outdoor relief policies and to claim that such policies would reduce indoor relief.[33] In London the situation was peculiar, in that the provisions of the Metropolitan Common Poor Fund established in 1869 made it financially more attractive for Guardians to offer indoor than outdoor relief; consequently London's rate of indoor pauperism was always higher than the outdoor, and higher than the national rate. At the same time improvements in Poor Law institutions which had taken place in the last two decades of the nineteenth century removed much of their deterrence in the eyes of the orthodox. Similarly, progressive changes in Local Government Board (LGB) policy, such as the Chaplin circular of 1900 on more generous relief to the aged, together with much writing of the Inspectors on the mischief of 'inadequate doles', could be used by a determined and political Board such as Poplar's to justify its own policies.[34]

Nationally, the earlier years of the twentieth century witnessed a steady increase in the cost of relief — starting in the 1890s — and a check on the fall in the number of those relieved which had occurred since the mid-nineteenth century. Particularly alarming to orthodox upholders of Poor Law principles was the increasing number of the ablebodied claiming relief, although they remained a minute proportion of the total. All of this suggested a weakening of the 'principles of 1834' and was the subject of much discussion in Poor Law circles.[35]

The labour group and its supporters on the Borough Council tried two distinct policies for dealing with unemployment during the depression of 1902–5, neither of them including generous out-relief. First, in the winter of 1902–3, when there was much distress in Poplar, press appeals were made, distress funds started and soup kitchens opened. In December 1902 the *East End News* Relief Fund raised £7,000, of which £2,500 was spent in Poplar. Meanwhile the Borough Council opened a labour register and decided to put in hand all possible public works; a total of 4,460 men were registered, of whom 2,458 received work, largely in periods of three days. In the following winter, 1903–4, distress reappeared and a more sustained attempt was made to use public works to combat unemployment. A municipal labour bureau was again opened, and 4,021 men registered and 3,300 were given employment in periods ranging from three days for the majority to three weeks for the lucky minority. As Pringle and Jackson commented in their report to the Royal Commission on the Poor Laws, the net result of this effort 'was a dole of about a sovereign apiece in employment relief to 3,000 of them (i.e. the unemployed) at a cost to the borough of £20,000'.[36]

The following winter saw the peak of the distress. The labour group adopted a different policy, entirely in accordance with current thinking about the evils of casual work and the need to regularise work offered by public authorities. A census taken by the Guardians revealed an unemployment rate of 24.12 per cent.[37] On 14 October 1904 Lansbury and Crooks, together with a number of leading philanthropists and Poor Law experts including Canon Barnett, William Vallence, the Clerk to the Whitechapel Guardians, and H.R. Maynard of the COS wrote to the *Times* asking that any work given to the unemployed should be on conventional lines. Lansbury argued strongly before the Davy Inquiry that the three days' work system was both too expensive and demoralising;

... this is the most pernicious system possible because you just tide these men over in exactly the same way you do with out-relief ... the men had no initiative to work because they knew they would have their three days whether or no.[38]

Hence work was now given in Poplar on a regular basis, i.e. a number of men were hired to do specific jobs, rather than sharing work amongst as many as possible.

In consequence only 129 men per week were given work by the borough council, compared with 700 in the previous year, though the work was for longer periods, and in some cases represented the largest continuous period of work the applicant had ever had. It increased pressure on the Guardians; their response caused a great climb in the outdoor pauperism figures from November 1904 onwards. This policy continued in the winter of 1905–6, by which time a statutory Distress Committee under the Unemployed Workmen Act had been established. This co-operated with the municipal labour register until July 1906 when the latter was taken over by the Central Unemployed Body. In all, 3,615 men registered between November 1905 and July 1906, of whom 631 were given temporary work, and 9 permanent. A total of 2,584 men were still registered in July 1906.[39] According to Sidney Buxton, the Distress Committee itself adopted a policy of referring men *en masse* to the Guardians, whilst it certainly found work for only 311 men, and emigrated a further 42.[40]

The second strand of Poplar's policy was that of the Guardians. Until the autumn of 1904, out-relief does not seem to have been regarded as a particularly suitable method of dealing with the able-bodied unemployed on a large scale. By the end of 1902, the workhouse was grossly over-crowded, though it is not clear how many inmates were unemployed. The Guardians bought the Well Street workhouse from the Hackney Union specifically for use for able-bodied men. In January 1903, 98 of the latter were moved into the new institution.[41]

Well Street was organised on traditional lines with nine hours' task work a day, including oakum picking for refractory inmates. But it was only a temporary solution, for in the summer of 1903 the Well Street lease expired. Thereafter the Guardians were concerned with Lansbury's hobby horse, the purchase of land in Essex from the wealthy American Joseph Fels, for use as a farm colony for the unemployed. Indoor accommodation was still limited and there was much discussion of alternative places for the unemployed, and of means of providing work; some were sent to the Lingfield and Hadleigh farm colonies.[42] Out-relief still played no apparent part in this discussion, and in November 1903 only four men received out-relief on the grounds of 'sudden or urgent necessity' which was the normal way of giving relief to the unemployed.[43]

In March 1904 the Guardians took formal possession of land at Laindon, Essex, leased by Fels on favourable terms. This was regarded as a farm colony by Lansbury, and is described as such in the Minutes of the Board, but the Local Government Board persistently regarded it as a branch workhouse.[44] Men were moved in the summer of 1904.

In October 1904 the Guardians drew up a resolution for the conference of local authorities, in which they again demanded a single London Union for the treatment of unemployment and stressed the need for work training and labour colonies. There was no mention of out-relief. By now the distress in Poplar was considerable and the Labour Guardians were heavily involved in the unemployed agitation which accompanied the development of the Long scheme.

The crucial events took place on 16 November 1904 when a deputation of the unemployed led by a Mr Salmon was received by the Guardians, and demanded assistance. Salmon had been appointed by the Poplar Trades and Labour Council to organise the unemployed, and according to W.G. Martley, the District Secretary of the Charity Organisation Society (who was surprisingly sympathetic to the Guardians) the deputation was part of a concerted effort to influence the Guardians to give out-relief to the unemployed.[45]

The Board discussed what to do in the presence of the men. A.A. Watts (an SDF member, later a founding member of the CPGB in 1920) moved a resolution — supported by a non-Socialist Guardian — that 150 acres of land should be bought for the purpose of setting men to work. Lansbury moved the purchase of another farm, and argued strongly that the Poor Law could deal *more* satisfactorily with the unemployed than Borough Councils, providing 'the disfranchisement clause could be got rid of'. He was clearly thinking of labour colonies, however, and argued that out-relief under Article 10 of the 1852 Relief Regulation Order was demoralising.[46] Eventually they decided to approach the LGB on the question of land, but as an interim measure decided to apply Article 10 to able-bodied applicants. Martley insisted that *all* the Guardians agreed to this.

It is difficult to judge how far the Labour Guardians deliberately intended to inaugurate a policy of out-relief, and how far they were pushed into it by events. The general evidence of the writings of Lansbury and Crooks in this period is that they saw out-relief as an unpleasant necessity, and certainly Lansbury was obsessed with labour colonies. J.S. Davy implies that the affair was designed by the Lansbury group to draw attention to Poplar, as a means of pressurising Balfour into holding an autumn session of Parliament. Again this is plausible. The pattern of unemployed deputations organised by sympathetic Guardians was to be systematically repeated in the 1920s.

In December 1904 the Board applied for the Modified Workhouse

Test Order to be applied in Poplar so that some of the unemployed
could be sent to Laindon, but in the same month the LGB refused to
allow the Board to buy land for the purposes of setting the poor to
work.[47] The Guardians were therefore left simply with the out-relief
policy and their farm at Laindon.

From this date onward the numbers on out-relief rose rapidly. Outdoor paupers on 1 January each year numbered 3,509 in 1903, 4,069
in 1904, 7,886 in 1905 and 7,330 in 1906. The ratio of outdoor paupers
(excluding vagrants and imbeciles) per thousand population rose from
19.2 in 1903 to 21.8 in 1904 and 35.9 in 1905. The only comparable
unions in the London area were Bermondsey, and the Canning Town
district of West Ham, but the increases there were confined to shorter
periods, whereas in Poplar they showed no sign of decreasing, even in
the relatively mild winter of 1905–6.[48]

There was a sharp political reaction to this turn of events, particularly
as the rates had increased from 6s 1d in the £ in 1885 to 12s in 1905.
In May 1905 a ratepayers' all-party grouping, the Municipal Alliance,
was formed; on 17 October it petitioned the LGB for an inquiry into
all the rate-supported local authorities. The Guardians were involved
in a correspondence with the Municipal Alliance, and in November
wrote to the LGB welcoming the chance to remove many misconceptions in a public enquiry.[49] The LGB finally decided to hold an enquiry
in spring 1906. They were influenced in their decision by reports from
the Essex police about the behaviour of the Laindon men, by a disallowance of out-relief in a test case brought by the District Auditor,
and a letter from the Finance Committee of the LCC querying the
financial viability of the Guardians.[50] It was eventually agreed that
the Inquiry should be public and that the Municipal Alliance,
representing 30 per cent of the rateable value of the borough, should
be allowed to produce evidence and cross-examine witnesses.[51]

The Enquiry

The Enquiry took place in the boardroom of the Poplar Guardians
between 7 June and 26 July 1906; 'Great interest was taken in the
proceedings throughout, and there was a large attendance daily of
Guardians, ratepayers and others[. . .'.[52] J.S. Davy, an assistant
secretary at the LGB was well known for his orthodox views on the
Poor Law, and the Labour Guardians claimed that he had prejudged
their case.[53] Before the enquiry he investigated conditions in the
district, attended relief committee meetings and drew up a statistical
memorandum which was attached as an appendix to his report.

Throughout the enquiry the Municipal Alliance was represented by counsel, E. Elvy Robb, and after the fourth day the Guardians by the radical barrister, Corrie Grant, and old friend of Lansbury's from his Liberal days.[54]

The enquiry covered both the administration of the workhouse – which was enlivened by the revelation of an affair between the master and one of the nurses – and the granting of contracts, but attention here will be confined to its treatment of policy towards the unemployed. It is worth emphasising, however, that Crooks and Lansbury were exonerated from any charges of corruption or misconduct as regards the workhouse scandals or the contracts, and that J. McCarthy, the Guardian apparently most involved in the workhouse scandals, was *not* associated with the labour group.[55]

It is not surprising that Davy criticised the policy of the Guardians as regards out-relief to the unemployed. From the viewpoint of orthodox Poor Law policy there was no defence possible. Both Crooks and Lansbury were on weak ground in attempting to argue that the special conditions of Poplar, rather than their administration, caused the high pauperism statistics. Clearly it *was* a matter of policy and administration. The labour group's rather defensive attitude at this stage contrasts with their more radical approach in the 1920s. Then they were prepared to admit that they were in effect manipulating the Poor Law.

Davy pointed out that from the third week in February 1906, when news of the enquiry was announced, the figures of pauperism fell, particularly for outdoor relief. He argued that this reflected the administrative nature of the crisis, quoting the evidence of a local schoolteacher of radical inclination, Miss Clara Grant, 'that the Guardians were showing a great want of moral courage in being affected by the fact that they were somewhat under a cloud'.[56]

Davy's Report is notable for its combination of Poor Law orthodoxy with strict fairness. Granted his lack of sympathy with this abuse of the 1834 principles, he at all times put both sides of the case. Thus, although highly critical of the direct pressure put on Relieving Officers by some Guardians, of the failure to report all departures from the Relief Regulations Order under Article 10, and of the automatic granting of out-relief to the unemployed, he admitted that some relief committees did their work carefully, citing that chaired by A.A. Watts of the SDF. Similarly he wrote that

some excuse for the policy of the Guardians may be found in the fact that many of them actually live among the applicants for relief, and know, or think they know, the individual circumstances of each case.[57]

The idea that the Labour Guardians were in close contact with the local community, that they had a definite policy as regards the poor, and were attempting to educate their followers was one of the most interesting things to emerge from the enquiry. In various ways, the evidence of Martley, of Miss Clara Grant, and of the Rev H.A. Mosley, the Rector, all confirmed this view of the Guardians. Martley indeed went so far as to argue that as a result of this policy 'revolutionary anarchism is now non-existent in Poplar and . . . the sense of citizenship has reached and is daily more and more pervading the lowest strata of the people'.[58]

Davy's general conclusion, probably rightly, was that the policy of the Labour Guardians had basically political aims. He made no definite recommendations for future policy, except in the case of the Laindon farm colony which he felt should be used only as a branch workhouse. The Report and evidence were given much publicity when published in October 1906. José Harris has argued that the criticisms of Laindon affected particularly adversely the Central Unemployed Body's plans to extend the farm colony movement.[59]

Post-Enquiry Policy

There has been little attempt to trace the subsequent policy of the Poplar Guardians. The unspoken assumption of historians has been that the 1906 enquiry was a defeat for the labour group. In fact, the decline in pauperism at the time of the enquiry was short-lived, and from autumn 1906 onwards there was a steady rise. The workhouse was overcrowded, and the Guardians were also concerned that their lease on Laindon was due to expire in March 1907. Consequently, they again adopted a policy of granting out-relief to the able-bodied, under Article 10 of the 1852 Order, in the absence of any further accommodation of the farm colony type.[60] Unemployed agitation revived and as the Guardians were at the same time involved in negotiations with the LGB about the purchase of another farm, it is possible that this was another attempt to put pressure on the Department. In April 1907, Crooks having resigned the Chairmanship, two Municipal Alliance members, A.W. Yeo and R.V. Broodbank, were elected Chairman and Vice-Chairman respectively. Despite a concerted effort by the Municipal Alliance in both the municipal and Guardians elections, the labour group was not swept away but remained a strong minority on both local bodies.[61]

The policy of granting Article 10 relief continued and was increasingly a cause of LGB concern, leading eventually to a special meeting in November 1907 between Oxley, the Poor Law Inspector for London, and the Guardians. On this occasion, the Guardians *opposed* the offer of the house to the unemployed because it meant breaking up families. A compromise solution, the adoption of the Modified Workhouse Test Order (MWTO), was recorded. This meant that whilst the men entered the workhouse their wives and families could remain at home.[62]

Out-relief figures continued to rise in the depressed year of 1908 however, and Oxley was critical both of the generous scale of relief given and the lax administration of the workhouses where the men were accommodated. Eventually the LGB took drastic action by subjecting Poplar to a Special Order (in October 1908). Under this order, relief to a family under the MWTO was limited to eight weeks in the year, and the men themselves were subjected to stringent workhouse regulations.[63] The next 18 months saw a policy of obstruction by the Labour Guardians, which was unsuccessful due to the striking victories won by the Municipal Alliance in the 1910 Guardians elections. By the spring of 1912 an insignificant number of able-bodied were receiving relief. Despite an upsurge in the outdoor figures in the summer due to the dock strike, the first phase of Poplarism was over.[64]

Poplarism in the 1920s

The coming of mass unemployment as a long-term feature of the economy at the end of 1920, and the granting of a fairly comprehensive unemployment insurance system, should not be interpreted as a radical new attitude towards unemployment and the unemployed in official circles. The circumstances had indeed drastically changed since the pre-war period, but there was much continuity in attitudes and policies. Pre-Keynesian economic orthodoxy dominated government policy, and unemployment insurance itself cannot be regarded as more than the price various governments were prepared to pay to maintain a degree of social stability. The view of the 1920s as a period in which substantial gains were made by the unemployed, has been modified by Alan Deacon in a recent article.[65] In the area of Poor Law administration, the inherent ambivalence towards the unemployed received clearest definition simply because in itself it represented the much older orthodoxy of nineteenth-century political economy.

Outdoor relief was now governed by the Relief Regulation Order of

1911, which simplified and consolidated all previous outdoor relief orders. It made no alteration in the 'broad principles governing the administration of outdoor relief by the Guardians', but tried to put into practice the recommendation of the Royal Commission on the Poor Laws that such relief should be given

> only after thorough enquiry except in cases of sudden and urgent necessity, when it should be adequate to meet the needs of those to whom it is given, and that persons so assisted should be subject to supervision.

In exceptional circumstances, relief to the able-bodied could be granted on performance of a work test, or the man could enter the workhouse whilst his family remained outside (the former MWTO) or, most momentously in the light of future developments, under Article XII the regulations could be departed from and unconditional relief in kind granted provided the departure was reported to the Local Government Board (after 1919, Ministry of Health) within 21 days. It was this loophole which allowed Poplar and other unions to pursue policies diametrically opposed to the principles of 1834.

From 1921 onwards the Poor Law reeled under the impact of mass unemployment, and the total figures of pauperism never fell below one million, reaching nearly 2½ million in August 1926, as a result of the combined effects of the General Strike and the miners' lockout.[66] Apart from the increase in numbers, the most striking change, compared with the pre-1914 period, is in the pattern of regional distribution. Before 1914 the rural areas of the south and west had maintained the highest rates of pauperism; the increases now were largely concentrated in the great industrial centres, above all the coalfields, and in London. The growth of pauperism in the 1920s suggests a breakdown in central control, and this in fact took place as soon as the flood of unemployment began to appear in the autumn of 1920. It cannot be specifically related to the influence of Poplar.

Gilbert has pointed out how working-class pressure and the fear of social disorder, particularly associated with ex-servicemen, influenced the decision to introduce both the Out of Work Donation of 1919 and the 1920 Unemployment Insurance Act.[67] A similar pattern can be seen as regards the Poor Law. In the autumn of 1920 numerous demonstrations of the unemployed were held in London and other big cities, often involving marches on local Guardians' offices and the demanding of relief. These were regularly reported to the Cabinet by Basil

Thomson who related them to disaffected left-wing elements and the Communists.[68]

Throughout the winter the situation appeared threatening, and the Boards of Guardians regularly appealed to the Ministry of Health for guidance. The Ministry officials were clearly taken by surprise, and from autumn 1920 began to recommend the granting of out-relief under Article 12 of the 1911 Relief Regulation Order. The danger of letting such an exceptional procedure become 'normal' was seen by some officials, but there was little they could do. H.W.S. Francis, Assistant Secretary in the Ministry, lucidly described the situation in November 1920:

> the Ministry have disclaimed responsibility for supervising the conditions of relief, and have even suggested that their view is that the Guardians would be well advised not to impose test ... it has been made clear ... that Guardians may grant relief in whatever form is convenient to them, and will not be checked by the central department.[69]

In the summer of 1921 the Ministry held lengthy discussions about the possibility of reimposing control, but decided against it on the grounds that several Boards would be likely to defy them, that public opinion would be against ex-servicemen having to enter workhouses, that the unemployed themselves might create disturbances and finally, that the Ministry of Labour wanted outdoor relief to continue as a supplement to insurance benefits.[70] Consequently it was decided to deal individually with unions granting too much out-relief by stressing the need for traditional Poor Law policies, and a circular to this effect was issued in September 1921.[71]

In Poplar the political position had changed. In the first post-war Guardians' election in 1919, the Labour Party gained 15 out of 24 seats. In the municipal elections of the same year they gained 39 out of 42 seats. The Municipal Alliance now formed the main opposition party. Lansbury dominated Poplar politics; he was editor of the *Daily Herald* until 1925, and was identified with the left of the Labour Party. Though not a Communist he maintained close links with the Party and both the Poplar Board and Council included Communist members. Both were dominated by manual workers and their trade unions, closely Thus reflecting the social composition of Poplar itself.[72]

Although the unemployed movement which began in autumn 1920 cannot be related directly to Poplar, Lansbury himself did much to concentrate its demands on the Poor Law. In December 1920 the *Daily*

Herald launched a 'Go to the Guardians' campaign in which Lansbury
argued that Poor Law relief was no more disgraceful than the dole,
pointed out that relief could be given simply by reporting cases to the
Ministry of Health, and advised the unemployed to go in groups of 50
and 100 to the workhouse if boards refused to give out-relief. His
article was issued as a free pamphlet for distribution amongst Trade
Unions, Labour parties and the Organised Unemployed Committees.[73]

The Poplar Board itself adopted a scale of relief for the unemployed
in November 1920, but at this stage the Ministry of Health, clearly
expecting trouble, thought the Guardians were behaving reasonably
well, and a special report stressed the genuine nature of the distress in
Poplar.[74] By the end of 1920 it is clear that the Poplar Council – which
overlapped in membership with the Guardians – realising that this was
to be a very severe crisis, was already thinking of drastic action on
the rates. The *Herald* commented that it was expected to refuse to levy
calls for the outside authorities, in protest at having to bear the burden
of unemployment. The Poor Law Inspector had already expressed
similar fears about the Guardians.[75]

It is not intended here to describe in detail the imprisonment and
subsequent release of the borough councillors, but simply to point
out its significance in Poor Law terms. In many ways it was the logical
conclusion of the demand for rate equalisation made by the Labour
group in Poplar since the 1890s. They brought matters to a confrontation in 1921, probably because they were then in a much stronger
position, because the situation was in many ways desperate and
because they themselves seem to have been radicalised by the post-war
crisis. In addition the growth of unemployment meant that the whole
subject of rate equalisation was again the focus of discussion by
London local authorities.

On 2 March 1921, the Clerk of the Poplar Board submitted his
financial estimates for the half-year ending 30 September 1921, which
included £80,000 for out-relief, over twice as much as in the current
half-year. At the same meeting the Guardians approved a resolution
of the London Trades Council and London Labour Party demanding
maintenance for the unemployed at a rate of 40s for a married man
plus dependents' allowances. This was followed by the refusal of the
Borough Council to include in its estimates the precepts of the LCC,
Metropolitan Police, Asylums Board and Water Board 'as a protest
against the indifference of the Government and central authorities
to the serious problems of local finance'.[76]

The imprisonment of the councillors in September 1921 came in the midst of a new outburst of unemployed demonstrations. By 7 October Alfred Mond, the Minister of Health, was urging on the Cabinet the necessity for settlement due to the threats of other London boroughs to follow Poplar.[77] The Ministry officials seem to have been considering rate equalisation, but this was opposed by the richer boroughs in two conferences held at the Ministry on 17 and 18 October. Instead, a suggestion by the Town Clerk of Westminster that outdoor relief costs should be equalised through the Metropolitan Common Poor Fund was accepted, despite the warnings of the Poor Law expert, H.W.S. Francis, that this amounted to a charter to grant outdoor relief for Poplar-type boroughs. Oddly, Lansbury's own scheme for a Central Board for the London unemployed, which he had been urging since the 1890s was rejected, though Francis argued that it was preferable.[78]

The new provisions were enacted in the London Authorities (Financial Provision) Act 1921, and Francis's worst fears proved quite justified. The arrangements enabled Poplar to finance most of its outdoor relief costs from the Metropolitan Common Poor Fund for the next seven years, by borrowing in the current half-year in anticipation of revenue to be received from the Fund. Unlike unions outside London they did not have to ask the Ministry for loan sanction. Hence the Ministry had no control except through the process of audit and surcharge. Successive Ministers were unwilling to force another confrontation because, as Joynson-Hicks put it, the Guardians 'ask nothing better than to become martyrs by being committed to prison for their principles'.[79] Hence successive disallowances and surcharges by the District Auditor were ignored by Poplar.

The Local Authorities (Financial Provisions) Act enabled the Minister of Health to draw up a scale of relief as a guideline for the London Unions. The Ministry scale — known as the Mond Scale — allowed 25s for a man and wife, 6s for the first child, 5s for the second and third, and 4s for the fourth or subsequent children. It was not ungenerous, but gave no rent allowances and the regulations governing it stated that the whole of a family's income must be taken into account when administering relief.

When it was issued in January 1922 the numbers of unemployed on relief in Poplar totalled 4,582 (28 January 1922) and the total of those on outdoor relief was over 21,000, a far higher figure than any other East London union.[80] The Guardians had already been subjected to pressure from the unemployed, some of them organised by Sylvia Pankhurst's Workers' Socialist Federation, which was to the left of the Communist Party and was critical of the 'moderate' Poplar Guardians.[81]

This pressure was crucial to the events of January 1922. Oxley, the Poor Law Inspector, thought that the Guardians were disposed to accept the Mond scale, but were intimidated by the force of unemployed demonstrations at board meetings on 19 and 25 January 1922. At the second of these, the demonstrators — numbering several thousands — imprisoned the Guardians in their office. In this heated atmosphere a scale considered ludicruously generous was voted, and was predictably rejected by the Ministry. The Board's delay in implementing the new scale — it was in fact *never* implemented — led to a crisis in their relationship with the unemployed, and to riots outside the Board's offices. Thereafter 'Poplarism' was so notorious that J.H. Thomas attributed to it Labour's setbacks in the local elections in April.[82]

A likely interpretation of this sequence of events is that the Guardians had hoped to achieve some modification of the Mond scale by organised demonstrations of the unemployed's potential force (the Municipal Alliance argued that the demonstrations of 25 January were 'fixed') but were then placed in a situation where there was a danger of being outflanked on the left.

This crisis, combined with financial difficulties which caused them to apply to the Ministry for a loan, led to the appointment of Mr H.I. Cooper, Clerk to the Bolton Guardians, to carry out another enquiry into Poplar's administration.[83] This commenced on 13 March and the report was published on 18 May. Predictably it was a savage indictment of Poplar's policies and its choicest examples of malingerers abusing relief were widely publicised. The Guardians retorted with their pamphlet 'Guilty and Proud of It' — the classic defence of Poplarism. Attempts made in the summer to reach a compromise over the Mond scale failed. In June, a second Poplar Order was issued under Section 52 of the 1852 Relief Regulation Order, restricting relief in Poplar to the Mond scale and ordering all departures to be reported.[84]

The Order was in practice ignored, and departures from it were reported in vast numbers each week. The Ministry was powerless, though surcharges were made by the District Auditor. In February 1924, one of the first acts of the first Labour Minister of Health was to rescind the Order and to remit all surcharges made under it. This caused a sensation and was interpreted by the press and Opposition as encouragement to Poplarism. In fact the legality of the Order was doubtful after the end of 1922, for when the Local Authorities (Financial Provisions) Act was renewed as the Local Authorities (Emergency Provisions) Act 1923, the Mond scale was replaced by a flat-rate payment for each person on relief. Ministry of Health officials thought that the Order had lapsed. The position was not clarified until 1924 when the Law Officers of the Crown decided that it had not.[85]

It is necessary in conclusion to analyse the main features of 'Poplarism', and to try to give some estimate of its influence and importance, if any, in the 1920s. 'Poplarism' was used as a term of abuse, to describe 'lax' policies of generous out-relief to the unemployed without the performance of any test. It was normally associated with Labour Guardians, but as the Webbs pointed out, numerous boards of varying political complexions found no other way of dealing with mass unemployment save by giving outdoor relief. Like most orthodox Poor Law experts they related the problem in part to the removal of the pauper disfranchisement in the 1918 Representation of the People Act.[86] The Webbs also noted that the Ministry of Health used 'Poplarism' almost as a technical term to define a form of Poor Law policy which they equated with the desire to implement the Labour Party policy of work or full maintenance, and that they distinguished between this ideological policy and others.

Neville Chamberlain listed the main features of 'Poplarism' as being the recognition by Guardians of a fixed, usually high scale of relief which was automatically granted at the maximum level, the refusal to consider in full the earnings or income available to the whole family (i.e. a refusal to adopt a stringent household means test) and the granting of clearly illegal relief, notably to persons involved in an industrial dispute.[87] A fourth principle was the violation of the doctrine of 'less eligibility' by granting relief in excess of local minimum wages. Other aspects of the policy were the granting of relief as a supplementation to casual or even low full-time earnings; the failure to discriminate between deserving and undeserving applicants; grants of small amounts of relief simply to bring an application income up to scale, and the granting of out-relief to single young men and women without dependents.

One striking feature of the Poplar Guardians' policy in the 1920s was their willingness to defend it on ideological grounds. Lansbury stated: 'If people starve on wages, there is no reason why they should starve on relief'.[88] On the family income question they argued that

the Guardians hold the view that it is not right to depress the standard of life of the whole family because single sons who ought to be out at work can find no employment.[89]

In short, this version of 'Poplarism' rejected the basic assumptions of the deterrent Poor Law; it refused to play the game by the same rules.[89]

Another significant characteristic of 'Poplarism' concerns the wider question of public control and response to outside pressure. Poplar's relationship with the unemployed organisations has been described, and a similar response to demonstrations can be found elsewhere, in, for instance, West Ham and Bedwellty. In such unions it seems likely that a militant group of Guardians would organise demonstrations to put pressure on the Board at crucial moments, when there seemed to be a danger of some weakening of policy. Another form of control was through local Labour Party and Trades Council direction of the policies of a local Board. The civil servants of the Ministry of Health constantly complained that the Labour groups in West Ham and Bedwellty held meetings prior to Board meetings, at which they in effect decided policy. In its most extreme form opponents of 'Poplarist' control alleged that it involved the direct corruption of the electorate, and could lead to the open intimidation of Relieving Officers by both Guardians and applicants.[90]

Behind public or political control lay the belief that government policy could be influenced by local activities. The most successful example was that of Poplar itself in 1921, when considerable concessions were gained by the action of the councillors. In the same year the Ministry of Health feared that the Bedwellty Board of Guardians might cease to function, in order to compel the central government to take over its administration. The Ministry related this to the demand of South Wales local authorities for a national policy for unemployment, or at the least, for Exchequer grants to help hard-hit areas.[91] The use of relief machinery in the General Strike and the miners' lockout of 1926 was interpreted by some civil servants as a conspiracy originating in Poplar designed to create financial chaos and precipitate the breakdown of local government.[92] It is certainly true that in mining areas the Guardians used the machinery at their disposal in the interests of their communities, and that this assisted the prolongation of the strike in some districts. Similarly, though arguments were put forward throughout the 1920s in favour of Exchequer assistance, it would be wrong to discount a simpler motive on the part of Labour Guardians, namely the desire to make the lives of the unemployed and the poor more tolerable in what must at times have been intolerable circumstances.

The actual number of avowedly 'Poplarist' unions was small — perhaps half a dozen in London, and slightly larger numbers in South Wales, Durham and parts of the West Riding and Lancashire, but greater numbers of boards gave relief which could not be justified, according to

Poor Law principles.[93] There were two main ways open to the Ministry of Health to reimpose control: the refusal to grant loans, and the procedure of disallowance and surcharge by the District Auditor. The usefulness of both was limited by the desire to avoid another confrontation of a Poplar type; hence from 1922 onwards the Ministry sought alternative methods. Bills providing for the suspension of recalcitrant boards were prepared between 1922 and 1925, but successive Governments shied away from introducing them. It was not until Chamberlain became Minister of Health that decisive action was taken.[94]

Chamberlain aimed to restrict the Poor Law to the relief of destitution, or what in a Cabinet memorandum he called 'a reversion to the Elizabethan Poor Law'.[95] This necessitated drastic action as regards 'Poplarist' boards. This was made legislatively possible in July 1926 when, following a crisis in West Ham precipitated by the General Strike, the Board of Guardians (Default) Act was passed, giving the Minister power to suspend boards which were unable or unwilling to function.[96] The Act did not include the reimposition of pauper disfranchisement, though the Poor Law department, to a man, advocated it, as it was considered politically too risky.[97] The Act was never applied to Poplar itself, though the West Ham, Chester-le-Street and Bedwellty Boards were suspended and replaced by Commissioners who cut down relief and administered the Poor Law in its pristine severity, at considerable social cost.[98]

The Audit (Local Authorities) Act 1927 which prohibited Guardians upon whom a surcharge of over £500 was upheld from serving on a local authority for five years, and the Local Authorities (Emergency Provisions) Act 1928 which placed the Metropolitan Common Poor Fund under the control of the Metropolitan Asylums Board and eighteen Ministry of Health nominees, completed the legislative framework which curbed 'Poplarism'. However, the other prong of Chamberlain's attack was through a tightening-up of the administration. From 1927 a deliberate purge of lax administrative methods was launched, the aims being a return to the Relief Regulations Order of 1911, with the very minimum of unconditional relief being granted.[99] The Inspectors visited all unions with even slightly unorthodox tendencies and their highly critical reports were widely published in the press.

This process extended to Poplar itself where between January 1927 and March 1930, when the Guardians were abolished, 'normal' methods of administration were reimposed by the Inspector and the District Auditor, and both the numbers of paupers and the costs of administration were drastically reduced. When the Communist Party attacked the Labour group in the 1928 Guardians elections for avoiding a confrontation on this issue, the reply was that opposition would be useless as it would simply lead to their suspension and the 'starvation policy' of the West Ham Appointed Guardians.[100] This acquiescence would seem to offer some corroboration of the Webbs' theory that Chamberlain's policy was part of a general counter-attack in the changed mood of the country after the failure of the General Strike.[101]

Is Poplarism of more than historical and parochial interest? The policy, although it obviously could lead to abuses — as can any welfare system — provides a rare example of the radical potential of local government machinery in a period in which central control over local government was still relatively slight. The conflict between local and central government, and its resolution via the Default and Audit Acts, is still a possibility, as the recent Clay Cross and Tameside affairs demonstrate. The granting of cash benefits by local authorities elected by claimants is no longer part of our social security system, but this example of such a system in action is of interest, either as an example or as a warning. The divergence between local bodies and the central authority, which re-emerged in the 1930s with the action of some of the Public Assistance Committees, was one of the major reasons for the centralisation of relief to the able-bodied which came with the establishment of the Unemployment Assistance Board in 1934.[102]

Finally, it remains worth emphasising, in view of the generally uncritical treatment of Chamberlain's policy, that in many ways he was attempting, in a period of acute economic difficulties, to return to the principles of 1834; that there is considerable evidence that in the mining districts at least these policies caused considerable suffering; and that Poplarism, at its best, represented a genuine attempt to help thousands of the poor, who have, incidentally, been much maligned in the conventional interpretation. To quote Mrs Julia Scarr, a Poplar Guardian, in an interview with Mond,

> In administering the scale I often feel ashamed to offer the people the amount we offer, taking into account the other few shillings that are coming in. I feel that the women cannot do what they ought to do for the children and the home. I can assure you that the people are careful people. We live among them and go among them, and there is not a shilling too much given in the scale of relief that we give.[103]

As in the earlier period, final judgement involves also a viewpoint on such questions as the role of social policy in an unequal society, and perhaps objectivity is neither possible nor desirable.

Notes

1. S. and B. Webb, *English Poor Law History*, Part II, Vol. II, pp. 825–35, 982–3.
2. See for example Bentley B. Gilbert, *British Social Policy*, 1914–39, pp. 214, 220 and 224; G.W. Jones, 'Herbert Morrison and Poplarism', *Public Law*, 1973, p. 24.
3. This information, together with much of the evidence on social structure, is taken from Francois Bedarida's valuable article, 'Urban Growth and Social Structure in Nineteenth Century Poplar', *London Journal*, Vol. I, January 1975.
4. Bedarida, op. cit., p. 161.
5. Ibid., pp. 167–8.
6. Ibid., p. 172. See G. Stedman Jones, *Outcast London* (Oxford 1971) for an analysis of the problems of the casual labour market in London.
7. Bedarida, op. cit., p. 181.
8. For Crooks, see George Haw, *From Workhouse to Westminster* and for Lansbury, George Lansbury, *My Life* and *Looking Backwards and Forwards*; Edgar Lansbury, *George Lansbury, My Father*, and Raymond Postgate, *The Life of George Lansbury*.
9. Bedarida, op. cit., p. 186.
10. British Library of Political and Economic Science. Poplar Labour Electoral Committee, First Annual Report 1891–92. See Paul Thompson, *Socialists, Liberals and Labour*, for the emergence of organised labour politics in this period.
11. See George Lansbury, *My Life*, pp. 76–8; Thompson, op. cit., pp. 118, 193; Poplar Labour Electoral League, Second Annual Report, 1892–93, and Tower Hamlets Central Reference Library, *Bow and Bromley Socialist*, October 1897, for SDF criticism of 'our Labour friends'.
12. See J. Harris, *Unemployment and Politics: A Study in English Social Policy 1886–1914*, p. 193; P. Thane, 'Working Class Attitudes to Welfare before 1914', unpublished paper. Royal Commission on the Poor Laws and Relief of Distress: Report.
13. Cmd. 4755. *Evidence of London Witnesses and Critics of the Poor Law*. Evidence of Harry Quelch as representative of the Social Democratic Federation.
14. British Library of Political Science. *Report of a Debate between George Lansbury and Harry Quelch, September 20th and 21st, 1910, on the Minority Report on the Poor Laws* (Twentieth-Century Press Pamphlet).
15. Twenty-Ninth Annual Report of the Local Government Board 1899–1900. Inspector Lockwood's report contains a sympathetic analysis of the Poplar old age pensions scheme.
16. See J. Harris, op. cit., pp. 236–43 for Labour thinking on unemployment. Also K. Brown, *Labour and Unemployment 1900–1914*, Chap. 1.
17. GLC Records Department. Minutes of the Poplar Board of Guardians, 3 October 1894.
18. See, for example, G. Lansbury, *Unemployment, the Next Step*, in W. Crooks, *Social Ideals* (undated), though Lansbury did always stress that the morally defective were a very small group.

19. Cmd. 4755, 1909. *Evidence of London witnesses and critics of the Poor Law*, Evidence of Harry Quelch.
20. See in particular, G. Lansbury, *Socialism for the Poor* (1909) on the Quelch/Lansbury debate, both dating from the period when Lansbury was supporting the Webbs' ideas in the Minority Report.
21. Cmd. 3274, 1906. *Transcript of the Shorthand Notes at the Public Inquiry held by J.S. Davy . . . into the General Conditions of the Poplar Union, its Pauperism, and the Administration of the Guardians and their Officers.* Evidence of W. Crooks.
22. Minutes of the Poplar Board of Guardians, 26 July 1893, 9, 23 August 1893.
23. Board of Works for the Poplar District, *Report of Unemployed Relief Works*, 1894. *Transcript . . . of Shorthand Notes*, Evidence of W. Crooks.
24. R.C. on the Poor Laws. Cmd. 4795. Report by Mr Cyril Jackson and the Rev J.C. Pringle on the effect of Employment or Assistance given to the Unemployed since 1886 as a means of relieving distress outside the Poor Law, p. 648.
25. Minutes of the Poplar Board of Guardians, 15 February 1895. Lansbury Papers, Vol. 1, for press cuttings on unemployed demonstrations.
26. Minutes of the Poplar Board of Guardians, 5 March 1895.
27. Lansbury Papers, Vol. I. Undated letter to W.C. Sewell.
28. Minutes of the Poplar Board of Guardians, 24 February and 7 April 1897, for C.O.S. complaints; 30 October 1901 for Ratepayers' Association protest; 8 February 1902, for an unfavourable report by Inspector Walsh on the casual wards.
29. This is documented in K.D. Brown, op. cit., Chaps. 1 and 2.
30. See for example, *The Star*, 6 November 1905: 'It was Poplar's day and Poplar's demonstration . . .'
31. Lansbury Papers, Vol. 2, Sidney Buxton to George Lansbury, 2 January 1905.
32. See Jackson and Pringle, op. cit., for a thorough examination of Poplar's unemployment policies.
33. *Twenty-Fourth Annual Report of the Local Government Board*, 1894–95. Reports of Inspectors Lockwood and Davy.
34. For Poplar's self-justification by reference to the Chaplin circular, see Davy Report, p. 24. For the Inspectorate's criticism of inadequate out-relief, see the *Annual Report of the LGB 1895.*
35. *Annual Reports of the LGB 1895–6, 1905–6, 1906–7 and 1907–8.*
36. Pringle and Jackson, op. cit., p. 650.
37. Cmd. 3240, 1906. *Report to the President of the Local Government Board on the Poplar Union by J.S. Davy*, p. 44.
38. *Transcript . . . of the Shorthand Notes.* Evidence of G. Lansbury.
39. Pringle and Jackson, op. cit., p. 653.
40. Lansbury Papers, Vol. 2, Sidney Buxton to G. Lansbury, 30 July 1906. Pringle and Jackson, op. cit., p. 653.
41. Minutes of the Poplar Board of Guardians, 10 December 1902. Ibid., 20 January 1903.
42. Ibid., 13 May 1903.
43. Ibid., 11 November 1903.
44. Ibid., 25 November 1903, 16 March 1904.
45. *Transcript . . . of the Shorthand Notes.* Evidence of W.G. Martley.
46. Ibid. Also Minutes of the Poplar Board of Guardians, 16 November 1904.
47. Minutes of the Poplar Board of Guardians, 7 and 14 December 1904.
48. Davy Report, p. 24. Also Appendix Tables B and H.
49. Minutes of the Poplar Board of Guardians, 8 November 1905. *Davy Report*, p. 4.

50. Ibid., p. 5.
51. Ibid., pp. 5–6.
52. Ibid., p. 3.
53. Ibid., p. 6.
54. Ibid., p. 4.
55. This statement is based on an analysis of voting. Minutes of the Poplar Union, 1905, passim.
56. *Davy Report*, p. 23.
57. Ibid., p. 23.
58. *Transcript . . . of the Shorthand Notes.* Evidence of W.G. Martley.
59. Harris, op. cit., p. 195.
60. Minutes of the Poplar Board of Guardians, 24 October 1906, 31 October 1906.
61. Lansbury Papers, Vol. 2, Letter in 'Justice' from Lansbury, 10 November 1906. Vol. 3, Series of letters to Lansbury, March 1907.
62. *Thirty-Eighth Annual Report of the LGB 1909.* Report of Inspector Oxley.
63. Ibid. Also Minutes of the Poplar Board of Guardians, 28 October 1908. Out-relief under Article 10 was normally given in kind, whereas the wives whose husbands accepted the MWTO received cash. This was one reason why Oxley felt the MWTO failed to deter applicants.
64. Minutes of the Poplar Board of Guardians, 26 May 1912 and July–August 1912.
65. A. Deacon, 'Labour and the Unemployed; the administration of insurance in the twenties'. *Bulletin of the Society for the Study of Labour History*, 31, Autumn 1975.
66. Webbs, op. cit., pp. 837 ff.
67. B. Gilbert, op. cit., pp. 66–7.
68. PRO CAB 24/112. Report No. 77 etc.
69. PRO MH 57/121/C. Memo 9 November 1920.
70. PRO MH 57/111/C. Memo 15 August 1921.
71. *Second Annual Report of the Ministry of Health 1920–21*. Circular No. 240 to Boards of Guardians, on Poor Relief to Unemployed Persons.
72. This brief survey of Poplar politics is taken from various sources, in particular newspapers of the period – *East End News, East London Observer, Workers' Weekly, The Communist*, etc.
73. *Daily Herald*, 18 December 1920.
74. PRO MH 57/121/C. Report of Inspector Haywood.
75. *Daily Herald*, 3 September 1920. PRO MH 57/121/C. Report of Inspector Haywood.
76. *The Times*, 10 March 1921.
77. PRO CAB 24/128. CP 3379. 7 October 1921.
78. PRO MH 79/307.
79. PRO CAB 24/162. CP. 416.
80. Parish of Poplar Borough. Report of a Special Enquiry into the Expenditure of the Guardians. Appendix, Table D. 1922, HMSO. Unemployment in Poplar was estimated at 25 per cent by the anon. authors of *The Third Winter of Unemployment* (London 1922).
81. See *Workers' Dreadnought*, 9 July 1921.
82. The description of these events is taken from reports in PRO MH 68/214.
83. Ibid.
84. PRO MH 68/215.
85. Various Ministry of Health Papers cover the rescission of the Poplar Order. PRO MH 68/225/226/227.
86. S. and B. Webb, op. cit., pp. 851–2.
87. PRO CAB 24/178. C.P. 50.
88. PRO MH 68/215.

89. MH 68/231.
90. For examples of intimidation in the coal lock-out see my article 'The Poor Law in 1926', in M. Morris, *The General Strike* (London 1976).
91. PRO MH 68/257. Ministry of Health memo, 30 December 1921.
92. PRO MH 79/303.
93. Webbs, op. cit. pp. 851–2.
94. The draft Bills can be found in PRO/MH 79/305. See also PRO CAB 24/178. CP 50, for Chamberlain's comments.
95. PRO CAB 24/173, CP 219.
96. For the West Ham crisis see PRO MH 68/81/82/83/84/85 and Webbs, op. cit., p. 926–9.
97. PRO CAB 23/53.
98. For criticisms of the new administration in the three Unions, see the *Poor Law Officers' Journal*, 1927, passim.
99. MH 57/110B. Memo to General Inspectors, 21 May 1928, for a summary of objectives.
100. Election addresses in the Guardians' Elections, 1928.
101. Webbs, op. cit., pp. 910–12.
102. See E. Briggs and A. Deacon, 'The Creation of the Unemployment Assistance Board', *Policy and Politics*, Vol. 2, No. 1, 1973.
103. MH 68/215.

NON-CONTRIBUTORY VERSUS INSURANCE PENSIONS 1878–1908

Pat Thane

The Old Age Pensions Act 1908 granted government financed non-contributory pensions to individuals aged over 70, subject to certain conditions. The health and unemployment benefits introduced in 1911 were financed on a contributory insurance basis. The Pensions Act was preceded by a long debate concerning the preferability of contributory or insurance pensions. The resulting non-contributory legislation ensured that future benefits would be contributory. Discussion of these issues centred around values central to late-Victorian and Edwardian society: should compulsion and dependence upon the state replace freedom and self-help, was redistribution of income desirable?

Serious discussion of the provision of state pensions began in the 1870s. At that time, workers could receive pensions from their trade unions, which had only 1.5 million members in Great Britain and Ireland, out of a population of 38 million, as late as 1892; or through friendly societies,[1] covering approximately 3 million of the population. Friendly societies existed primarily to provide sickness benefits. They had fallen accidentally into old-age provision due to the increasing proportion of aged members who claimed permanent sick benefit when too old for work. Higher longevity among members than anticipated caused a crisis for the societies, whose contributions were not calculated to cover this contingency. The resulting pressure on their funds led many of them, by the end of the 1870s, to consider separately funded pension schemes for new members.[2] Some were launched; none was successful.

But a major weakness of both forms of provision was that neither covered women,[3] whose life expectancy was longer than that of men; nor did they include the low-paid and irregularly employed who were not unionised and were rarely members of friendly societies. The high and growing numbers of the aged receiving poor relief drew attention to old age as a social problem.

Serious discussion of alternative forms of state provision for the aged began at the end of the 1870s, with Canon Blackley's proposals for compulsory insurance against old age and sickness. Blackley proposed that the state should counter these two important causes of poverty by

enforcing payment of contributions, to a total of £10, from every
member of the population between the ages of 18 and 21. They would
be paid into a fund, from which would be paid to all 'wage-earners' — to
be distinguished from 'wage-payers and leisured and salary earners' who
would contribute but not benefit — 8s per week sick pay until the age
of 70; 4s per week pension thereafter. The role of the state was to
enforce payment, but to contribute nothing. The system would be
financed by the beneficiaries and by redistribution from those who
would contribute but not benefit.

Blackley's motives for this first serious national insurance proposal
in Britain were explicit. He was concerned with two problems, which
he believed concerned two distinct strata of the working class: firstly,
the difficulties faced by the respectable and hard-working in attempting
to protect themselves against occasions when sickness and old age
prevented their providing for themselves by work. For this he blamed
what he saw as the instability of the friendly societies. He strongly
criticised the friendly societies for their inability to prevent respectable
people too often ending their days on poor relief, condemning them
as 'nine out of ten in the kingdom insolvent and the average insurer
being unable to select a safe one'. This was a fair criticism of small,
local societies, which had funds too small to meet the needs of aged
members and were sometimes bankrupted as a result, but not of the
large national societies.

Secondly, he was anxious to relieve the burden which he believed
was suffered by the rest of society, from the feckless underclass which
did not attempt to save, who, he believed, turned without conscience
to the Poor Law, at the ratepayers' expense, when in need. He argued
that there were

> instances as I can give from my personal knowledge, of young
> labourers by the dozen, without a change of decent clothes continually
> and brutally drinking, living almost like savages while earning fully £1
> a week ... For it is the plain failure of good government that an
> enormous class of people should be allowed to ignore the first duty
> of every loyal citizen, and it is a political crime of the gravest sort
> that they should be, as they are, encouraged in their belief that the
> grosser their waste, their sensuality, their ignorance and their selfish-
> ness, the stronger claim they establish to support and aid from their
> fellow men ... I do not see for an instant why we should mince this
> matter. If everyone can make his own provision and will do so, let

him be shown how; if he can and will not let him be compelled.[4]

Blackley proposed to solve both problems by his compulsory insurance scheme. This, he believed, would provide absolute security for the provident whilst compelling the improvident to recognise the virtues of regular saving. He expected by this means to eliminate the Poor Law, which he condemned as a major cause of fecklessness by its provision of free benefits for the destitute. He wrongly assumed that old age and sickness were the major causes of pauperism, neglecting such problems as involuntary unemployment and low pay.

His scheme showed shrewd appreciation of the fundamental obstacles to working-class self-help. Men found great difficulty in saving once they had the responsibility of a family. Women presented greater problems of sickness and survival into old age; yet often their only opportunity to save was the period between starting work and the birth of their children. Hence his proposal that all contributions should be paid before the age of twenty-one. This also provided many years of compound interest before the period of greatest need.

Blackley also recognised, but did not solve, the problem of the casual worker which bedevilled later national insurance proposals. Since these labourers — navvies, builders' labourers, dockworkers and many more — changed employers frequently, it was, and is, difficult to ensure their regular contribution to any compulsory scheme. Yet they were the group least likely to save privately, with the highest sickness and mortality rates. Blackley proposed that each employer should be responsible for ensuring that some part of the contribution was paid. This solution, however, presupposed the cooperation both of workers and employers, which could not be assumed to be infallibly forthcoming.

He was unhappy about certain details of his scheme. He thought the age of 70 too old to begin payment of pensions, and 65 a closer approximation to the age at which physical powers failed, as indeed it was, but that pensions at 65 would necessitate a higher contribution than many could afford. A more serious difficulty was that Blackley's scheme presupposed the availability of work for all. One of its advantages, he argued, was that since contributions were compulsory, work too would become compulsory in order that contributions could be paid. Failure to contribute through failure to work was to be punished by labour in the workhouse, until all contributions had been paid off — which assumed, in unresolved contradiction to his aim of abolishing it, the continuation of at least a residual, punitive, poor law.

Blackley argued that since only three years of contribution were required early in life, few would be unable to meet the obligation. For many men this was probably a reasonable assumption, though it evaded the question of whether unskilled wages averaging 13s p.w. in 1880 and often irregularly available, left a margin of over £3 6s a year. Women, for example in the major, and low-paid, occupation of domestic service and in others paying only about 6s per week, for whom the problem of old age was equally real and often acute, posed problems which he did not solve.[5]

Blackley's proposals were opposed, notably by the official investigation into them, the Select Committee on National Provident Insurance, 1885–7, for their compulsory nature, which implied a considerable extension of the power of the state over the individual. This they regarded as bad in principle, and deeply harmful to 'the self-taught habits of thrift and self-help which prevail among the working classes to a considerable extent'; they also disliked the element of redistribution, not because it was believed wrong for the rich to help the poor, which was entirely consistent with mid-Victorian conceptions of the social obligations of the wealthy, but because it was compulsory. Charity should be voluntary; compulsion might diminish the instinct for voluntary giving, and would in any case be strongly opposed by the rich.

His proposals for sickness insurance were rejected because, the Committee argued, the friendly societies already made adequate provision for the provident, and the improvident should be encouraged to follow their example. The friendly societies, with good reason, objected to his criticisms of themselves. The larger ones were aware of, and tried hard to solve the problem of aged members. They prided themselves on never allowing a member to fall on to poor relief. They could not, however, solve the problem of those who dropped out of membership due mainly to unemployment. These were one of the causes of Blackley's concern.

Blackley replied before the Committee to some of their objections that, in certain circumstances, state compulsion might be the only means to achieve necessary social improvement. The state, he pointed out, already exerted a great deal of compulsion, e.g. to pay rates and taxes; the need was not to reject it, but to distinguish between right and wrong occasions for it. He also argued that exhortations to the poor to practise self-help had manifestly failed and should be replaced by compulsory education in self-help through contributory insurance. He failed to sway the Committee. They were especially opposed to sickness insurance, which they felt that the friendly societies provided quite adequately, but they

were prepared to accept the possibility that a pension scheme was
desirable, and that a more acceptable one might be devised in the future.

Blackley's proposals were rejected in Britain, at about the same
time that Bismarck introduced social insurance in Germany. However,
the German example aroused little enthusiasm in Britain, initially
because it was inimical to so many influential values. *The Times* pointed
out on 19 June 1889:

> Natural as free individual development is to the English in their
> island home, equally necessary is for Germany a rigid, centralised,
> all pervading state control ... how exceptionally is Germany
> fitted to be the scene of this great philanthropic experiment. No-
> where is the ponderous, plodding, incorruptible bureaucracy so
> effective and so cheap. ... Self-help and spontaneous growth are
> better suited to Englishmen but (we are) ready to believe and
> willing to hope, that state initiative and socialistic science and self-
> conscious statesmanship may be adapted to other circumstances
> and other habits. ... the German is accustomed to official control,
> official delays and police supervision from the cradle to the grave ...
> whereas ... self-help and spontaneous growth are better suited to
> Englishmen.

Later, weaknesses were detected in the German scheme. As the Board
of Trade pointed out in 1899, it was far from an ideal means of helping
the very poor. There remained in Germany a class of casual labourers
earning less than M300 p.a. (about 7s per week), who were excluded
from state insurance because they were irregularly employed and poorly
paid. It excluded the poorest. The benefits for those in the lowest
income grade were pitifully low. A man disabled early in working life
might receive as little as 2s 2d per week. Even allowing for lower German
living costs this did not approach a subsistence rate.[6]

The debate about the respective merits of contributory or non-
contributory pensions, however, continued in Britain until the introduction of the Pensions Act of 1908. The central problem on which the
debate focused was the difficulty of helping the poorest, while providing
the incentives widely thought necessary for the encouragement of self-
help and independence of the state. Discussion of pensions could not
evade the problem of relieving the needs of the very poorest; the aged
included many of the most absolutely destitute poor. It was plain from
the Report of the Select Committee of 1885–7 that very many of the
destitute aged were not guilty of feckless waste, but had succeeded in

maintaining a perilous independence throughout working life in conditions of low pay and irregular employment. They had been unable to save a surplus to provide for old age, a hazard of unpredictable length.

It became increasingly clear, however, that insurance pensions seemed unsuited to the needs of the respectable destitute aged who were already past, or approaching the end of, their working lives; there was no means by which they could contribute. Blackley's scheme did not attempt to provide for them, indeed would have provided no pensions for fifty years after its introduction. Contemporary optimistic about social progress assumed that, by then, problems of poverty would be solved. He assumed that the scheme would be 'fully funded' according to orthodox insurance principles, that the contributions paid early in working life would accumulate interest sufficient to pay the full cost of the benefit.

For many critics the outstanding objection to insurance pensions was this apparent impossibility of their providing for existing need, without a large transitional subsidy from taxation, or by some other method of redistribution from the generation of working age to those past work. Any such provision, as already in operation in Germany, was believed to be objectionable for encouraging dependence upon the state.

Contributory pensions might meet the needs of younger generations, but it was questionable to contemporaries whether their need in old age would be as great. It was argued that their higher pay and more regular work compared with the experience of the older generation, would enable them to make voluntary provision, whilst a state insurance scheme might provide a disincentive to such desirable self-help.[7]

Hence, by the end of the 1880s, Blackley's scheme was widely believed to be impracticable. When Joseph Chamberlain took up the campaign for pensions in 1891 he was aware of the major deficiencies in Blackley's proposals. He pointed out in 1891: 'I have never yet seen how you can apply compulsion to any but persons in regular employment whose contributions can be deducted from wages through employers.' He was, rightly, more pessimistic than Blackley about the ease with which the casual labour market might be eradicated. Chamberlain initially met the problem, equally unrealistically, by arguing that the lowest paid, the casual workers, and the feckless poor, were least likely to survive to old age, and might therefore be ignored.[8]

He was not satisfied with this solution for long. Plainly many of the lowest paid during working life did survive, and he had ignored the question of women. But Chamberlain, like Blackley, was convinced that 'a non-contributory scheme might lead to a re-introduction of all the evils against which the Poor Law is supposed to guard us'. And, unlike

Blackley, he was opposed to compulsion.

These incompatible principles prevented Chamberlain from developing any widely acceptable proposals capable of dealing with the problem of poverty in old age. His suggested escape route from the dilemma was evolutionist and mildly redistributive. He told the Royal Commission on the Aged Poor of 1895:

> I have never been able to see how you are to benefit the lowest class in the community except by raising the class above them . . . raise the highest and gradually the lowest will rise to the position of the second lowest and so on . . .

This, he believed, would necessitate some redistribution to the respectable, regularly employed working class through a subsidy from taxation to a voluntary insurance scheme, established either directly by the government or through subsidies to friendly societies:

> The two classes who will contribute to this out of all proportion to the benefit they will receive are the thriftless, who will indirectly contribute through their taxes to the pensions of the thrifty, and the rich who will contribute without corresponding advantage. But that is part of our social arrangements. It is Christian socialism at any rate and it is the basis of a great deal of our present taxation. They may say, however, that indirectly they get an advantage. The foundations of property are made more secure when no real grievance is felt by the poor against the rich.[9]

More explicitly than Blackley, Chamberlain believed that partially redistributive voluntary contributory pensions were among the measures which could contribute significantly to maintaining social stability. Chamberlain believed that this was threatened by the re-emergence of labour militancy in the 1880s, but not irremediably. In 1893 he was 'convinced that my fellow politicians immensely exaggerate the influence of labour . . . it can easily be overcome by a political leader with genuine sympathy with the working class and a practical programme'.[10] His 'practical programme' included proposals such as voluntary contributory pensions designed to alleviate real grievances among more secure workers without removing incentives to self-help.

But by the end of the decade he was less optimistic. He believed that it was impossible to help the poorest quickly enough, by the means he had proposed, and remove their potentially explosive grievances. Those in greatest need, he then argued, could only be helped by a small non-contributory benefit, paid solely to those who had saved to help themselves, but had been defeated by inadequate wages and employment opportunities. He hoped that such a measure would be a first step towards a more comprehensive, contributory pension scheme.[11]

He had become more aware of the involuntary nature of much poverty, and now saw this as the only, if unsatisfactory, solution to the problem. He was trapped between his humane recognition of the needs of the destitute aged and his awareness that social welfare institutions could play an important role in the maintenance of social order. He was anxious to gain the advantages of a scheme which encouraged self-help and social stability whilst modifying economic relationships only in minor ways. He was unenthusiastic about the implications of any scheme which encouraged dependence upon the state, and feared further pressure for large-scale redistribution through taxation. Growing recognition in the 1880s and 1890s of the reality of underemployment and low wages confronted supporters of the existing social order with the limits of the principles of self-help and minimum government intervention to maintain the status quo.

In the 1890s not only was it difficult to propose a plausible insurance scheme designed to solve the problems of the aged poor, but insurance principles were opposed by some of those likely to need help in old age. Trade unionists and other labour activists persistently opposed contributory pensions, emphasising the problems of casual and female workers.[12] Amy Hurlston, of the Womens' Trades Union League, put the case for women workers with exceptional clarity to the 1895 Royal Commission. She summarised the major obstacles to contributory pensions for women as:

(1) Intermittent employment; (2) low rate of wages now current; (3) marriage; (4) actual inability of married women to contribute anything during the earlier years of marriage and the upbringing of children, save only in exceptional cases; (5) the frequent cessation from work through physical or domestic necessities.

The need for state pensions for women was undoubted. Miss Hurlston pointed out that many women, married or unmarried, worked in seasonal jobs, such as felt hat making, or silk weaving, where wages were irregular. All of them, with very rare exceptions, earned half to one-third of average male manual wage: 4s 6d to 9s per week. Very few, she argued, could save as much as 50s even before marriage, indeed, few could hope to do little more than 'pay her way honestly and dress respectably'. Where possible, they belonged to saving clubs but a major priority for saving was that 'every sixpence earned is of necessity to be stored away where it can be withdrawn at any given time when wages have sunk so low as to fall short of necessary expenditure'. The more so, since, she argued, women who worked at all were likely to marry men with the least secure employment prospects.

This was true of female factory and domestic workers with whom she was familiar, less so of the growing numbers of women in white-collar employment. The latter remained, however, a minority of working women up to 1908. Working women in the Midlands, to whom Amy Hurlston had spoken, had no objection in principle to compulsory contribution, which they felt was certainly preferable to the Poor Law, provided that they could afford to contribute, and they felt that they could not. They suggested, rather, that employers might be compelled to contribute towards women's pensions, since they took every chance to substitute female for male labour, to increase their own profit. This, she said, 'they would regard somewhat in the light of a law of compensation'.[13]

The problem was increased by the longer life expectancy of women. There was general agreement with Miss Hurlston's assumption that lower-paid men could not afford a double insurance contribution to cover their wives. This was never seriously proposed.

Male trade unionists, especially in the skilled trades, found the principle of insurance appealing, since it would confer upon contributors an inalienable right to benefit. They recognised, however, that such a scheme could help neither the existing aged, nor poorer workers.

It has been suggested that friendly societies were influential opponents of contributory pensions, due to the fear that workers forced to contribute to a state scheme would abandon them.[14] Their attitudes were, however, more complex. As already pointed out, they were largely opposed to Blackley's scheme, since it was premised on a blanket condemnation of themselves. It is less obvious that they were overwhelmingly opposed to all state insurance proposals, or motivated so completely by the desire for self-preservation as is sometimes suggested. Even in evidence to the Select Committee of 1885–7, some friendly society witnesses were in favour of compulsory state contributory sickness benefit and pensions for the poorest and the chronically sick, whose need was undeniable and for whom they were unable to provide without imposing unacceptably high premiums, in view of the higher sickness rate of |poorer workers.

They also however questioned the likelihood of any scheme's obtaining contributions from the lowest paid men and from women.

The friendly society witnesses were divided on the principle of state insurance, compulsory or not. They were generally, understandably, fearful that it might harm their own operations, but were uncertain of its likely effects. Many of them were willing to support alternative proposals which would relieve real need among the poor, without harming the societies. Among witnesses from the largest friendly societies, the Manchester Unity of Oddfellows and the Ancient Order of Foresters, were those who favoured a voluntary state scheme which would compete with the friendly societies, but bring the poorest and the 'bad risks' the advantage of a large fund and lower premiums, due to the evening-out of risks. They recognised that this might destroy their weaker competitors, but, provided that contributions were paid early in life, as Blackley proposed, it would leave stable societies the role of supplementing the small proposed state benefits for the more provident workers, who already comprised most of their membership, and who would desire higher incomes when unable to work. Others supported a compulsory scheme for the poorest only. None totally opposed any state action.

The view that there was nothing for sound friendly societies to fear even from a compulsory contributory scheme was largely rejected by the official representatives of the societies, but several local officials, who gave independent evidence, insisted that it was increasingly the view of rank and file members. One Past Provincial Grand Master of the Manchester Unity asserted that even if a scheme such as Blackley's, which he supported, caused the contraction of his Society's business

provided it would, as we (members of the Southampton district) believe, benefit the whole community, we would not wish to see the Manchester Unity stand in its way. The Manchester Unity exists for the benefit of its members, and we do not believe that it will interfere with it at all; but we do believe that it will raise the moral condition of the people generally.

Many members and officials clearly suffered real tension between their appreciation of the needs of the poor and the desire to perpetuate their own institutions.

The second largest of the affiliated orders, the Ancient Order of Foresters, most consistently and for the longest period opposed state pensions. Its reasons are interesting, as they were expressed by its leading members in journals, conferences and newspapers: that the proposals of middle-class politicians like Chamberlain should be treated with suspicion, for they were means of evading the just demands of the working class for higher wages and regular work. Employers and middle-class politicians supported social reform because it was cheaper than increasing wages, the more so because it would be paid for by the working class themselves. The latter, they argued, were the main contributors to government revenue, more of which, they argued, was derived from indirect taxes on tea, tobacco, alcohol and cocoa, which were paid disproportionately by the working class than from the income tax and death duties levied on the wealthy. If there had to be pensions or other reforms, the Foresters preferred them to be financed by local rates, which, at least in theory, were progressive taxes levied according to the value of property.

Successive editorials in the *Foresters Miscellany*,[15] their monthly magazine, urged members to oppose state pensions and all forms of state 'welfare'. Instead they should support trade unionists in their struggle for higher wages, which would enable workers to save independently for sickness and old age. Thus they would retain their independence, in preference to increasing dependence upon and control by a state which operated in the interests of an opposing class; this would also, of course, enable the friendly societies to survive.

In particular, collective action of this kind could help the impoverished masses outside the friendly society movement, towards whom the Foresters expressed a particular responsibility, as fellow members of the working-class. They recognised that their wages and conditions of work currently made it impossible for them to save systematically. They opposed state pensions but not due entirely to self-interest, or fear of state competition. These opinions were those of the leaders of the AOF, though they received repeated support and acclamation at conferences and local meetings.

By 1904, however, the Foresters had changed their views and supported preferably non-contributory state pensions. Their suspicion of the motives of state 'welfare' legislation had not lessened, but they had to recognise the extent of need and that it was unlikely to be alleviated by any other means in the foreseeable future.[16]

There were also, of course, influential members of leading friendly societies who upheld the orthodox opposition to compulsion and dependency upon the state. Others, however, supported state action on the grounds that the state had a duty to support those who worked to sustain it; these were likely to advocate redistributive taxation for the financing of non-contributory pensions.[17]

Clearly, friendly society opinion was divided, and cannot be described as unified pressure against state insurance pensions.

The labour movement, as it became increasingly organised in the 1880s and 1890s, demonstrated similar divisions of opinion to those among and within the friendly societies, from opposition to any state welfare as a means of undermining the labour movement and maintaining social inequality, to the acceptance by many trade unionists and supporters of the political labour movement that state pensions by improving the condition of the poor could only be beneficial. Many had reservations about a measure which they interpreted as a substitute for providing the higher wages which would enable working men to retain their independence, but recognised, like the Foresters, that by no other means would destitution in old age be alleviated in the short run, and that many poorer people wanted and needed pensions.

By the end of the 1890s pensions were supported, for a variety of motives, by almost all sections of the labour movement; most supported non-contributory pensions as a just reward for a working life, necessitated by the probable difficulties of casual workers and women in making contributions to a self-help organisation, or to state insurance. In general, they supported universal non-contributory pensions of 5s p.w. for all above the age of 65. This age was chosen as the assumed age at which most became incapable of regular work, although it was argued that workers in such heavy occupations as mining and dock labouring were unable to work past 55.

From 1899 the labour-based National Committee of Organised Labour for the Promotion of Old Age Pensions took a major part in the pressure for non-contributory pensions.[18] This organisation was inspired, and the case for non-contributory pensions much strengthened, by the intervention of Charles Booth. Booth discovered from his early poverty surveys the extent of poverty among the aged. So that all in need would be adequately and immediately supported he advocated in 1891 a universal non-contributory pension of 5s per week at 65. He opposed insurance pensions on the grounds that no scheme proposed allowed payment of pensions for several years.[19] He stopped short, however, of extending his 'universal' scheme to those who had been paupers (as John Brown points out). His proposal was attacked as 'ruinously expensive'.[20] Blackley described it as 'a form of universal pauperisation'.[21]

Opposition, especially to the cost of his proposal (estimated at £30m) led Booth in 1899 to propose a higher pensionable age of 70, but a higher pension of 7s. His research into poverty suggested that 5s was an inadequate weekly sum for subsistence.[22] Rowntree, in his later York survey of 1901, also estimated that 7s p.w. was the subsistence minimum for a single adult. Despite this, the National Committee of Organised Labour did not alter its claim for a 5s pension. Booth estimated that his latest proposal would involve a 'socialistic transfer' of some £20m per annum.[23]

The movement for non-contributory pensions was also encouraged by their introduction in Denmark in 1891 and in New Zealand in 1898, by a Lib-Lab government, although both were on a restrictive basis.[24] The New Zealand Act gave up to 7s per week to those over 65, who could prove in a magistrates' court both their destitution and their good character. Similar legislation was passed in New South Wales in 1900 and in Victoria in 1901. The Danish scheme was also strictly means-tested.

The National Committee rejected such restricted schemes. But it was argued elsewhere that Britain was larger and had a proportionally larger problem of poverty than these other countries and hence could not afford schemes even so bold as those introduced abroad.

However, the possibility that any form of pension scheme would be introduced in Britain had seemed to be dashed by the report of a committee set up by the new Conservative government in 1896 chaired by Lord Rothschild. Its purpose was to reassess the negative conclusions of the Royal Commission of 1895. The majority report of this much divided Commission had concluded that the number of aged poor was declining, hence future provision was unnecessary, but that the Poor Law should treat the existing aged with more consideration.[25] The Commission had heard all points of view and concluded that the time was not ripe for state pensions.

The Rothschild committee, however, was directed to examine schemes designed to encourage the working class in 'thrift and self-reliance', and means of securing friendly society co-operation. Hence the Committee examined only contributory pension schemes, and failed to find a feasible one. Its report, too, was quite negative.[26]

The Conservative backbenches contained both active supporters of state pensions, such as Lionel Holland MP, for the large working-class constituency of Bow and Bromley, who supported limited non-contributory pensions, and opponents of any gesture which sought to increase the burden of rates or taxes upon the middle class. The Cabinet was similarly divided. Chamberlain was Colonial Secretary. He was already moving towards his last great political campaign, for protection of the imperial economy by tariffs, both to encourage the further expansion of British industry and to provide revenue for necessary reforms. However, he retained his belief in the necessity for a limited non-contributory pension scheme. Two Cabinet Ministers, Balfour and Henry Chaplin, the President of the Local Government Board, were sympathetic to his ideas.

The Prime Minister, Lord Salisbury, was largely indifferent to social reform. The Minister who held the ultimate veto over any increase in national expenditure, the Chancellor of the Exchequer, was Sir Michael Hicks-Beach – of whom Salisbury wrote despairingly: 'The influence which the Gladstonian garrisons of the Treasury have upon Hicks-Beach's mind is very disastrous'.[27] He was most unlikely to welcome expensive social reform.

Nevertheless, the combined influence of Chamberlain and his colleagues, with widespread disappointment with the Rothschild Report, led to the setting up of a select committee in 1899, to study the question yet again. It was chaired by Henry Chaplin.

This Committee rejected insurance pensions, due to the inability of the poorest to contribute, and to the assumed time lag before pensions could be paid. After examining the Danish and New Zealand schemes, the Report proposed legislation similar to that of both countries: a means- and character-tested pension of between 5s and 7s per week, payable at 65, to those with incomes of under 10s per week. Bad character was defined as imprisonment or receipt of poor relief within twenty years of the claim, or failure of a claimant to have done his 'best to provide for himself and his dependents'.[28]

The Chaplin Committee succeeded in devising a scheme which was both non-contributory and appeared to contain stimuli to self-help. Its total annual cost was estimated at £7½m. It left the assessment of pensions claimants to Poor Law Guardians. Despite his dislike of this association with the Poor Law, Chamberlain was satisfied. He wished, however, to add a voluntary contributory scheme to the basic pension proposed to the Committee.[29] When the Chaplin Report was followed by a civil service interdepartmental committee, chaired by a permanent secretary at the Treasury, to cost the Chaplin proposals, legislation seemed imminent.

The Cabinet discussed the possibility in November 1899. Balfour proposed legislation on the lines proposed by the Chaplin Committee, but suggested replacing assessment by the Poor Law Guardians with that of specially constituted committees to remove any association of pensions with the Poor Law.[30]

The Treasury tried hard to dissuade the Cabinet from such a course. A Treasury memorandum rejected contributory pensions on the familiar grounds that they could not cover those in real need, including women, because they could not afford contributions, and because of the long time-lag before pensions could be paid. Transitional arrangements were too expensive for them to contemplate.

Universal non-contributory pensions were rejected by the Treasury as 'proposals which could never have been recommended by a government to parliament'. The Treasury found the Chaplin proposals equally unacceptable, but more insidious.

> It is a grant made without the condition of destitution which is a safeguard of the Poor Law . . . it would be an inducement not to thrift but to fraud, both in statements of income and in assignments of property; it would lead to the reduction of wages and pensions now given to old people by their employers and to the withdrawal of help now given to the aged by their relatives or by charities. And the socialistic principle on which it rests, that the 'soldiers of industry' who have not a certain 'living wage' of their own shall be pensioned by the state, if once adopted is certain to be extended.

The Treasury feared that any moderate pensions measure would be under pressure for extensions the government could not afford. The memorandum recognised that it was politically impossible to do nothing for the aged. It recommended therefore, as the 1895 Commission had done, more generous treatment of the aged by the Poor Law.[31]

No more was heard from the Cabinet of pensions legislation; instead, in 1900, a circular was issued to Poor Law Boards suggesting better treatment of the aged.[32]

The opening of the Boer War in 1899, and its greater intensity and cost from 1900, rescued the Conservative cabinet from further consideration of the issue. The cost of the war, the government claimed, left no surplus for financing social reform. Chamberlain's ministry was closely involved with the war. Most of the population seemed more concerned with the war than with demands for reforms. The National Committee of Organised Labour found it almost impossible to arouse interest in pensions.[33]

When the war ended in 1902, Labour pressure for non-contributory pensions revived. The Conservatives, now led by Balfour, set up another select committee, which in 1903 produced a report almost identical to

that of the Chaplin Committee.[34] But it was obvious when a private
member's Bill on the lines it proposed was introduced in 1904 that
Conservative backbench opposition was very strong. Members were
convinced that existing rates and taxes were causing ruin especially in
agricultural constituencies and nothing should be done to increase
them. Sir Carne Rasch, from Essex, opposed the Bill because he 'did not
want his agricultural friends and himself to be compelled to retire to
the workhouse'.[35] The Treasury insisted that there could be no increase
in government expenditure.

So the situation remained until the Liberal victory of January 1906.
Campbell-Bannerman, the new Prime Minister, and Asquith, the
Chancellor of the Exchequer, were soon under pressure to introduce
pensions from the larger number of 'new' Liberal radicals in the
Commons after the 1906 election,[36] and from the need to counteract
the new attraction of Labour to working-class voters. They faced
deputations of Labour supporters demanding pensions. The necessity for
pensions was one of the issues on which most Liberal radicals and Labour
supporters were united.

Once persuaded of the need for pensions in some form, Asquith
faced the real problem of shortage of government revenue. The Treasury
still insisted that the growth of ordinary government expenditure was
outstripping the growth of revenue. Most serious in the long run, in the
Treasury's view, were the apparent limitations on the potential growth
of revenue. Direct taxation, from the flat-rate income tax, could be
increased either by increasing the flat-rate levy, which was judged to be
impossible without harming those taxpayers with incomes immediately
above the £160 p.a. lower limit of taxable income, or by introducing a
graduated income tax, which was flatly rejected by Treasury,
Conservatives and many Liberals as a solution seriously advocated only
by socialists. Indirect taxation could be significantly increased only by
extending important duties and taxes on foodstuffs, which raised the
spectre of tariff reform. They also repeated their objections of 1899 to
any form of pension.[37]

Asquith chose to risk the taint of socialism in preference to that of
tariff reform. In 1907, after much Treasury opposition, he began the
gradual introduction of a graduated income tax.

Once this solution to the financial problem was in sight, Asquith set
a Cabinet committee to devise a scheme of pensions. A determined
Chancellor could override Treasury objections. He was convinced, after
reading a speech made by Chamberlain in 1895, of the necessity for non-
contributory pensions, believing that this was the only way to help the

poorest. He saw no need for universal benefits which he, like many others, rejected, as giving needlessly to the rich, despite Charles Booth's assurance that it could be recouped through taxation.

Labour support for universal pensions continued, while the Conservatives moved towards official support for contributory pensions, on the grounds that it was the cheaper scheme and did most to encourage self-help.

The most clearly formulated arguments for contributory pensions at this time were expressed by William Beveridge, in a series of articles in the *Morning Post* early in 1908, following a visit to Germany. He was convinced that no government would be prepared to pay the cost of an adequate subsistence-level universal non-contributory pension, but would resort instead to a limited means-tested scheme.

Means-tested benefits were, he believed, inefficient for detecting need and administratively wasteful. He added, not entirely seriously, that if the scheme was to be limited there was a great deal to be said for restricting it to women in the first instance: the test of qualification was simple and unmistakable; the need was undeniable since few women earned enough to save for old age; and the total cost would be halved.

An extensive study of trade union retirement pay convinced him that the majority of workers required superannuation at the age of 65, but that the age of physical incapacity for work varied considerably among individuals and occupations. He was also convinced that 'to make the old age pension payable only on proof of poverty, is at once to deprive it of its honourable character and to give it not as deferred pay for valuable services, but as alms in alleviation of failure'. For this reason, he was impressed by the German system of invalidity pensions which 'gave not pensions at a fixed age, but pensions whenever invalidity began'. He was convinced that only an insurance scheme could fulfil this need.

Beveridge was convinced of the need for a grand design of welfare such as Germany had carried out, and conceived of pensions as the first instalment of a wider ranging programme of remedies for the major categories of need. Beveridge's preference for social insurance derived partly from his belief that it was the most efficient means of caring for the poor, but more centrally from his belief at this time in the capacity of social reform to promote social integration and cohesion in place of conflict. He believed that social insurance, in particular, could foster interdependence, social solidarity, and feelings of identification with a benevolent state, by teaching employers to contribute to the support of 'workers' who were unable to work, rather than to exploit and antagonise them, and by encouraging co-operation by employers and workers in insurance administration.[38]

He was, however, curiously blind to the real difficulty of providing insurance for the casually or irregularly employed. He dismissed the problem, with 'surely they waste more than 2d per week on drink, let them contribute that . . . How can a man better prove that he needs and deserves a pension than by paying for it?' His approach was, however, influenced by his optimistic assumption that 'their whole working life is one which will not be allowed to continue permanently in a well organised state'. This difficulty could not, however, be so easily dismissed and remained a major obstacle to the implementation of contributory pensions.

Asquith gave no further consideration to such arguments. He was assured of such articulate support as that of the Liberal businessman, Alfred Mond. Mond, the founder of Imperial Chemical Industries, voiced during the passage of the Pensions Bill through the Commons the support, he claimed, of many employers in Chambers of Commerce for non-contributory pensions. Having studied the German scheme, which many Conservatives advocated during the debates, and having discussed it with German employers, he was convinced that it was unnecessarily costly and cumbersome and that the same results could be achieved more cheaply through a system financed directly from taxation. He

did not believe himself from his experience of workmen that their moral fibre was of such very small calibre that the question as between a contribution of one-third and nothing was going to make all the difference between pauperisation and thrift. He thought it was an absurd idea.

Its supporters, he pointed out, often forgot that the German scheme included character tests. Claimants could be refused pensions if they had made themselves incapable of work due to 'drunkenness, sexual excess and a whole number of other things'.

In his experience, all employers who had taken an interest in the question — 'and nearly all large employers had to face the question one way or another' — supported non-contributory pensions. Those who had tried to develop occupational pensions met the difficulty that they could not afford to give pensions to workers who joined them late in life, 'and gave the best years to another firm'. Yet they recognised the injustice of employing only younger men. They were unwilling to introduce contributory schemes because they could not guarantee permanent employment to any worker. State pensions would remove this burden from employers.

Mond was, perhaps optimistically,

> perfectly certain, if money was wanted for these schemes, employers on the whole would be quite favourable to paying some kind of tax on wages which would go towards helping to solve this question.

In his view,

> the employer had a most direct benefit in the work of his workman during his life and, therefore, he would willingly give more than the ordinary taxpayer in order to see his workman decently well off in his old age. No employer with any feelings at all liked to feel that when his workman was getting old, he had no alternative before him except the workhouse.

Mond repeated Bismarck's defence of the German Insurance Bill in the Reichstag:

> That the veterans of labour are entitled to a pension as much as the veterans of war.

He was in favour of restricting pensions to the 'industrious':

> It might be a little difficult to apply, but he was perfectly convinced that if they allowed the wastrel, the well-known village drunkard, the recognised loafer, who was turned out of his union because of his chronic laziness, to come in with the men who had lived decent honest lives, they would do a great deal of harm.

The means test would help to increase economic growth and hence would ultimately diminish the need for pensions:

> One thing which stopped increased prosperity was the enormous burden the young generation had to carry on their shoulders for the support of the old ... if the burden of life was taken from the young and they were given a full chance to do for themselves, in one or two generations the working classes in this country would not want a pension at all.

The philanthropic soap manufacturer, W.H. Lever, 'heartily' supported
non-contributory pensions. He opposed contributory insurance because
he believed that not all workers could afford to contribute throughout
life, but the experienced businessman added the less commonplace
reason that it was a

fallacy that there would be investments available for the funds contributed, without entirely destroying and breaking up the very
foundation on which the investments in this country rested.

It was better, he argued, that pensions should be paid from 'just and
fair' taxation. In his view the existing system was unfair, since, though
the working class did not pay income tax, they paid a higher proportion
than the wealthy of their income in tax through indirect taxation, a
system which justly caused resentment. He supported the introduction
of a graduated income tax.

Pensions, he believed, would stimulate industry; 'the old would
receive their pensions and on that basis they would build up a sounder
Britain than we had today'.

He opposed character tests because they would be unjust to 'people
who had lived lives which ought to entitle them to esteem and respect'.
Any member of parliament, he pointed out, would resent such an
inquisition into his own affairs, and they ought not to impose it upon
others who were equally respectable.[39] This would omit many in need,
but would be much cheaper.

The Treasury insisted that it could allow no more than £7m p.a. to
be spent on pensions. Hence the Bill was preceded by a long discussion
in the Cabinet committee as to the qualifications for pensions which
could be introduced to keep the scheme within the financial limit.[40] The
major new restriction which resulted from the Treasury limit was the
raising of the pensionable age from 65 to 70.

The resulting Bill gave 5s per week pension at the age of 70, to those
with income of less than £26 p.a. (altered during the committee stage to
a sliding scale giving pensions of 1s–5s p.w. to those with incomes
between £21 and £31 10s p.a.), provided that they did not receive poor
relief after 1 January 1908, had not been imprisoned for any offence,
including drunkenness, during the ten years preceding their claim, were
not aliens or the wives of aliens, and could satisfy the pensions authority
that they had not been guilty of 'habitual failure to work according to
his ability, opportunity, or need, for his own maintenance or that of
his legal relatives'. It was a pension for the very old, the very poor and

the very respectable.

The pauper disqualification was removed, after parliamentary clamour, in 1911. The 'habitual failure to work clause' appears not to have been implemented. Throughout the passage of the Bill through the Commons there were demands to extend its scope. Hence the fear was confirmed that, once implemented, limited reform schemes would be under pressure to take further expensive steps.

In all, 490,000 of the very old and very poor received pensions in January 1909. The experience of this legislation had at last convinced the Treasury that non-contributory welfare benefits might in the long run be more costly than they had anticipated. This was also clear to Lloyd George, who succeeded Asquith as Chancellor in April 1908 and guided the Bill through the House of Commons. He was already considering legislation for health benefits. The need to refuse desirable improvements in the pensions Bill, due to the financial constraint, convinced him that more effective future legislation would need the other sources of finance available to a national insurance scheme. He was also fully aware that the Treasury was unwilling to accept further non-contributory social legislation. Hence, immediately after the pensions Act became law, he visited Germany to investigate the previously maligned health insurance scheme.[41] From this trip emerged the health insurance legislation of 1911.

It was also arguable that the insurance approach was better suited to health benefits and to Churchill's unemployment measures of 1911 than to pensions. Pensions were needed by those already past work and past the capacity to contribute. Health and unemployment benefits were needed by those, even the better paid, who could still work. The problem of women and the underemployed remained, and despite some efforts to include them, they gained little from the health and unemployment insurance legislation of 1911.

The emergence of national insurance did not take the form of the natural evolution sometimes supposed; rather it resulted from the Treasury's refusal to pay for more comprehensive non-contributory benefits, after the experience of the Pensions Act.

Notes

1. Estimate. The true figure is difficult to calculate due to the lack of suitable contemporary returns.
2. B. Gilbert, *The Evolution of National Insurance in Great Britain* (1966).
3. Pat Thane, 'Women and Welfare in Victorian and Edwardian Britain', *History*

Workshop, forthcoming, 1978.
4. H.L. Blackley, 'National Provident Insurance', *Nineteenth Century*, November 1878, p. 850.
5. Ibid.; M.J.J. Blackley (ed.), *Thrift and National Insurance as a Security Against Pauperism (1906)*; Blackley's evidence to the Select Committee, H.C. 270 1885, H.C. 208 1886, H.C. 257 1887.
6. Board of Trade (Labour Dept), *Report on Provision for Old Age by Government Action in Certain European Countries*, C.9414, 1899.
7. Based on evidence to the Select Committee 1885–7; and the Royal Commission on the Aged Poor 1895.
8. Quoted A. Wilson and G.S. Mackey, *Old Age Pensions* (1941), pp. 21–2.
9. C 7684 1895 Qn. 12.342.
10. Jos. Chamberlain MMS. Letter to Sir Charles Dilke, 21 April 1893.
11. *Hansard* (4th series) Vol. 60. 22 March 1899, Vols. 74–5.
12. Trade Union Branch Resolutions submitted to the Chaplin Committee 1899.
13. C 7684 1895 Qn. 16,296 ff.
14. B. Gilbert op. cit., p. 178 ff.
15. E.g. Jan., Sept., Nov., Dec. 1892; Sept., Dec. 1893; April, May, Sept., Nov. 1895; July 1896; April, Sept. 1897.
16. Ibid., Oct. 1904.
17. *Oddfellows Magazine*, Aug., Sept., Oct. 1891; Jan. 1893; Jan. 1894; Jan. 1899.
18. See *Annual Reports*, National Committees of Organised Labour for the proportions of old age pensions.
19. C. Booth, 'The Enumeration and Classification of Paupers – State Pensions for the Poor'; *Journal of the Royal Statistical Society* 1891; *Pauperism – a Picture, and Endowment of Old Age, an Argument* (1892); *The Aged Poor – condition* (1896).
20. T.W. and M.B. Simey, *Charles Booth* (1960), p. 162.
21. J. Lister Stead, 'Friendly Societies and Old Age Pensions, a Reply to Mr Chamberlain', *National Review*, XXV (March 1895), pp. 59–60.
22. C. Booth, *Old Age Pensions and the Aged Poor – a Proposal* (London 1899), pp. 37, 70.
23. Ibid.
24. F.H. Stead, *How Old Age Pensions Began to Be* (1910), pp. 11–14.
25. C 7684 1895. Report.
26. C 8911 1898. Report.
27. J. Chamberlain MSS. Chamberlain to Salisbury, 24 October 1894.
28. Parliamentary Papers 1899, Vol. XCII.
29. J.L. Garvin, *Life of Joseph Chamberlain*, Vol. 3, p. 627.
30. Public Record Office CAB 27/51/57, 15 November 1899.
31. CAB 37/51/89.
32. *Thirtieth Annual Report of the Local Government Board, 1901*, App., pp. 18–19.
33. F.H. Stead, op. cit., p. 88.
34. H.C. 276 1903. *Select Committee on the Aged Pensioners Bill.*
35. *Hansard* 1907, Vol. 134.
36. H.V. Emy, *Liberals, Radicals and Social Politics* (1973); Peter Clarke, *Lancashire and the New Liberalism* (1970).
37. Public Record Office CAB 37/51/89.
38. See José Harris, *William Beveridge* (1977).
39. Asquith MMS. Sir Samuel Welby to John Burns and other members of the Cabinet Committee, 4 November 1907.
40. Ibid., Correspondence with Meiklejohn 1907. Burns MMS., John Burns diary, 10 July 1908.

41. Sir H.N. Bunbury (ed.), *Lloyd George's Ambulance Wagon, Being the Memoirs of William J. Braithwaite, 1911–1912* (1957).

EMPLOYERS' ATTITUDES TO SOCIAL POLICY AND THE CONCEPT OF 'SOCIAL CONTROL', 1900–1920

J.R. Hay

The term or concept of 'social control' is difficult to use. Not least because the senses in which it has been used have varied enormously, but also because the range of phenomena to which it has been applied extends from whole societies over many stages of change, to marginal adjustments within a functioning society in assumed equilibrium. The term has been used by Marxists and by non-Marxists, by conflict theorists and consensus or convergence theorists. It has been seen as the central concern of sociology and as a useless and vague encumbrance in the literature best disregarded by any serious scholar.

At its broadest, social control shades off into the concept of 'socialisation', which has been defined as 'the continued process of adaptation by the individual to his physical, psychological and social environment through "transactions" (direct or symbolic) with other people'.[1] Such a definition, with its overtones of Freudian psychology, emphasises the role of the individual in the process of socialisation and in a similar way there are those who see 'social control' as being concerned very largely with self-control, though the focus is extended by analogy to social groups.

According to Janowitz, the classical use of the term 'social control' referred to the capacity of a social group to regulate itself according to desired principles and values.[2] He was referring here largely to an American tradition and to an attempt to reconcile sociology and social philosophy. He argued that this use of the term did not necessarily imply a conservative political outlook, and that social control is not the achievement of collective stability, He suggested that it was largely an empirical question whether 'the processes of social control are able to maintain the social order while transformation and social change take place'.[3] This seems to me to beg several questions, not least whether we can define a social order independently of the principles and values which may be assumed to be changing in the process of transformation. I cannot see how this idea of social control can be divorced from assumptions about an inherent set of forces in society tending to bring about cohesion — a Durkheimian *conscience collective* perhaps.[4]

Indeed the central question would seem to be whether social control precedes, or is predicated upon, some tendency in societies towards cohesion. There does seem to be a clear distinction between those who accept consensus or equilibrium models of society, no matter how great the allowance they make for disparities of power and access to resources, and those who start, as do Hobbes and Marx, from very different perspectives, with the notion that existing society is the product of antagonism, resolved by the power of certain groups or individuals.

To Marx the conflict between the classes over the control of the means of production is fundamental to the development of society and the process of social change. It is, therefore, essential for the ruling class in any society to possess a battery of economic, social, political, legal and ideological controls to maintain their hold over the property on which their position depends.

The most powerful of these controls, in capitalist society, are the economic ones which stem from the need for survival and which force the vast majority to sell their labour in order to do so. Workers must do this on the capitalists' terms, in so far as they cannot change the terms of the bargain by their own collective organisation and effort. But if this naked economic control were all that existed, then effective collective action would surely be forthcoming in each capitalist crisis. It is necessary, therefore, for the economic controls to be reinforced by the political and coercive controls exercised by the state. Even so, the power of the state would regularly be challenged were it not possible for both capitalists and the state to achieve some degree of legitimacy in the eyes of the proletariat by ideological means. This is what I take Gramsci to mean by bourgeois hegemony – the degree to which the working class accepts the dominance of the bourgeoisie as legitimate.[5]

Marxist 'social control' is a continuous process of change and adaptation under capitalism, not a series of occasional responses to departure from equilibrium. However, it has been argued that Marxists should not use this term, since it has been developed by consensus writers. Its rigorous use, according to Stedman Jones, involves taking over unspecified elements of functional analysis and the ideological assumptions of this form of sociology.[6] Short of coining a new phrase to describe the processes by which society is preserved from disruption, this is a danger which can be met by clear definition and consistent use of the concept of social control.

Here the term 'social control' is used solely to encompass the activities, actions and influence of the ruling class of Britain, by which they attempted to retain the existing basis of social relationships. It is used throughout to apply to conscious action, though it is clear that there is a whole range of unconscious activities, ideological influences and relationships which tend to preserve capitalism as a social system, independently of the conscious volition of members of its ruling class at any particular time.

Social control is a social process occurring continuously within capitalist society, and is a product of the class antagonisms of that society. Social control is not static but dynamic. Each attempt at modifying the existing basis of control is a response by the ruling groups of that society to new forms of challenge to the existing controls. Such responses themselves may help to inhibit challenge and integrate or incorporate dissident groups and individuals, but, inevitably, they do more. They alter the basis of existing controls and create in so doing the potential for new challenges, as the subordinate groups come to experience, appreciate and transcend the new forms of control. The process of control is ongoing and continuous, it is a true dialectical relationship.[7]

This can be illustrated by the analysis of G.R. Askwith in a Cabinet paper on the industrial unrest in 1911. He argued that Britain was in the midst of periodic unrest, such as that of 1833–4. Each change in the organisation of the workers had led to corresponding changes in tactics on the part of employers. He denigrated the idea that the current difficulties were purely cyclical and could be allowed to pass away naturally, and pointed to the growth in scale, organisation and coherence of the labour movement. Labour men, like others, had learned from experience. He concluded:

These being our views of the general situation, we are driven to the conclusion that some effort should be made to maintain control. Successful as the Board of Trade may generally have been in finding a solution of difficulties which appeared almost insurmountable, it must be remembered that these difficulties are becoming daily greater, and one failure may mean the letting loose of forces which would seriously damage our trade and commerce.[8]

There remains another fundamental criticism of the concept of social control, namely its breadth and ubiquity. If all policy involves control then the concept is so broad as to be valueless.[9] To this there are several possible replies. Firstly, if one accepts that all institutions and policies involve social control it is still necessary to delineate the forms of control operating and the specific aspects of their contradictory nature – the ways in which these controls do both control and create social unrest. The latter contains the seeds of further challenges to the existing controls and hence to the functioning of the system *on the basis of the existing controls*. Furthermore, certain forms of control seem specific to certain social formations or stages of society and these require analysis in relation to social change. Social control can be exerted in different ideological forms from repression to the pure liberal individualism so common in the early twentieth century, which supposed that the free rational and non-dependent person would choose something very like capitalism in one of its many forms, given an unfettered choice.[10]

How then did employers view welfare in relation to this idea of social control? First, social control was only one motive for employer interest in welfare. Considerations of economic efficiency and cost – opposite sides of the same coin – were often much more important in the minds of employers, though the arguments concerning efficiency and control were regularly used simultaneously. Indeed, it is often difficult to distinguish where efficiency ends and control begins. The creation of a docile labour force, which responds swiftly to economic incentives, involves both control and efficiency. However, employers did, on occasion, separate the two concepts clearly enough, and when they did so, it is evident that efficiency and relative costs were often of greater concern than social control.[11]

Secondly, welfare was not the only means by which employers attempted to exert control, and it was probably not the most important method of doing so. The wage system itself was a more vital element. Beyond that, however, employers had a whole range of strategies towards the labour movement which included, but did not stop at, welfare. Employers wanted militant unionism curbed, but, in this period, they were increasingly prepared to strengthen moderate unionism as a means of control.[12] Co-partnership schemes were a direct response to union militancy, and also seen as a form of control.[13] Finally, employers were clear on the need to mount an ideological campaign in support of capitalism as a social and economic system, and did so on public platforms, through the press and through politics, as well as within the firm.[14] Welfare was only one part of a broader employer approach to labour between the 1880s and the 1920s.

If one can accept that one powerful motive behind employers' interest in welfare was the desire to extend economic and ideological control over workers, then there is another and equally important question of how far they were able to influence state policy. This raises both theoretical and empirical problems about the relationship between employers as a class, or more accurately as part of a class, and the state in capitalist society. In principle, there are three ways in which this relationship between class and state can be analysed.

Firstly, there is a strong Marxist tradition that the relationship between class and state is an objective one. It is a defining feature of capitalism that the ruling class are the owners of the means of production and that the state is no more than 'a committee for managing the common affairs of the whole bourgeoisie'.[15] Therefore, the interests of class and state can be identified as being identical in ultimate essentials given the objective relationship between them. There may be apparent differences, but these are short-term, concerned with inessential problems, and arise out of 'accidental' and temporary circumstances. This I take it is what Poulantzas means when he argues

> the relation between the bourgeois class and the state is an *objective relation*. This means that *if* the function of the state in a determinate social formation and the interest of the dominant class in this formation coincide, it is by reason of the system itself.[16]

This approach, however, defines many of the interesting problems about the relationship between class and state out of existence and it would seem to be somewhat ahistorical or at least too abstract for much historical analysis. Engels certainly allowed for some degree of independence for the state when he argued that:

> The state is a power arisen out of society but placing itself above it, and alienating itself more and more from it.[17]

Though he had earlier qualified this by saying that the state is a power 'seemingly standing above society'.

There is a wide gap between superficial appearance and reality. Moreover, the relationship should be seen as an organic rather than a mechanical one, though there is continual interaction between the ruling class and the state. Marx himself, in his historical analysis, used a much more sophisticated approach than the crude formulation of the Manifesto might suggest. For example, in examining the origins of factory legislation he discussed the positive contributions of government inspectors, 'progressive employers' and the landed aristocracy.[18] Similarly he dissected the roles of financial and non-financial elements within the bourgeoisie in his treatment of the class struggles in France.[19] Therefore any reliance on purely definitional criteria is not sufficient. Moreover, as Miliband has pointed out, such reliance makes it very difficult to distinguish between various forms of state in capitalist societies, between, say, liberal democracies and Fascist states.[20]

A second approach is that adopted by Miliband himself.[21] If members of the ruling class and the state are drawn from the same social groups in society, are subject to the same socialisation and educational process (and derive their incomes from similar sources), then they are likely to share the same fundamental assumptions and interests and, in a crisis particularly, they are likely to behave in ways which tend to preserve their common interests – i.e. the maintenance of bourgeois hegemony in a capitalist society. This approach relies on probabilistic assumptions about behaviour by certain social groups according to their position in class society, especially those who make up the ruling class and the state. But do groups drawn from the same strata necessarily share common assumptions? What exactly is the nature of these assumptions? They do not stand in identical relationships to the means of production. Does this imply a possibility of divergent interests? This type of analysis is an essential, though insufficient, way of treating the problem.

Finally, one might examine the views, attitudes and policies of the ruling class, or by groups within it, and relate these to the policies adopted by the state. If a regular coincidence can be demonstrated – in the range and type of policies selected, and in those rejected – then it may be possible to indicate the nature of the relationship between class and state, and the degree of autonomy or independence which remains with the state can then be determined. Analysis along these lines requires the presentation of the objective historical situation which is to be examined. This should be followed by an account of the attitudes and policies of the ruling class and those of the state. Finally, the links between class and state which led to the adoption of policies have to be demonstrated.

Dahl made suggestions along these lines for adjudicating between Marxist and pluralist analyses of society.[22] He suggested we should look at a series of major political decisions and consider whether Marxist or pluralist explanations gave the more coherent account. But there are serious objections to proceeding solely in this way. According to Urry there is a prior question to be answered.[23] Why is it that certain issues

become matters for decision in the first place? If a ruling class exists
it may be able to prevent certain items ever reaching the political
agenda, or it may determine the form in which they do.

It would seem, therefore, that there are objections to each approach,
certainly if used in isolation. I would argue that it is necessary to combine all three to bring about any satisfactory analysis of the relationship
between class and state. Consequently the rest of this paper, which is
concerned primarily with the formation of policy, is deficient to the
extent that it does not bring out the definitional or the structural
elements in the relationship. Some of the problems of definition have
been touched on already. The reasons for limited attention here to
structural questions is, in part, that at the present stage of research it
is impossible to go further.

What then was the nature of the relationship between employers and
the state over the issue of welfare? Clearly, social legislation extended
into new fields before 1914, and even after the war expenditure on
social services continued to rise despite employer opposition. This
expansion might be explained by postulating a considerable degree of
state 'independence' from the views of the owners of capital and
employers. Alternatively, it might, in part, be accounted for by the
extent of divisions within the latter groups over the role of welfare.
Governments and civil servants were able to choose from policies which
would find favour with certain employer groups, though perhaps unacceptable to a numerical majority of employers. In either case, it
remains to be determined whether the introduction of a specific policy
represented the adoption of the employers' views or was the product of
independent pressures within the civil service or from other influential
social groups, such as the growing number of professionals in charitable,
statistical and welfare activities.

Over the period 1880 to the 1920s, it has been argued that employers
were able to influence social policy to an increasing extent. Employer
organisations became more directly involved with government during
and after the First World War. These changes gave employers new
opportunities for direct influence on the process of social legislation
and administration, though this influence was often less than employers
collectively might have wished.

Perhaps the most effective direct links between employers and government before 1914 consisted of a relatively small number of individuals,
who were within the Liberal Party or were consulted by leading
politicians or their senior civil servants on important issues. The full
extent of this interchange will probably never be known. However, the

private memorandum on 'Labour Unrest and Liberal Social Policy' submitted to the Cabinet Committee on Industrial Unrest in May 1912,
by a group which included three members of the Rowntree family,[24]
called for an enquiry into railway nationalisation, establishment of the
general principle of a minimum wage, accompanied by a reduction in
the burden of taxation on the trading classes. All three elements were
part of Liberal policy by 1914, or were implied by that policy.[25]

Before embarking on what turned out to be the contentious unemployment section of the National Insurance Act, the Board of Trade
consulted leading employers, including Sir Benjamin Browne and H.T.
Holloway.[26] Though both had reservations, neither opposed the idea
in principle, and this, coupled with the lack of critical response by
employers' organisations between the announcement of proposed
legislation in the 1909 Budget and the publication of the Bill in 1911,
may well have convinced both Churchill and his officials that
employers would not object to unemployment insurance.[27]

By its very nature, this direct contact, often on a purely personal
basis, was unknown to the mass of employers and this helps to
explain the many complaints about lack of consultation over national
insurance. Such complaints were not new, however. It was the
expressed lack of effective organised influence which was the
justification for the foundation of the Employers' Parliamentary
Council in 1898.[28] This body failed to become the central co-
ordinating body for employer opinion, and when it moved sharply to
the right during the industrial unrest of 1910—14, Sir Charles Macara
departed and formed the Employers' Parliamentary Association, which
capitalised on the rank-and-file backlash among employers, particularly
in Lancashire, against the National Insurance Act.[29]

Evidence of divisions of opinion among employers turns attention
again to the basic problem of analysis in class terms. Such an analysis
poses questions as to what constitutes a class view and how it is
formed. It is one of the most common criticisms of class analysis to
argue that there are conflicts among the groups who make up the ruling
class and wide differences among members. Such observations form the
starting point for the pluralist or elitist alternatives to Marxism, yet
there is little in Marx's writing to indicate that conflict within classes
as well as between classes does not exist, rather the reverse. Whether this
conflict is best explained, as Stedman Jones does, by postulating the
existence of differing modes of production within a social formation
or, more simply, by the necessity of competition between individual
capitalists for the existence and development of capitalism, is something

which needs further study.

It is very clear that in the period 1880–1920s there was no single employer view on social control or on the role of welfare in relation to social control. Rather this was a period during which employers began to struggle towards common approaches in the face of the internal and external challenges facing the British economy and society. Before 1914, however, there were significant groups, like the Association of British Chambers of Commerce, which for a brief period was the only national inter-industry organisation involving British employers, and important individual employers, who supported certain forms of welfare as a contribution to economic efficiency and social control, and who were able to bring influence to bear on the formation of social policy.[30]

Even at this time, however, though the examination of the evidence is only just beginning, it would appear that the majority of employers were hostile or lukewarm to most state social policy and preferred private welfare or none at all. By the 1920s the weight of organised employer opinion was being thrown against welfare, as those groups who had supported welfare before 1920 moved into opposition because of the costs involved and the apparent failure of welfare to provide the much trumpeted improvement in efficiency.[31]

How then were the views of individual employers and employer organisations formed? It has been suggested that some form of economic determinism was at work. Mathias argued that employers in consumer goods industries producing for the domestic market favoured welfare, while those in capital goods, heavy industries and mining were opposed.[32] Evidence to hand so far is probably sufficient to modify any crude generalisations about the relationship between particular forms of production and attitudes to, or the development of, welfare. There are many examples of quite sophisticated employer welfare/control schemes in heavy industry, including the Shipbuilders and Engineers Foreman's Mutual Benefit Society.[33] The reaction of the Lanarkshire Coal Masters Association to the National Insurance Act of 1911 is also interesting. Far from cutting back their existing medical benefit scheme, in conjunction with the doctors and the Miners Federation, they extended it to the wives and families of insured workmen, who were, of course, not covered by the Act. The scheme was financed by workers' contributions, with employers meeting the administrative costs.[34]

So there is evidence to suggest that employers' views on welfare were governed by more than their narrow concerns at the point of production. Therefore when it is argued that welfare schemes were intended to reinforce the existing systems of incentives and controls within the firm, this is not meant in any simple, narrow or crude sense. The structure of what Baldamus calls 'effort controls' at the point of production (e.g. piecework, incentive schemes, bonuses, etc.) was so much more efficient at relating effort to rewards for the worker that it would have been senseless to try to duplicate such systems by welfare.[35] The purpose of welfare was, rather, to reinforce incentive and control schemes by influencing the environment in which the worker laboured and lived. It helped justify the existing hierarchy of enterprises, their unitary ideology and behind these, of course, the unequal distribution of power and property.

Hence welfare was a system of ideological control at least as much as an economic control. For example, the practice of holding annual junketings, which were usually graced by speeches from the entre-preneurs stressing the need for common effort, harmony of interests and shared sacrifices, was a popular and inexpensive form of company welfare, much indulged in the textile towns of the Scottish borders.[36] Some of the spirit of these occasions, though with an element of melodramatic tragedy, is captured in a mining context in Lawrence's *Women in Love*.

If welfare was a system of ideological control, it was also a system of institutional control. The form of this control changed in quite important ways in the late nineteenth and early twentieth century, in response to the changes in British capitalism. This change has been characterised in various ways. Most recently, John Foster has dealt with the problem in his analysis of the changing process referred to as the 'labour aristocracy'.[37]

Foster argues that there was a switch from bribery through the market to bribery through institutions, what he terms Lloyd Georgeism and welfare. It seems to me vital not to see this as a one-way unidirectional process inevitably leading to the further incorporation of the labour aristocracy or of a wider section of the working class. As James Hinton has shown, the sectional craft consciousness of engineer-ing workers could spawn a defensive and economist response to dilution and other forms of government pressure, which eventually turned into the basis of the (near) revolutionary shop stewards movement by the end of the First World War.[38] Bob Holton has also demonstrated the way in which syndicalism transformed existing institutions in a wider attack on trends in wages, government policy and the incorporation of workers' leaders in the period before 1914.[39] Indeed it is not too fanciful to see in the whole period from 1890 through to the 1920s not simply the imposition of new forms of institutional control but a war for institutions, or a war between different concepts of institutions, going on among employers as well as between classes.

The early stages of the development of imperialism or monopoly capitalism had produced a considerable increase in the scale of economic organisation, even in Britain. Consequently to face this the labour movement also had to organise on a larger scale. So workers needed institutions to organise their common action. Whether these institutions should take the form of trade unions or political parties was one major issue which was debated throughout this period, with emphasis shifting in one direction then the other in response to the development of theory and practical experience. It is important to stress both aspects, because historians of the left and the right have often failed to grasp the way in which there was a symbiosis of theory and practice in these years, which created a series of novel working-class reactions to attempts by the ruling class and the state to impose their forms of control. As has been indicated already, this is something of which governments and employers at the time were well aware.[40]

New institutions posed new problems of control and the struggle for control went on inside and between institutions throughout this period, in the friendly societies,[41] over the idea of labour colonies[42] and over school boards.[43] As a result when welfare institutions were created in the period after 1906 particularly, great care was taken to ensure that they were organised in such a form as to ensure working-class participation on ruling-class terms. Take the case of labour exchanges which the left wing of the labour movement castigated as institutions for the control of labour supply in the interests of employers, rather than a means of reducing unemployment. Working-class participation was absolutely essential if labour exchanges were to operate, and for this to be obtained the official leadership of organised labour had to be offered a role in their administration. On a liberal interpretation this would indicate an honest attempt to ensure fair and impartial running of labour exchanges through the equal representation of equally powerful interests. It was not so interpreted by participants. One can ignore for the moment the objections of the left wing of labour, but what are we to make of the reaction of Shackleton, pillar of TUC, Lib-Lab and the absolute archetype of the incorporated labour aristocrat? Faced with the proposed composition of Advisory Committees he replied,

If there is a committee of 20 with an independent chairman, that is a sufficient minority for us. The independent chairman will probably be a man looked upon as of independent thought and absolutely impartial, but he will be drawn from a class which is on the employers' side — there is no doubt about that.[44]

Faced with this type of analysis, Churchill had to agree in the end that what he described as

all the questions of war that are at issue between labour and capital will go to an absolutely equal committee, on which the real combatants are represented on each side.[45]

The language in which the concession is presented is almost as interesting as the decision itself.

Employers, concerned with similar problems of control, seem on the whole to have preferred private welfare schemes under which they, or responsible committees of workers, could discriminate between efficient, deserving and respectable workers and the others. Even a liberal employer like W.H. Lever, who argued on one occasion that it was unsuitable for him to own his workers' houses since it created opportunities for improper influences over them, nevertheless in practice interfered very considerably in the lives of his employees, directly and indirectly. Workers were not allowed to cultivate their own front gardens, it had to be done by the firm, and women wishing to bring partners to company dances had to have the latter vetted by the social committee.[46] Unlike the German employer von Stumm, he did not, however, as far as I know, forbid what he considered unsuitable marriages by company employees.[47]

Lever was by no means an isolated example in Britain. The Engineering Employers' Federation instituted the Foreman's Mutual Benefit Society as a means of removing their key employees from the influence of trade unions by providing the welfare benefits, which the unions offered. Foremen had to be non-union men to join the society. Engineering employers consequently wanted to keep skilled workers and supervisory grades out of state insurance schemes as far as possible.[48]

Nevertheless, as has been indicated above, some employer organisations, groups and individuals were in favour of state welfare provided it contributed to efficiency and exercised discriminating control. When any form of state welfare was proposed, from whatever source, it was often assessed in these terms. Legislation which imposed burdens or failed to discriminate either had to be opposed or amended.[49] State welfare with its essentially bureaucratic rules and inflexibility was always a potential danger.

The attempts to modify proposed legislation to secure a greater degree of control can be illustrated in the case of the National Insurance Bill of 1911. Standard histories of this Bill make little mention of employer interest and their influence in the process of amendment. Gilbert, for example, concentrates solely on the pressure group activities of the friendly societies, the doctors and the industrial insurance companies.[50] Employers, nevertheless, secured major amendments and modifications to both sections of the Act. The Engineering Employers' Federation, for example, like many other employers wished the Bill delayed for greater consideration, but refused to countenance root and branch opposition which was being orchestrated in Glasgow by their former secretary, Thomas Biggart.[51] His successor, Allan Smith, wrote on 7 December 1911:

> I am desired by the Chairman of the Parliamentary Committee to report that this Bill has now been given a Third Reading, and to say that in Committee or in Report Stage, practically all the amendments framed by your sub-committee, to which importance was attached, have been adopted by the Government and are now incorporated in the Bill.[52]

The amendments referred to included the direct representation of employers on local insurance committees and limitations on the role of these committees in determining settlements made under the Workmen's Compensation Act.[53] Many other amendments, designed to reduce the cost of administration or recover a proportion of employers' contributions in the case of short-time working, were also carried following EEF pressure.[54]

More sweeping alterations in the Bill were achieved by a range of employers' organisations, and similar bodies including the Association of British Chambers of Commerce. Initially, the health insurance proposals had been designed to operate through existing agencies in the field of sickness insurance, pre-eminent among these being the friendly societies. The majority of friendly societies were originally spontaneous working-class organisations, but by the early twentieth century a large number of employer-sponsored or supported associations were registered as friendly societies. These provided sickness benefits and/or pensions for employees in return for contributions, usually paid by the employees themselves, but occasionally also supported by the employers.[55]

Employers' organisations were able to ensure not only that these quasi-friendly societies were accepted under the Act, but that 'shop clubs' were also granted approved society status subject to certain conditions. Shop clubs were employer-controlled sickness or accident funds, of which membership was a condition of employment. They were already the subject of registration under the Friendly Societies Act of 1896 and had to be certified under the Shop Clubs Act of 1920. Many employers wanted to see shop clubs recognised as approved societies as they stood, but this would have been quite intolerable to the trade unions or even to the friendly societies, since it would have given employers power to insist that benefits under the Act were channelled through agencies under their own control. There was the further practical objection that many shop clubs were very small, involving under a hundred workers, whereas the idea of the approved society had been to make use of larger organisations in which pooling of risks was possible.[56] In the end, Section 25 of the Act permitted the approval of shop clubs provided that compulsory membership was withdrawn and rights of transfer between societies were allowed. Employer representation on the committees of such clubs was limited to one quarter of the total membership, and subject to the employer accepting either responsibility for the solvency of the fund or making a contribution to the funds of the society beyond those prescribed under the Act.[57] To get round the point about small societies, a minimum membership of 50 was set and employers were allowed to combine for the purpose of setting up joint societies.

The virtues of shop clubs as agencies of social control were outlined, in his presidential address to the Association of Chambers of Commerce, in March 1912, by Lord Brassey.

(1) The Society would, generally speaking, consist of picked lives.

(2) The workers would manage it and have a personal interest in its efficient administration.

(3) They would impose a severe check upon malingering.

(4) The employer would contribute in excess of his statutory liability.

(5) He would be increasingly interested in providing anything conducive to the better health of his employees.

(6) The spirit of friendly co-operation and more intimate contact thereby obtained would result in a kindlier spirit and a closer relation all through the works.[58]

Brassey objected to the obligation imposed under point 4, but he argued that works societies (or shop clubs) would be of considerable benefit in linking capital and labour in joint organisation. He was worried, however, that the Act would tend to benefit the well-to-do sections of the working class rather than the very poor, but his only specific suggestion for assisting the latter was graduated contributions, rather than the Act's flat-rate scheme.[59]

In practice, the administration of national health insurance through the ex-shop clubs seems to have been highly successful from the employers' point of view. The following account is taken from the Departmental Committee on Workmen's Compensation in 1920:

> 31 of us in Sheffield, mainly the largest firms, got together, and we formed our Approved Societies ... The employers took a great interest in these Societies, which were continuations of the Yard Sick Clubs ... We do not interfere in the administration of the Health Societies of our own Works ... Friendly Society experience is the experience running these Societies ... We have provided considerable extra benefits ... The very best medical skill in the town is available that cannot be obtained under the panel doctor. I suggest that the administration of this Association ought to be investigated. It has a double effect, which is very interesting, because we have found that in a certain proportion of cases, when a man under a panel doctor is ordered to go and see one of the best specialists in the town, he returns to work sooner than face the specialist. The first experience we had of that was that out of 130 cases which had accumulated to be sent to the specialist 79 returned to work.
> ... The workpeople are keenly interested to see that their own scheme is not robbed, and if they suspect anyone of malingering, their own visitors from the Works are pretty drastic in their reports to their own Societies.[60]

But if some employers were reasonably satisfied with the results of the National Insurance Act of 1911, it appears that many more were concerned that social legislation had failed either to yield gains in productivity or to control the labour movement. Moreover, the cost of welfare had risen, according to the National Confederation of Employers' Organisations, to a level far exceeding that of Britain's competitors.[61] Consequently the weight of organised employer opinion was increasingly thrown against state welfare in the inter-war period. The change in opinion seems to centre on 1919—25. In the early stages of the Industrial Conference of 1919 proposals for extended state welfare came from employer groups;[62] thereafter, wage cuts and higher levels of unemployment became the more common means of control. Whether this apparent change of opinion results from focusing on the views of different groups of employers, or whether it represents a common movement to the right of employers as a class, is something which needs further investigation.

My conclusion in the light of this discussion would be that the concept of social control is a useful one for analysing the motivation of employers in relation to welfare within the firm and at the level of the state. It is valuable because it brings out certain aspects of welfare which employers considered important, and it directs attention to some of the characteristics of welfare which employers insisted state schemes should reinforce. It thus helps to explain employer support for state welfare at certain periods in British history. By extension, the concept is also valuable in the analysis of social welfare in Germany in the Bismarckian era and, probably, in the USA in the 'Progressive' period.

However, social control is not the key to all problems. It is not the only reason for employer interest in welfare, nor, often, the most important reason for such interest. Efficiency and cost considerations were often more important. It is far too early to be sure but I would tentatively suggest that there are cycles in employers' attitudes to welfare. There are 'optimistic' periods when influential employers seem to believe that extensions of private and state welfare can serve their interests and those of society. By contrast in other periods the 'costs' of welfare seem to outweigh any possible benefit. These attitudes seem to alternate, and far from having an onward and upward view of welfare, there are wide swings in employer opinion and consequently in the direction of employer influence on welfare. It is really another story, but I would suggest that the pro-welfare periods are the 1830s—40s, the 1890s—1919, and 1945—70. The anti-welfare periods are the 1850s—70s, 1920—40s, and the period we are living in now.

Notes

1. H. Brown, *Socialisation* (Open University, 1975), p. 16.
2. M. Janowitz, 'Sociological Theory and Social Control', *American Journal of Sociology*, 81 (1975), pp. 82—108.
3. Ibid., p. 85.
4. S. Lukes, *Emile Durkheim* (1973), pp. 4—6. For a recent survey of the

literature on social control see C.K. Watkins, *Social Control* (1975).
5. K. Marx and F. Engels, 'The German Ideology', cited in M.C. Howard and J.E. King, *The Political Economy of Marx* (1975), p. 7; A. Gramsci, *Selections from the Prison Notebooks* (1971), pp. 12–13.
6. G. Stedman Jones, 'Class Expression or Social Control.' An unpublished paper delivered to the Labour History Society meeting on Leisure at Sussex in 1975. A brief resumé appears in *Society for the Study of Labour History Bulletin*, 32 (1976), p. 17.
7. There is also the possibility that certain forms of control may collapse because they become unacceptable to the controllers. For example, the rising cost of welfare as a means of control leads to reappraisal by members of the ruling class and attempts to transfer to less expensive forms. See pp. 121–2.
8. PRO Cabinet Paper, Cab. 37/107/70, The Present Unrest in the Labour World, 26.7.1911.
9. This point was raised forcefully at the conference by Dr José Harris.
10. H.H. Asquith, 'Liberalism', 20.1.1893, in *Speeches* (n.d.), pp. 23–4.
11. J.R. Hay, 'Employers and Social Policy in Britain: The Evolution of Welfare Legislation, 1905–14', *Social History*, 4 (1977).
12. E. Wigham, *The Power to Manage* (1973), pp. 66–71; H.A. Clegg, A. Fox and A.F. Thompson, *A History of British Trade Unions since 1889*, Vol. 1, 1889–1910 (1964), pp. 362–3.
13. E. Bristow, 'Profit sharing, Socialism and Labour Unrest', in K.D. Brown (ed.), *Essays in Anti-Labour History* (1974).
14. Glasgow City Archives, Clyde Shipbuilders Association, *Minute Book* No. 8, 25.2.1913; Wigham, op. cit., p. 54; Engineering Employers' Federation, T. Biggart to L. Field, 29.6.1897.
15. K. Marx and F. Engels, *The Communist Manifesto* (various eds.).
16. N. Poulantzas, 'The Problem of the Capitalist State', in J. Urry and J. Wakeford, *Power in Britain* (1973), p. 298. Originally published in *New Left Review*.
17. F. Engels, *The Origins of the Family, Private Property and the State*, quoted in V.I. Lenin, *The State and Revolution* (Moscow, 1969), p.8.
18. K. Marx, *Capital* (Moscow, 1961), Vol. I, pp. 278–97, esp. pp. 281–3.
19. K. Marx, *Class Struggles in France* (1936), pp. 33–40.
20. R. Miliband, 'The Capitalist State: A Reply in Nicol Poulantzas', in Urry and Wakeford, op. cit., p. 312. Also from *New Left Review*.
21. R. Miliband, *The State in Capitalist Society* (1969).
22. R. Dahl, 'A Critique of the Ruling Elite Model', *American Political Science Review*, 52 (1958), pp. 463–9.
23. J. Urry, Introduction to Urry and Wakeford, op. cit., p. 7.
24. Lloyd George Papers, C/21/1/17, Labour Unrest and Liberal Social Policy, 20.5.1912.
25. H.V. Emy, *Liberals, Radicals and Social Policy, 1892–1914* (Cambridge, 1973), p. 271; for discussion of the extent of Liberal commitment to a general minimum wage see J.R. Hay, *Origins of the Liberal Welfare Reforms 1906–14* (1975), p. 53.
26. J.R. Hay, 'Government Policy towards Labour in Britain, 1900–14: Some Further Issues', *Scottish Labour History Society Journal*, 10 (1976).
27. PRO, Lab/2/211/LE.500. Typescript report of conference with Engineering Employers' Association and Shipbuilding Employers' Federation, 18.8.1909. Churchill set out the merits of a contributory insurance system and the end to 'handing out doles on a great scale . . . these contributory insurances are quite a new step, the workmen have never been ready to do it before; we have never been able to get them so far as that before'.

28. *Textile Mercury*, 24.12.1898, cited from pamphlet in possession of Dr Howard Gospel, University of Kent.
29. Hay, 'Employers and Social Policy', op. cit.
30. Ibid.
31. See pp. 121–2.
32. P. Mathias, *The First Industrial Nation* (1969), p. 375. A full critique of this view depends on work on employers' internal welfare schemes being conducted by Joe Melling.
33. Wigham, op. cit., p. 65.
34. Scottish Record Office CB.8.2. Lanarkshire Coal Masters Association, Annual Reports of Executive Committee, 1912.
35. G. Baldamus, *Efficiency and Effort* (1961).
36. *Hawick Express* and *Hawick Advertiser* in January of each year 1906–14, passim. Copies in Hawick Museum.
37. J. Foster, 'Imperialism and the Labour Aristocracy', in J. Skelley (ed.), *The General Strike* (1976), pp. 20–1.
38. J. Hinton, *The First Shop Stewards Movement* (1975), and 'The Clyde Workers' Committee and the Dilution Struggle', in A. Briggs and J. Saville (eds.), *Essays in Labour History* (1971), pp. 152–84.
39. R.H. Holton, *British Syndicalism, 1900–1914*; see also R.H. Holton, 'Daily Herald v. Daily Citizen, 1912–15: the struggle for a labour daily in relation to labour unrest', *International Review of Social History*, 19 (1974), pp. 347–76.
40. Public Record Office, Cabinet Papers, Cab.37.110.62 & 63, 13 & 14. 4. 1912 and Cab. 37.107.70, 25.6.1911.
41. Pat Thane, *Society for the Study of Labour History Bulletin*, 31 (1975), pp. 6–8.
42. J. Harris, *Unemployment and Politics, 1886–1914* (Oxford, 1972), pp. 135–44.
43. I owe this point to Callum Brown, a research student in the Department of Economic History, University of Glasgow.
44. PRO, Board of Trade Papers, Lab.2.211.LE.500. Second Conference with Parliamentary Committee of the Trades Union Congress, 8.7.1909, 30.
45. Ibid., p. 32.
46. C. Wilson, *A History of Unilever* (1954), Vol. I, p. 148.
47. W.M. Simon (ed.), *Germany in the Age of Bismarck* (1968), pp. 204–7.
48. Engineering Employers' Federation, Minutes of Foremen's Mutual Benefit Society and Dyer Memorial Fund.
49. In June 1910 the EEF wanted Employers Liability and Workmen's Compensation Acts consolidated in a single scheme together with the government's new insurance proposals. EEF, Minute Book No. 6, 16.6.1910.
50. B.B. Gilbert, *The Evolution of National Insurance* (1966).
51. Engineering Employers' Federation, circular letters to local associations, 17.11.1911, No. 235.
52. EEF, Microfilm Records, I(8)11, 7.12.1911.
53. EEF, Microfilm Records, I(8)2, 19.7.1911. The necessary amendments were moved by the Attorney General and 'one of the Government's own supporters'.
54. EEF, Report of Parliamentary Committee for 1911, pp. 1–5.
55. E.W. Brabrook, *Provident Societies and Industrial Welfare* (1898). I owe this reference to Joe Melling. See also Annual Report of Chief Registrar of Friendly Societies for 1911, House of Commons (123), 1912–13, pp. 65–7.
56. Gilbert, op. cit.
57. A.S. Comyns Carr, W.H. Stuart Garnett and J.H. Taylor, *National Insurance* (1912), pp. 213–15.
58. Association of Chambers of Commerce of the United Kingdom, Report of

Proceedings at Autumnal Meeting (1912), pp. 17–19.

59. The Second Schedule of the Act did introduce lower rates of contribution for employees earning less than 2s 6d per working day. No employee contribution was due on earnings of less than 1s 6d per day. Comyns Carr et al, op. cit., p. 140.

60. British Parliamentary Papers, Departmental Committee on Workmen's Compensation, Minutes of Evidence, Vol. II, Cmd. 909 (1920), Q.14690, evidence of A.J. Hobson, representing Association of Chambers of Commerce of the United Kingdom and various companies in Sheffield and Birmingham.

61. PRO, PIN/7/73. N.C.E.O. Memorandum on Widows, Orphans and Old Age Contributory Pensions Bill, 8, 14.5.1925.

62. Department of Employment, National Industrial Conference, Sub-Committee 3, Unemployment. Memorandum submitted by employers' representatives, 18.3.1919.

SOCIAL CONTROL AND THE MODERNISATION OF SOCIAL POLICY, 1890–1929

John Brown

Social control is an ambiguous concept because it has been used of so many different types of constraint, from the enforcement of law, through religious and other cultural influences which can in a sense be freely accepted or rejected, to the socialisation of children within the family.[1] A concept which can draw equally easily on studies of institutional bureaucracy and on psychological theories of personality, is a vessel into which very different definitions might be poured. Its value lies in the general questions which it raises about the nature of social policy, and which tend to miss systematic examination in historical discussion. Here the predominant language has been of rights and freedoms. Though there has not been much borrowing from the social sciences, a considerable debt, whether acknowledged or not, has accumulated to T.H. Marshall's discussion of citizenship and social class. His description of a move away in the twentieth century from a narrow concern with property and political rights to a new concern with social ones, and of a growing sense of citizenship which reduces the importance of class inequalities, makes explicit assumptions which lurk behind many general histories of modern social policy, even though some recent research cannot very easily be accommodated within Marshall's model.[2]

The language which historians use mainly derives from the new attitudes to social policy which emerged around the turn of the century, and it reflects some of the ambiguity which these displayed. One major concern was to humanise and liberalise social administration. In a memorandum, which has often been quoted since it was first published in 1957, Lloyd George wrote in 1911 that the trouble with the Poor Law was not that it failed to meet need but that it did so under conditions 'so harsh and humiliating that working-class pride revolts against accepting so degrading and doubtful a boon'.[3] The new attitudes also stressed the possibilities of what now might be called social engineering. When Alfred Marshall in 1890 called for hard work over a number of years to remedy the defects of the census, or when Canon Barnett in 1902 implored the TUC delegates not to import the language of warfare into industrial relations,[4] they were expressing two aspects of the belief that research could solve social problems provided political and legislative processes were not distorted by the force of emotion and class hostility. Beatrice Webb in 1906 told the Sociological Society that the social and physical sciences shared a common scientific method and that although the former could not experiment in the same way as the latter, a change in public administration on the basis of previously tentative courses of action constituted 'an experiment of a kind'.[5] This vision of objective research and expert opinion as arbiters of policy could seem authoritarian even to contemporaries. But very few thought that there was any real conflict between a scientific and a humane policy. The seductive notion of a national minimum, which once it was established could be progressively raised, lulled any suspicion that the needs which were collectively acknowledged by the state might fail to coincide in any major respect with those which were subjectively experienced within society.

The equation of scientific policy with an informed consensus produced an impulse towards the accommodation of practical differences; it is also possible to detect in the consensus, which limited and contained debate on specific proposals, an implication that modernisation involved some loosening of traditional controls. In 1909 both the Majority and Minority Reports of the Poor Law Commission abandoned the principle of a deterrent Poor Law in the sense that they accepted that those in need must be persuaded to apply for relief as early as possible, certainly before their cases became hopeless. It was believed from the start of national insurance that its impersonal functioning, its uniform obligations and guarantees, and its contributory basis, created a sense of right or entitlement among those within the scheme. Where means testing and personal enquiry continued to have a central role, in poor law, local government and charitable services, it was felt that skilled casework would legitimise their use, provide a valuable element of discretion, and prevent the clients of these agencies from suffering any unjustifiable shame and demoralisation.

What is needed is a perspective which places this concern to respect personal dignity (both as an end in itself, and because a failure to do so could render policy ineffective), and a wider discussion of rights and status, in the same context as other, very different aspects of legislation and administration. The cluster of associations around some meanings of social control provides this.

In its 'paradigm sense', according to Lukes, Durkheim's concept of *contraint social* describes 'the exercise of authority, backed by sanctions, to conform to rules'.[6] This definition, whatever further questions it raises, draws attention to what T.H. Marshall's approach neglects, in spite of its concentration on legal changes. The rights or entitlements in legislation cannot be separated from the restrictions, obligations and disqualifications. Both form part of a single code of authoritative rules. All social policy is therefore a series of statements and reinforcements of what is considered socially appropriate. In the case of the legislation which, from at least 1908, clearly broke with the past, the central moral values were the maintenance of family obligation and of the need to work.

The continuing social control function of social policy is most obvious in the coercive power of the law. Legislation created new and complex legal obligations, and a substantial body of precedent arose from decisions in the ordinary courts or by administrative tribunals. More intangible constraints on conduct, powerful though difficult to trace, came from contact with the bureaucracies which administered the new policies. An awareness of these ran through the pages which the 1909 Majority Report of the Poor Law Commission spent on the training and qualifications of officials, on their pay, working conditions, career prospects and chances of mobility, on the methods by which money should be dispensed, on the suitability of women rather than men for certain tasks, and on many other details. It is more commonplace now than it was then to analyse the way in which experience of clients at the hands of agencies of social administration can influence the way they see themselves and their place in society, and how social policy can either diminish or generate stigma — the situation in which an individual feels, or is considered by others to be, disqualified from full social acceptance;[7] but there is a certain continuity of discussion. In theory two processes, one formal and the other relatively informal, can be distinguished. It is probably meaningless, however, to draw a strong contrast between behaviour altered by the force of external sanction and alterations which arise from subjective experiences — the first produced by legal requirements and the second by administrative procedures — for an unemployed man at the labour exchange, or a family whose children were fed at school, could scarcely very easily distinguish between the two.

A complication is that policy can have unintentional effects, or its intentions can be ineffective and unreal. This last point is made by Barbara Wootton when she describes the history of social policy as needlessly littered with devices 'born of the fear that the "working classes" would belie their name'.[8] If these provisions only reflect irrational fears, an examination of them leads mainly to a study of legislative pathology. However, when another contemporary observer of

what is now called officially 'voluntary unemployment' writes that 'the
problem of stigma may be seen in its most tragic form among those
who appear to feel it least',[9] this comment on an unintentional consequence of policy goes against the grain of Barbara Wootton's remark.
Moreover, it carries echoes of the fear which was frequently expressed
before 1914, that the expansion of new social services would call into
being a class of dependent clients, no matter what devices were designed
to avoid this danger. Attention, therefore, cannot be confined to
explicit statements of legislative and administrative intent. In places
any study of social control moves into the area of largely unacknow-
ledged motives and unspoken assumptions. In others it moves into an
exploration of unforeseen repercussions of policy.

This definition draws attention to two particular features of the new
policies which had developed by 1929. The first is the nature of the
legal requirements and disqualifications which were written into
legislation. The second is the administrative use of means testing,
personal enquiry and discretionary decisions. Though no doubt wider
definitions of the process by which social control operates would be
possible, this one has the advantage of being manageable and of relating
clearly and directly to the choices made in developing policy.

Around the turn of the century the complex attitudes towards the
ways in which the existing system of relief punished its recipients
were obscured rather than revealed by the frequent tendency to con-
demn it in generalised terms. It is very difficult to divide opinion
clearly into 'progressive' and 'reactionary' camps even over the issue
of the need to preserve or limit a punitive element. In the 1890s, for
example, Charles Booth's demand for universal old age pensions (that
is, for a system which made them available to everyone over a certain
age without any test of means) arose from a concern to prevent stigma,
but on a specific and limited front. His concern was to preserve the
morale of old people who had previously led independent lives from
a humiliating enquiry into personal circumstances. He was not much
concerned about those whose lives before old age had been punctuated
by the intervention of the Poor Law. He admitted to Alfred Marshall
in 1892 that his insistence that a pension should be granted on
application clashed with the 'reasonable' demand that people 'be
treated according to deserts', and as a solution he publicly proposed
that the Guardians should become the trustees of old age pensions for
those who had previously been on poor relief. This was to be the
preliminary to an elaborate categorisation, which would free some
from tutelage, allow others to live outside the workhouse but 'still

receive their pensions from the relieving officers' hands under supervision', and compel the rest to enter the workhouse, where a further
process of sorting out would take place. Booth believed that the
value of this proposal lay in the wide scope it gave 'for just discrimination, and that to some extent the discrimination would extend backwards if it was known that the cause of any lapse before sixty-five would
be considered . . . ' .[10]

A similar example of the complexity of a 'progressive' outlook, on
the role of punishment and deterrence in social policy, can be found in
W.H. Beveridge's views on pauper disenfranchisement. In 1905 he
followed up a sample of men, those living in Stepney, who had been
unemployed in 1903–4, and who as a consequence had received
assistance from the Mansion House Fund, to find out whether they
were on the 1904 or 1905 electoral register. About a third in fact had
the vote, but they were not those whom casework among applicants
to the Fund had labelled as the most sober and regular workers, and
Beveridge therefore reached the conclusion that the franchise 'was not
distributed with reference to merit'. He regarded this as a very important
issue. In a sense he condemned disenfranchisement because of the way it
worked, but he saw nothing wrong with the principle behind it.

> 'In the first place', he argued, 'men who cannot in ordinary circum-
> stances support themselves in independence are not citizens in
> fact, and should not be in right . . . In the second place it is
> dangerous to let recipients of public relief elect its dispensers.'[11]

The 1908 Old Age Pensions Act neatly combined the strong feelings
about the need to maintain both family obligations and the obligations
to work. It disqualified anyone who had 'habitually failed to work
according to his ability, opportunity and need for the maintenance and
benefit of himself and those legally dependent on him'. A.V. Dicey's
complaint that this provision was disregarded in deciding pension claims
has the merit of drawing attention to the fact that in practice it seems
to have excluded no one.[12] It raised awkward problems, to put it
mildly, of enquiry and judgement, but the local pensions officers and
committees were given virtually no guidance in its interpretation by
the circulars and regulations in the wake of the Act.[13]

In the wider context of the Act's other disqualifications, however,
this particular one does not appear as an empty gesture. The difficulty
of applying it had been foreseen, and it had never been expected to
have any very substantial effect. It had been pointed out well before

the passage of legislation that the number of old age pensions applicants who would be excluded by an investigation into their characters and past histories, would depend upon the accuracy and depth of enquiry, and that because of the huge total number involved and the difficulties of obtaining information, there could be no elaborate enquiry.[14] This did not seem to matter much because the test of industry and family responsibility in practice seemed to overlap with another of the Act's disqualifications, the exclusion of paupers.

The use of poor relief to determine status had a long history. Its appearance in the 1908 Act was controversial, but this was because of its precise form, rather than because of any deep objection in principle. In the long previous debate it had been accepted that a major problem lay in deciding the boundaries other than age and income to any old age pensions scheme. A poor law disqualification in some form or another appeared in almost all proposals, as part of a general attempt to discriminate between socially responsible and undesirable conduct. For example, the Chaplin Committee, whose report in 1899 had seemed to mark a breakthrough towards some practicable scheme, had recommended that pensions should begin at 65; and that anyone should be disqualified if in the twenty years before pension age he or she had received poor relief (other than medical relief) unless 'under wholly exceptional circumstances'.[15] How this suggestion could work in practice was never clear. The 1908 Act did something much more straightforward and excluded all those who received non-medical poor relief from 1 January 1908 until 31 December 1910. This was easily administered, and it immediately disqualified in England and Wales about 284,500 potential claimants. Since the 1890s, however, it had been known from analyses of the pauperism statistics that within the population aged between 60 and 80 or more, a higher proportion of each successive five-year age group was on poor relief.[16] The Chaplin Committee's wish to examine conduct during later middle age, and to turn a blind eye to occasions when poor relief had been accepted in exceptional circumstances, was not in conflict with what was known about the close connection between ageing and loss of financial dependence. The 1908 Act's penalisation of paupers over 70 was controversial because it ignored this research; and on its expiry at the end of 1910 it was not renewed. The general notion that it was possible to use the operations of the Poor Law as tests of personal responsibility was not directly at issue in the controversy.

The Act's final major test of responsibility also fell apart, although beforehand it had seemed to present no problems whatsoever. This was the disqualification of all those who were imprisoned without option of a fine during their period in gaol and for ten years after their release. In 1907 this seemed an uncontroversial, watered-down version of the Chaplin proposal to disqualify those imprisoned without option of a fine at any time during the twenty years before they reached pension age.[17] Beatrice Webb, writing privately to Reginald McKenna to indicate thinking within the Poor Law Commission, suggested that 'of course' a disqualification on the basis of a criminal conviction would be acceptable in any pensions scheme provided that it was 'nothing less than a judicial conviction'.[18] The Home Office warned that each year imprisonments resulted from 'some very trifling cases to pay fines',[19] and presumably to avoid this problem the 1908 Act only disqualified those found guilty without option of a fine. But other variations in sentencing existed, which were only dragged into light by this provision. In some cases it led to considerable hardship when short sentences of a few days, or until the court rose, prevented some people from qualifying for a pension.[20]

In 1911 amending legislation reduced the period of disqualification from ten to two years after release from prison, and the Local Government Board warned against using the formula of imprisonment without option of a fine as a disqualification from insurance benefit.[21] In insurance disqualification from benefit ran only for the period of imprisonment, but uncomfortable anomalies were not avoided, since after a test case anyone simply detained in custody was disqualified.[22]

Though the moral judgements behind this and similar provisions seemed largely unimpeachable, and they were not a source of controversy, in other areas than legislation they were not so confidently nor so inflexibly applied. One of the Charity Organisation Society's defences against the charge of prejudice was its principle of not automatically refusing to help families of prisoners; and in practice a conventional field of voluntary action lay in aiding these families and in trying to rehabilitate those discharged from gaol. The available criminal statistics told very little about the nature of crime. In 1907 only the number of prisoners over 60 was known during the framing of the pensions legislation, not their offences, nor the lengths of their sentences. Very few of them could have been in the official category of 'habitual criminals', who lived wholly or partly by crime. This definition was so loose that police forces could not make uniform returns, but in any case in 1907 the estimated number of habitual criminals in England and Wales was only just over 4,000.[23]

The 1908 Act is only one instance of a tendency to reinforce responsible patterns of conduct. In general the provisions in legislation concerned with family obligations reflected a very powerful but confused set of assumptions and values. The penalisation in the 1908 Old Age Pensions Act of those who had failed to maintain themselves and their legal dependents added to existing obligations in private law which arose from blood relationship or marriage. These were much more extensive in Scotland than in England and Wales. Under Scots law there was a very wide obligation to aliment relatives, which had been intimately bound up with the development of poor relief.[24] There was no equivalent interaction in England because of the common law's narrow vision of the duty to maintain relatives, and as a consequence the Poor Law developed as a separate system of family law for the destitute.[25]

The role of new social policies in this situation was never clearly defined, partly due to ignorance of the precise ways in which the family functioned as a social unit. Social surveys, especially those of A.L. Bowley, showed the complex composition of working-class households, most though not all of whose members were relatives, living together in greater or lesser degrees of dependency and to some extent pooling income. But what this signified in social terms was open to different interpretations.

In the 1890s some attempts had been made to discover the extent to which parents in their old age were supported by their sons and daughters,[26] but even after the introduction of pensions in 1908 very little was known about the personal circumstances of old people. There was considerable anxiety at the low level of the pension; but how many old age pensioners lived with relatives or near them, rather than in social and financial isolation, was never clear.[27]

In the controversy over school meals, which began around the turn of the century, it was not certain how much malnutrition in children resulted from ignorance or neglect rather than a family income so low that in choosing food everything had to be sacrificed to cheapness.[28] School meals were attacked on the grounds that they encouraged working-class parents to neglect responsibilities which they could fulfil; they were defended by the claim that poverty (rather than parental indifference and irresponsibility) made it necessary for the public to provide what the family could not. Both sides tended to assume that responsible parents would withdraw their children from school meals immediately they could afford to do so. During the 1914–18 war the number of children being fed at school dropped remarkably, and this coincided with a rise in real wages. This change was seen by

the official enquiry into working-class living costs in 1917 as retrospec-
tive justification for the theory that the family accepted its responsibilities whenever it could manage to do so.[29] In fact local authorities
provided school meals under a wide variety of schemes, but they all
had in common personal enquiry and means testing, and this comment
neglected the deterrent element in the service from which parents were
withdrawing their children.[30] Since their conduct was likely to be influenced by the stigma attached to aspects of this system, it proved
little directly about family concepts of responsibility.

Casework theory, which found its fullest expression in the 1909
Majority Report, was untroubled by this lack of systematic knowledge,
since it stressed the variety of family life and circumstances. Its
emphasis was not strongly challenged. The Webbs were often
accused by casework theorists of neglecting the net of kinship which
enmeshed individuals; it would be truer to say that they always aimed,
wherever possible, to take account of family relationships, though often
in a purely negative way. A key position in the Minority plans was
held by the Registrar of Public Assistance, a local authority officer
whose staff was to be concerned with recovering as much as possible
of the cost of the new specialised services from those who used them.
The Majority pointed out that such a powerful emphasis on means
testing, especially in the case of illness, threatened to deter those in
need from applying.[31] Bernard Bosanquet criticised it as negative in
a somewhat different way. He argued that if the Registrar were given
suitably trained and skilled staff and responsibility for the treatment
of cases, he could perform a positive role, which would bring the
Minority proposals very near to the Majority ones.[32] Here lay the seeds
of the reconciliation of two 1909 Reports, which was achieved by the
1917 committee of the Ministry of Reconstruction. The fruit of
reconciliation was the proposal for a Home Assistance Committee, concerned with family casework, at the local authority level.

These plans were not implemented, but neither was the thinking
behind them completely set aside. Change conformed very broadly to
what they considered desirable. Increased co-operation between
charities and the state, greater specialisation, and family care, however,
developed in a much less systematic way than they envisaged.

In practice, from before 1914, a range of new services developed,
where those who were assisted remained in their own homes.[33] These
were all means tested but had little else in common. No uniform
scales of assessment existed, and even the same local authority used
different ones for different purposes. There was no agreed definition,

either of a family or a household, of the unit which should properly be assessed. By the 1920s the anomalies created by the procedures were the subject of severe criticism. There was scarcely any agreement, however, about the principles upon which rationalisation should be based. The English Poor Law confined obligations to near relatives, whereas households might contain relatives only distantly related.[34] The introduction of dependents' allowances into unemployment insurance led to further definitions of 'dependent relative', and of whether the relative was 'mainly maintained' by the claimant.[35] Different assumptions about the pooling of income by wage-earners within the same family or household could lead to considerable differences in estimates of general poverty.[36] Argument tended to move uneasily between the actual and the theoretical. On the one hand, there was the discussion of the extent to which family co-operation reduced existing need, and on the other, of the extent to which it might be properly forced to do so.

It might be possible to trace an incomplete and uneasy transition between the 1890s and 1929 from the notion of family ties as weak and in need of reinforcement, to an acceptance of their value and strength; but this would be a very fleeting and uncertain theme to take. The fear that the family was threatened, which appeared in the 1890s in the debates on old age pensions and school meals, arose partly from an exaggerated respect for the protection which it offered its members against the hazards of life. In general, social policy never managed clearly to define the family which was so often the focus of concern, nor to decide whether the main task lay in ensuring the observance of ties which were in danger of neglect, or in supplementing an effective net of kinship and help.

By comparison, legislation unequivocally stated the obligation to work. The fear of encouraging malingering was especially powerful during the framing of national insurance and left its marks in devices to prevent the abuse of health and unemployment benefit. The compulsory nature of the scheme did not to most contemporaries seem to set it apart from other legislation. The indignation against compulsion often simply cloaked the demands of interest groups, especially those of the British Medical Association. There was some relatively disinterested feeling in favour of a voluntary official scheme, but what this might amount to, other than the payment of subsidies from taxation to trade unions and friendly societies, was never clear.[37] In any case the 1911 Act was not totally compulsory, since both its parts contained major elements of voluntary insurance; and the indirect administration of the health scheme through 'approved societies' seemed to safeguard the interests of voluntary organisations.

It was difficult to delineate the precise boundaries of the 1911 insured industries. Initially there was a significant amount of under-insurance through the failure of employers and workers to realise their obligations, and almost half of the claims disallowed during the first year were on the grounds that the claimant had not worked the requisite twenty-six weeks in the insured trade over the previous five years. The scope of unemployment insurance in its expanded form of 1920, like that of health insurance from the start, was determined largely by income and contract of service. Though certain occupations, such as nursing and domestic service, were specifically exempted, by the 1920s almost everyone covered by one scheme was also in the other. National insurance did not, of course, comprehend a fixed section of the population, since, quite apart from those who had exhausted their right to benefit, there was a continuous movement into and out of insurance because of changes in age, income, occupation and other personal circumstances. On the whole, the strains experienced by this system were not internal, but arose because of the categories who were outside. Certainly features of insurance were disliked, but from the first there is evidence of its popularity; caseworkers, for example, remarked on how much the wives and families of the insured seemed grateful.[38]

The dangers of national insurance, both to its framers and its original critics, seemed to lie precisely in its attractiveness. Alternative methods of dealing with the social consequences of illness and unemployment, which had been discussed extensively by the Poor Law Commission in 1909, all involved much greater disciplinary supervision. The Minority proposals on maintenance and training for the unemployed would have meant, if they had been implemented, a conditional system of relief, discriminatory and backed by penalties for disobedience; the Majority had also wanted discrimination, differential treatment and close supervision. With regard to health the Majority had confined itself to suggesting cautious improvements in the existing medical services, but the Minority had proposed to set up a new and coercive system of public medicine. Its patients would have had no choice of doctor; could have found themselves denied domiciliary treatment even where it was practicable, if they had shown any recalcitrance in following the prescribed regimen; and could have found themselves removed against their will to a suitable place for treatment.[39]

In contrast to all these proposals national insurance seemed to be a system of relief which was largely beyond control. Beatrice Webb

pointed out that there was no means of controlling the way benefit
was used once it had been granted, and that the tendency for it to be
seen as a right meant it was very difficult to secure 'a kind of return in
the form of better conduct'.[40] The supporters of insurance did not
disagree that it might allow people to malinger outside the labour
market, pretending to be ill or unable to find work; but they believed
it was possible to control this danger. As a result the 1911 Act contained provisions, which were not necessary on any actuarial grounds,
to limit the payment of benefit in various ways. When the scheme in
the 1920s largely lost its actuarial shape, these conditions and
restrictions, slightly altered, remained to guard against abuse.

In 1911 there was very little relevant evidence to allow assessment
of the speculation and assertion which clouded the discussion of
malingering. Friendly society and trade union insurance had never
brought to light any appreciable amount of fraud, but this was held
to have no significance on the grounds that a compulsory scheme
would work quite differently from the voluntary ones of the past.
What little relevant evidence there was, seemed to come mainly from
the operations of workmen's compensation. Sir John Collie, the chief
medical expert on compensation, lent his authority to the view that
this experience showed that under national insurance malingering was
likely 'necessarily [to] increase and become more frequent', though
this was a controversial interpretation of the available statistics. Even
in 1917, after a much longer experience of the legislation, Collie was
still insisting that the rising number of non-fatal accidents was due
to workmen making the most of any injury, in the face of the Home
Office conclusion that the figures only showed an increasing knowledge
of the 1906 Act's provisions.[41] The other claim in 1911 was that in
Germany compulsory insurance had increased malingering 'by leaps
and bounds'.[42] Again this was not backed up by any close analysis,
but it was quickly noted that in Britain under health insurance the
average period of illness was longer than in Germany.[43]

The scheme also worked in certain ways to raise income during
unemployment and sickness above the flat rate. In unemployment
insurance the subsidies to voluntary schemes within the insured
industries increased benefit in a way which was strictly controlled,
since the subsidies were withdrawn if the total benefit was above a
certain amount. Within the health scheme the pre-1911 membership
of friendly societies almost universally continued to pay their existing
voluntary contributions, and large numbers of new members also
became voluntary contributors.[44] There was nothing to limit or.

prevent this and other kinds of double insurance. This seemed to create a potentially serious problem, and certainly it was difficult to see precisely what the consequences of double insurance were. It was claimed that it was 'not uncommon' for an insured person to have when sick a sum in excess of his normal wage, or at least to enjoy an income so near to this that there was 'no prick of poverty' to induce a return to work.[45]

In fact the administration of national insurance quickly supplied new information about unemployment and illness, which contradicted most of the suppositions on which the fears of malingering were based. Unemployment was very low during the first six months when benefit was paid out, and many claims never matured because new work was found within the first week of waiting which had to elapse before benefit started; in only one per cent of cases were men still unemployed after benefit had ended.[46]

In contrast, sickness claims were found to be running at an unexpectedly high rate. It was clear, however, that excessive sickness was concentrated in the membership of a few approved societies, especially those with a large proportion of women. The Act had in fact uncovered illness of various kinds in certain social groups, particularly women of child-bearing age, on a scale of which there had been little previous awareness. There was no evidence of any appreciable amount of fraud, and nothing to support any of the generalisations about the prevalence of malingering.[47]

This kind of conclusion was repeated from this time until the end of the 1920s by various private and official enquiries (except that, as health insurance dropped into even routine administration, the findings were mostly reached by examining unemployment benefit). A typical one was that of the *New Survey of Life and Labour*:

> The behaviour of the unemployed in searching for new employment gives no evidence that the possibility of drawing unemployment insurance has retarded the efforts of the unemployed to get back to work. It has removed the cutting edge of desperation which otherwise might have attended the search.[48]

These conclusions, however, failed to dissolve the anxiety that compulsory insurance would sap the will to work. They related to the operation of a scheme which had incorporated devices to guard against this danger, and the view of motivation which had produced the devices in the first place was not easily open to empirical debate, because it arose so much from *a priori* assumptions about human psychology and personality. As Collie put it, 'a very dark side of human nature' was under examination;[49] but the process of scrutiny often revealed more about the observer than the observed. The proposition that idleness was a very powerful, demoralising and corrupting force was often treated as a self-evident truth. According to a Fabian Tract of 1915, for example, there was

> Hardly any character . . . strong enough to stand up against dependence on alms . . . the mere expectation of [the dole] deadens all initiative and enterprise . . . unaccustomed idleness, with its evil loitering and inevitable gossiping, is . . . demoralising.[50]

Of course, deeper psychological penetration than this was sometimes shown. The Webbs and Collie were not wrong to describe how illness could produce a dependence upon drugs for reassurance, money wasted on patent medicines, an exaggeration of symptoms, irrational fears and even a certain childish recalcitrance.[51] They were wrong to isolate these traits of behaviour and to give them such emphasis at a time when there was widespread ill-health among those actively at work, and when financial need often put a premature end to convalescence. A darker side of human nature than the one to which Collie referred, was shown in the persistent and extensive belief, not confined to any particular class or social group, unamenable to the evidence of successive enquiries, and capable of surviving largely on hearsay, that malingering was extensive and that many people gained a living from national insurance without working.[52]

By the 1920s the question of the reform of the health scheme had become largely an academic exercise. The initial discussion of double insurance and the fear that high benefits might produce a disinclination to return to work quickly disappeared. Many approved societies increased the rates of sickness and disablement benefit by additional cash grants, as they were allowed to do if they were profitable, while others continued to pay only the basic rates. In the 1920s the unemployment scheme paid statutory allowances for dependents, but health insurance did not follow suit, and it was recognised that even for a single person the basic rate of disablement benefit was insufficient for maintenance, while for sickness it was dangerously near the margin.[53]

Between 1912 and 1914 claims were made that the panel doctors were lavishly granting medical certificates on very flimsy grounds. These came mainly from friendly society circles where considerable disquiet and resentment existed over the loss of the right to choose and dismiss a contract doctor. It was said that panel doctors had too many insurance patients to give each adequate attention; that if they failed to grant medical certificates, they lost patients to less scrupulous colleagues; and even that they were revenging themselves for their previous bondage to the friendly societies.[54] No approved society, however, collapsed under the weight of heavy sickness claims, though there were initial fears that some might. By the 1920s the tendency was to exonerate GPs from any criticism and to emphasise their responsibility; the 1926 Royal Commission, for example, found no evidence that panel and private patients were treated differently.[55] And in these circumstances malingering as a serious issue in health insurance faded into limbo.

In 1911 the actuarial requirement in the unemployment scheme that every week's benefit must be covered by five weeks of contributions, and the week of waiting before it became payable, were expected to expel the habitual malingerer. The legislation on unemployment insurance between 1920 and 1929 continued to base the payment of benefit upon a number of contributions within a fixed period, but the relationship between the two lost any actuarial validity. 'Unconvenanted' and later 'extended' benefit was in theory paid in advance of contributions until 1928; although published figures never separated the two, most claims were clearly to it rather than 'covenanted' and 'standard' benefit.

The Blanesburgh committee, and the 1927 Act which was based on its recommendations, in a sense linked unemployment insurance more firmly to a concept of need by not limiting its duration, and by abolishing the distinction between two kinds of benefit. It proposed, however, that at each three-monthly review, claimants must be able to show that they had had 30 weeks' insurable employment within the preceding 104 weeks, and that they were 'genuinely seeking work'. Since the effect of the 30 weeks' proposal would have been to expel at once large numbers from insurance, the continued payment of 'transitional benefit' was allowed until 1930, when by an arbitrary piece of optimism it was calculated that unemployment would have fallen markedly.

A curious and puzzling concept of right accompanied these changes. In theory extended and unconvenanted benefits were discretionary payments, but after Blanesburgh even transitional benefit was stated to be 'a right'.[56] In practice the destruction of the actuarial basis of the scheme threw into greater prominence the other requirements which had always been attached to the payment of benefit. Blanesburgh's requirement of 30 weeks' insured work was intended as a simple arithmetical test which could be easily applied. In fact the proposal that claimants should also show that they were 'genuinely seeking work' added to potential disqualifications which depended largely on administrative decision. What was noticeable in the 1920s was that the numbers on unemployment benefit seemed to vary because of changes in administration rather than in formal legislative requirements.[57]

Once a claim had been correctly lodged, it could be disallowed for a number of reasons. Some grounds for disqualification were minor and uncontroversial, but others were not. A claimant could be disqualified if his unemployment arose through a trade dispute, or if he had left work without just cause, or been dismissed for misconduct. The 1927 Act revised the definition of a trade dispute for the third time since 1911; it still resulted in a number of complicated appeals to the umpire, the final arbiter of disputed claims. It was always difficult to say who precisely was involved in a strike or lockout, and to a lesser extent to settle when one had begun or ended. The umpire ruled that disputes between employees over demarcation or black-legging were stoppages of work where disqualification applied, as were sympathetic strikes or lockouts. He decided that the 1926 General Strike was not 'a trade dispute'.[58]

Misconduct was not easily defined either. Cases arose from a wide variety of circumstances, such as absence from work, refusal to carry out certain tasks, refusal to comply with shop rules and conditions, negligence, insolence, swearing and drunkenness. It was held that peaceful persuasion to cease work or to insist on trade union membership was not misconduct, but that intimidation was.[59] Often the very different acts in question seemed 'the final stage in a personal tension between an incompatible employer and workman which has been developing for weeks'.[60] The men who were disqualified on the grounds of misconduct or leaving work without just cause, often suffered from a strong sense of grievance. Their disqualification arose initially from the statement which the employer supplied to the labour exchange, and Bakke believed that unless the statement was 'contradictory or confused the worker has an almost impossible burden of proof laid upon him'.[61]

Disqualification could also arise from a refusal to accept suitable employment, and after 1927 from a failure genuinely to seek work. In the first case, statute offered only a negative definition; it laid down the unsuitable circumstances, where employment had become available because of a trade dispute, or where wages and conditions were not the ones which could reasonably be expected in the district. This still left a grey area of doubt which was partly filled by the umpire's decisions. For example, it was held that the blacklisting of an employer by a trade union was not sufficient to justify the refusal of work, and that it was only justifiable to decline a job at works where a strike was going on, if the vacancy was due directly to the stoppage.[62] In the second case, the suspicion that a claimant was not genuinely seeking work led him into nerve-racking, harassing and periodic interviews with labour exchange officials. The umpire ruled that crucial to any decision was the claimant's 'state of mind'. But, as one comment put it,

> The state of a man's mind may be a matter of fact, but it is a fact of a kind on which two neutral and unbiased observers might reach opposite conclusions after the most careful consideration of the evidence available to them for forming a judgement.[63]

Decisions of this order were taken by labour exchange officials; on appeal cases came to local courts of referees, containing representative workmen and employers, meeting under an impartial chairman, and finally to the central umpire, who was a lawyer. Judgements were reached by a judicial process, which in theory and practice differed from casework procedure on the one hand, and administrative actions which maintained an element of discretion on the other. Legislation seemed to aim to make the kind of decisions, based on consideration of motives as well as actions, which were theoretically the province of the lengthy, skilled, persistent and relatively informal interviewing of trained case-work. The juridical framework arose from an attempt to set out rights clearly, so that there would be no demoralising uncertainty about what treatment to expect from official agencies, and to put decisions beyond dispute. But legislation also used as a basis for discrimination the categories which casework methods tended to dissolve. Where casework was used in policy, it did not label individuals clearly, but on the contrary tended to show them as 'ordinary men, neither incorruptible or unhelpable'.[64]

When Beatrice Webb before the Sociological Society in 1906 exalted the interview as a powerful scientific weapon, she met with the criticism that bias could destroy its usefulness.[65] The role of value judgements in decision making was raised most fully at this time by the attacks on the Charity Organisation Society, and the Webbs were among its most persistent opponents in spite of the central place of interviewing in its work. The COS, however, rather than its critics, defined the problems involved in casework, and established the role of the interview in policy. It stressed the need for training and for fixed principles and procedures in arriving at decisions, in particular the need to record information fully and to cross-check decisions. Doubts remained, since procedures for sifting individuals naturally lay themselves open to accusations that they are inquisitorial, but the COS stressed that any enquiry had to be conducted with sympathy, flexibility and a lack of haste. The victory for this philosophy came when it was widely accepted that social workers as a group could be drawn upon to strengthen a local administration run by amateurs and staffed by an inadequately trained bureaucracy.[66] By the 1920s, this was a conventional opinion. The full impact of this shift, at least on central government, was delayed until the 1930s.

The further development of casework had important consequences for the ways in which controls were transmitted through policy; it is not possible to discuss these here. By 1929, however, with the introduction and extension of national insurance, the remodelling of public assistance and the evolution of social work, the process of modernisation had already reached a major stage of completion, without policy becoming scientific, in Beatrice Webb's sense of the term, or conforming to T.H. Marshall's model of change.

Notes

1. Its ambiguities are similar to those inherent in Durkheim's concept of 'social constraint', which have been analysed by Steven Lukes [*Emile Durkheim* (London, 1973), pp. 12–34]. As a sociological term 'social control' seems to have originated in America. For an account of its history see *The International Encyclopedia of the Social Sciences* (The MacMillan Co. and the Free Press, 1968), Vol. 14.
2. T.H. Marshall, *Citizenship and Social Class* (Cambridge, 1950). The influence of this interpretation is difficult to trace fully, partly because it provides a general framework for detailed discussion, which need not be explicitly acknowledged, and partly because it draws upon a stream of thought which was already present in political debate and historical commentary.
3. Sir H.N. Bunbury (ed.), *Lloyd George's Ambulance Wagon, Being the Memoirs of William J. Braithwaite, 1911–1912*, (London, 1957), p. 122.
4. *Report of the Committee ... to enquire into ... the Census, Evidence,* PP, 1890 (C. 6071), LVIII, p. 68; *Toynbee Record*, October 1902, p. 5.
5. Beatrice Webb, 'Methods of Investigation', *Sociological Papers*, 1906, III, pp. 345–54.
6. Lukes, op. cit., p. 13.
7. Erving Goffman, *Stigma* (Harmondsworth, 1973), is an extensive discussion of this concept.
8. Barbara Wootton, *Social Science and Social Pathology* (London, 1959), p. 41.
9. Olive Stevenson, *Claimant or Client?* (London, 1973). p. 17.

10. Booth papers, Charles Booth to Alfred Marshall, 3 May 1892.
11. W.H. Beveridge, 'Unemployment in London. V – The Question of Disenfranchisement', *Toynbee Record*, March 1905, p. 102.
12. A.V. Dicey, *Law and Opinion in England in the Nineteenth Century* (London, 1962), p. xxxiv.
13. The government had accepted an amendment to the original Bill to the effect that voluntary payments over ten years to insure against sickness, unemployment and old age were evidence that the requirement had been met. A later regulation specified the minimum benefits which had to be secured (*Regulations, dated 15 Oct. 1908*, PP 1908, LXXXVIII).
14. *Tables which have been prepared in connection with the Question of Old Age Pensions, with a Preliminary Memorandum*, PP 1907 (Cd.3618), LXVIII, p. 14.
15. *Report from the Select Committee on the Aged Deserving Poor*, PP 1899 (C. 296), VIII, p. 9.
16. Charles Booth, *Pauperism a Picture, and the Endowment of Old Age an Argument* (London, 1892), p. 52, and *The Aged Poor in England and Wales* (London, 1894), p. 1; *Report of the Royal Commission on the Aged Poor*, PO 1895 (C 7648), XIV, pp. xiii–xiv.
17. *Select Committee on the Aged Deserving Poor*, p. 9.
18. Passfield papers, Beatrice Webb to Reginald McKenna, 30 Pr. 1907.
19. PRO PIN 3/1, Home Office Memorandum, 6 Nov. 1907.
20. PRO PIN 3/3, Sir Hector Munro to Llewellyn Smith, 8 April 1911. This is a covering letter for the Local Government Board notes on draft clauses of the unemployment insurance bill, headed 'Unemployment Insurance Bill, 1911'.
21. Ibid.
22. H.C. Emmerson and E.C.P. Lascelles, *Guide to the Unemployment Insurance Acts* (London, 1939), p. 118.
23. PIN 3/1, Home Office Memorandum, 6 Nov. 1907.
24. *Scottish Law Commission, Memorandum No. 22, Family Law, Aliment and Financial Provision (Vol. 2), 31 March 1976, Appendix A, The Historical Development of the Law*, pp. 330–51.
25. O.R. McGregor, *Family Breakdown and Social Policy, Maccabean Lecture in Jurisprudence to the British Academy* (London, 1973); O.R. McGregor, L. Blom-Cooper and C. Gibson, *Separated Spouses* (London, 1970), pp. 151–67.
26. Charles Booth, for example, had canvassed rural clergy and urban charity organisation groups to try to discover the extent to which parents in their old age were supported by their offspring. His findings, published in *The Aged Poor*, were scarcely more than very broad third-hand generalisations. This was by far the weakest of his investigations, and illustrated the virtual impossibility of surveying large geographically dispersed populations in the absence of sampling techniques. The London COS co-operated in spite of doubts about the value of the work (COS Administrative Committee, Minutes, 27 July 1893).
27. PRO T. 170/3/2, Bradbury papers, Departmental Committee on Old Age Pensions Statistics, minutes, 5 Jan. 1910; *Report of the Departmental Committee on Old Age Pensions, 1919* (Cmd. 410), XXVII, p. 8.
28. Phyllis D. Winder, *The Public Feeding of Elementary School Children* (London, 1913), p. 13; Mrs Pember Reeves, *Round About a Pound a Week* (London, 1913), p. 93.
29. *Report of the Working Class Cost of Living Committee*, PP 1918 (Cd. 8980), VII, p. 9.
30. M.E. Bulkley, *The Feeding of School Children* (London, 1914), describes the operation of the various school meal services in detail. She brings out the

elements of stigmatisation in the system.

31. *Report of the Royal Commission on the Poor Laws and Relief of Distress*, PP 1909 (Cmd. 4499), XXXVII, pp. 290–2.

32. Bernard Bosanquet, 'The Majority Report', *Sociological Review*, II (1909), p. 122.

33. *Ministry of Reconstruction, Local Government Committee, Report on the Transfer of the Functions of the Poor Law Authorities in England and Wales*, PP 1917–18 (Cmd. 8917), XVIII, passim.

34. Ford attempted a systematic calculation of the difference between the size of the household and the number of its members who were relatives with a poor law obligation for maintenance, on the basis of household samples taken from before 1914 until the 1930s. This involved reworking A.L. Bowley's surveys among other things, and it is not always possible to follow quite how this has been done. For the results see Table IV in P. Ford, *Incomes, Means Tests and Personal Responsibility* (London, 1939).

35. H.C. Emmerson and E.C.P. Lascelles, op. cit., pp. 120–33.

36. H. Llewellyn Smith (ed.), *New Survey of London Life and Labour* (London, 1932), III, pp. 93–6; P. Ford, *Work and Wealth in a Modern Port* (London, 1934), p. 123, and *Incomes, Means Tests and Personal Responsibility*, p. 10.

37. In 1912–13 the Unionist opposition discussed very inconclusively the conversion of national insurance into a voluntary scheme. The Bonar Law papers contain a number of letters dealing with this matter.

38. *Charity Organisation Review*, XXVI (July–December 1914), p. 127.

39. The most accessible account of these views is contained in Sidney and Beatrice Webb, *The State and the Doctor* (London, 1910).

40. Passfield papers, Beatrice Webb to Lady Betty Balfour, 18 Dec. 1910.

41. Sir John Collie, *Malingering* (London, 1913), pp. 280–1, and second edition (London, 1917), pp. 585 and 591. Collie became a member of the government advisory committee to assist the Insurance Commissioners. *New Statesman*, 17 Jan. 1914, gives an account of his position as a leading medical authority on insurance.

42. Collie, op. cit. (1913), p. 281.

43. *Charity Organisation Review*, XXVI (July–December 1914), p. 218.

44. Lloyd George papers C/18/8/1. Memorandum by A.W. Watson on number of insured persons and increase in membership of friendly societies, 23/5/12.

45. *Report of the Departmental Committee on Sickness Benefit Claims under the National Insurance Act*, PP 1914–16 (Cd. 7687), XXX, pp. 11–12.

46. *Report of First Proceedings of the Board of Trade under Part II of the National Insurance Act, 1911*, PP 1913 (Cd. 6965), p. iii.

47. *Report . . . on Sickness Benefit Claims*, pp. 10, 15–16, 47–51 and 79.

48. Llewellyn Smith (ed.), op. cit., III, p. 143. The Ministry of Labour's special enquiries of the 1920s into the characteristics of those on unemployment benefit are summarised in R.C. Davison, *The Unemployed* (London, 1929), pp. 170–1.

49. Collie, op. cit., p. 1.

50. *Fabian Tract No. 178, The War, Women, and Unemployment* (1915), pp. 14–15.

51. Collie, op. cit., pp. 3 and 7–8; S. and B. Webb, *The State and the Doctor*, pp. 133, 145 and 230–1.

52. The prevalence of these rumours is discussed in Davison, op. cit., p. 127, and E.W. Bakke, *The Unemployed Man* (London, 1933), pp. 83–4. Bakke found that one exchange with 8,000 on its live register received on average two anonymous letters every day. But in the 1920s, in the average year, out of every 4,000 claimants, 11 were suspected of fraud and 2 were prosecuted.

53. *Report of the Royal Commission on Health Insurance* (Cmd. 2596), XIV, pp. 25–6.
54. 'Medical Service under the Insurance Act, I. The Evil Effects of Personal Competition', *New Statesman*, 1 Nov. 1913.
55. *Report of the Royal Commission on Health Insurance*, pp. 33–4.
56. Davison, op. cit., p. 147.
57. For example, Davison (ibid., pp. 117–18) felt that the fluctuations in disallowed claims could not be explained solely in terms of changes in statutory requirements: 'It seems clear that in 1925, quite independent of any changes in legislation, there *was* a tightening up of benefit administration.'
58. Ibid., pp. 153–4; Emmerson and Lascelles, op. cit., pp. 89–100.
59. Emmerson and Lascelles, op. cit., pp. 101–3.
60. Ford, *Incomes, Means Tests and Personal Responsibility*, p. 52.
61. Bakke, op. cit., p. 91.
62. Emmerson and Lascelles, op. cit., pp. 107–17. Bakke commented (op. cit., p. 92) that if a worker disputed his disqualification on the grounds that he had refused employment, it was very difficult for him to present any evidence which would tell against the labour exchange officials, no matter how strongly he felt that the job had been unsuitable.
63. *Report of the Committee on Procedure and Evidence for the Determination of Claims for Unemployment Insurance Benefit*, PP 1929–30 (Cmd. 3415), XVII, p. 19.
64. This quotation is from a discussion in *Toynbee Record*, Dec. 1905 (pp. 36–8) of the experience of trying to use casework to discriminate among applicants for unemployment relief in London in 1904–5.
65. *Sociological Papers*, III (1906), p. 352.
66. *Toynbee Record*, March 1908, pp. 78–9; Passfield papers, Lord George Hamilton to Beatrice Webb, 3 Jan. 1918, and Lancelot Phelps papers, Lord George Hamilton to Phelps, 17 Jan. 1918 (these both give some indication of the private thinking behind the Ministry of Reconstruction's Local Government Committee, whose report advocated the use of social workers by local authorities); Clement Attlee, *The Social Worker* (London, 1920), passim.

UNEMPLOYMENT AND UNEMPLOYMENT POLICIES IN GLASGOW 1890–1905

J.H. Treble

During the years 1890–1905 the problem of unemployment appeared under five different guises within the city of Glasgow. In the first place there were periodic crises of confidence, associated with the downswing of the trade cycle, which invariably produced a high level of unemployment in those industries – heavy engineering, shipbuilding and iron and steel – whose fortunes determined both the prosperity of the local economy and the buoyancy of the demand for skilled male labour on Clydeside generally. Crises of this nature occurred in 1892–3 when 'a very considerable depression' was characterised by 'singularly dull' conditions in 'the iron industry, shipbuilding and its allied trades', and in 1903–5 when all the available social and economic indicators pointed to the existence of widespread and protracted social suffering which affected all sections of the workforce.[1]

Nevertheless, if unemployment on this scale was primarily the creation of exogenous constraints upon demand in international and internal markets, it is still not possible to explain the phenomenon exclusively in terms of trade cycle theory. Sharp, but usually ephemeral, rises in Glasgow's workless population could also be produced by adverse climatic conditions, such as occurred in January–March 1895 when a combination of low temperatures and snow heavily reduced employment outlets in the outdoor trades, and in the early months of 1903 when it was claimed that the fundamental cause of 'a good deal of idleness' lay in 'the weather conditions being unfavourable to all kinds of outside work'.[2] Similarly, major strikes in one of the staple industries in the west of Scotland would, if of sufficient duration, have adverse multiplier effects upon employment prospects within the broad spectrum of Glasgow's trades. Pre-eminent among such disputes were the troubles which convulsed the Scottish coalfields in October–December 1893 and June–October 1894 when, in the words of the Factory Inspector for the Glasgow District, 'the blast furnaces with the exception of two or three, were shut down. Many large works were closed, and most were on short time'.[3]

Finally, in the context of this discussion, the influence of the building cycle must be considered, not only because the building industry

147

was in itself an important employer of local labour, but also because the chonology of its cycle, with its long twenty years' swings, diverged markedly from the seven to ten years' swings of the conventional Juglar model. In Glasgow itself the evidence relating to the downswing phase of this attenuated cycle is quite unambiguous; after a period of sustained activity between 1892 and 1902, there was thereafter a sharp decline – lasting almost until 1914 – in the number of new dwellings approved by the Dean of Guild Court.[4] Nor was such an outcome surprising because the scale of overbuilding in the previous boom had meant that as late as 1907 there were still 14,000 unoccupied houses and dwellings in the city,[5] although the dimensions of this problem were clearly exacerbated by the siphoning off of the whole of the natural increase in Glasgow's population in the opening decade of the twentieth century. If, therefore, it must be concluded that the contours of the building cycle during the post-1902 period were powerfully shaped by the deep mood of pessimism which prevailed in the staple industries in 1903–5 and 1907–10, it is still necessary to treat it as one more variable affecting the volume of work in a vital sector of the labour market.

In addition to this type of unemployment, there was also a well defined, and easily discernible, seasonal pattern of working in certain of the city's trades. The salient characteristic of this pattern – the extreme contrasts in the annual labour requirements of employers between the good and 'dull' months – can perhaps best be illustrated by that broad range of occupations which collectively comprised the building industry, where brickmakers, sawyers, certain categories of workers in wood, a wide variety of labourers, bricklayers, masons, painters, causewayers, paviours, and decorators invariably experienced a decline in the length of their working day and an absolute diminution in employment outlets during a period running roughly from late October to early March. Other groups whose slack season occurred during wintertime included seamen, dockers, workers in such consumer-oriented industries as lemonade and jam making, and tailors in both the ready-made and bespoke sectors of the trade. But since the overwhelming majority of seasonal workers encountered the problems of unemployment and underemployment at roughly the same point in time – among men, only gasworkers, and among women, only certain kinds of domestic workers, experienced a falling demand for their services in the summer months – the opportunity for successfully 'dovetailing' jobs within the seasonal labour market was always strictly limited.[6]

Thirdly, there existed, alongside the seasonal question, a pervasive underemployment which was one of the hallmarks of the market for casual labour. As the *Glasgow Herald* pointed out in February 1907,

> the main feature of casual employment is that instead of either being completely in work or completely out of work, the workman gets only two, three or four days a week. The evil is too familiar to require proof; and among certain classes of labourers it is the rule, and not the exception.[7]

Socially, however, it is immensely difficult to draw the outer parameters of the casual market itself, for whereas at one level those who were dependent upon short engagements, whether by the hour or by the day, merged imperceptibly into the ranks of the seasonal workforce, at a lower level there was a minority which was readily identified by contemporary opinion with the 'unemployable' or 'loafer' class.

Since this paper is more concerned with the problem of unemployment rather than with the market *per se*, it is necessary to make here only two general points. Firstly, because the bulk of casual workers, both male and female, were unskilled, largely untouched by trade union organisation, and often of poor physique — in itself an eloquent commentary on the searing poverty of their lives — few of them had any hope of securing continuity in employment in a city which always had a surplus of 'hands', even at times of peak demand. In addition, virtually every industry which used unskilled labour on a large scale, had attached to it a pool of chronically underemployed workers. Thus while most commentators dwelt at length upon those who belonged to what was styled the 'Third Class' of dock labourers, the more perceptive were quick to acknowledge that casual work patterns also formed an integral part of the life-style of important elements among the porters in Glasgow's fruit and fish markets; carters; barbers; tailors; and those who were employed by bread, jam, lemonade and boot and shoe manufacturers. Elsewhere a similar picture can be discerned among charwomen, washerwomen and those sweated occupations — umbrella-covering, shirtmaking, box and paper-bag making — which were largely the preserve of female labour.[8]

Fourthly, unemployment could be the social sequel to structural and technical changes within industry. This process could of course damage the employment prospects of those without specific skills, as in the docks, where in a growth area of the local economy the increasing use of machinery raised productivity but, in the long term, produced a deceleration in the rate of demand for unskilled labour.[9] None the less it is clear that it wreaked its maximum social destruction upon disparate groups of individuals who unmistakably belonged to the skilled sector of the labour market, although the chronology and dimensions of such change varied sharply from industry to industry and, on occasion, from firm to firm within a single industry. As early as the mid-1880s, for example, ropespinners were compelled to abandon their union largely because their hold on the trade had been successfully challenged by 'the introduction of machinery and the consequent employment of boys and girls'.[10] Less than a decade later it was the turn of certain categories of male handworkers in Glasgow's pottery factories to be replaced by power-driven equipment operated by women, while bakers and masons were two other groups to complain that mechanisation posed a threat to employment prospects within their respective trades.[11] By the early 1900s this process had spread to affect clay-pipe workers; male handloom weavers of wirecloth whose livelihood was being undermined by the power-loom manned by cheap juvenile labour; and ship's painters who argued that the introduction of paint-spraying techniques reduced the length of their working season.[12]

On the other hand, compared with these examples, technical change proceeded at a more gentle pace and innovation was much less systematically applied within certain, but by no means all, of the traditional staple industries, although even here the local factory inspector felt compelled by 1902 to draw attention to 'the extended use of pneumatic tools, especially in shipbuilding yards and engineering and boiler shops. Jobs formerly done by journeymen can now with these tools be undertaken by apprentices'.[13]

Nevertheless, if, despite the rise of the semi-skilled machinist, it can be accepted that in this context gradualism was the general rule, there were a few narrowly demarcated work-groups to which such a conclusion is particularly inappropriate. Prominent among them were sailmakers who were direct victims of the rise of the iron and steel shipbuilding industry upon Clydeside, and to a lesser extent, shipwrights who, in the era of the wooden sailing vessels, had laid down the wooden hull, but who by the 1890s were forced to compete with joiners for the drastically reduced amount of wooden work available in the iron ship.[14] Again, in the iron industry millmen pointed to the fact that 'the introduction of machinery' had by the 1890s produced, within their ranks, an indeterminate number of individuals 'who are employed in this sense, that they have no regular work to go to, but look about the works, and get an odd day here and there where they can have it'.[15] Lastly, within the engineering workshops, W. Mosses, General Secretary of the United Pattern Makers, argued that rising unemployment among his members in December 1908 was the product of 'standardisation' which

> is playing havoc with our trade in marine centres, machinery is being introduced to an extent we would not acknowledge a decade ago, whilst we are about the most overstocked trade in connection with the engineering industry.[16]

The cumulative impact of such changes, therefore, was to create either short-term hardships or more intractable, long-term problems among a not insignificant section of the artisan class. Of those worst affected, some were to be absorbed into the ranks of the semi-skilled. Others faced a more uncertain future in which the threat of prolonged unemployment or chronic underemployment loomed large for the first time in their working lives, while a small minority, encountering considerable difficulty in obtaining new jobs in established trades after they had attained the age of fifty, might join the ranks of the permanent unemployed. Finally, as I have argued elsewhere, there remained 'a residual element of craftsmen who were the direct casualties of innovation, and who over time added to the city's pool of unskilled labour'.[17]

Fifthly, unemployment could be the direct consequence of the personal deficiencies of the individual. In its mildest form this was depicted as essentially a moral problem, afflicting the shipbuilding industry in particular, where over-indulgence in drink led to brief, but reasonably frequent, interruptions in the work rhythms of the 'black squad'. In the early 1890s, for instance, the Shipyard Helpers' Association complained bitterly that the incomes of a section of its membership were unnecessarily depressed because of the folly of hard-drinking platers.[18] A decade later the Boilermakers' Society joined the debate when it tacitly accepted that absenteeism among its members should in part be laid at the door of intemperance. But such failings were not of course solely restricted to the skilled.[19] Riveters and platers could equally well be exposed to this kind of involuntary unemployment through the non-appearance of holders-on, rivet boys, and platers' helpers.[20] On the whole, however, it must be conceded that this problem was neither as endemic nor as serious within Scottish industry — the *Glasgow Herald* was one of several sources to commend the thrifty habits of shipyard workers[21] — as the more clamant voices of the Temperance lobby implied.

On the other hand few contemporaries doubted the significant role played by 'physical weakness' in helping to perpetuate intermittent work patterns among the unskilled, although even then it was not always possible to isolate this social phenomenon from the drink question since in many cases attempts were made to establish a causal relationship between alcohol and physique. Among those, for example, who suffered from the ravages of underemployment in Glasgow's docks, poor physique and 'unsteady habits' were singled out as prime determinants of their inability to secure regular employment.[22]

But in its most extreme manifestation the majority of those who were placed in this category were defined as 'the unemployable'. Covered by this amorphous term were vagrants, discharged prisoners, beggars and a relatively homogeneous group of loafers who were 'morally lacking', frequently addicted to drink, and who, in the striking phrase of one critic, congregated 'at street corners and shop doors, especially on Sundays, expectorating all over the pavements'.[23] Above all it was this class, it was alleged, which most frequently benefited from the different initiatives taken in Glasgow to alleviate the distress of the 'deserving' unemployed. In 1895 James Motion, with typical hyperbole, argued that the applicants for relief to the Lord Provost's Fund were drawn 'entirely [from] this loafing class'.[24] In similar vein, the Superintendent of Parks, commenting upon those who had participated in the projects mounted by his Department in 1903—4 for the unemployed, emphasised that

> the larger proportion were of that indifferent class who never can keep any situation for any time — coming late to work, skulking, drinking, and exhibiting general indifference as to whether the work was done quickly or creditably.[25]

Almost inevitably, the vast majority of the city's articulate middle classes came to regard 'the unemployable' as a problem of exclusively moral dimensions, which was by its very nature hermetically sealed off from the broader socio-economic issues of the labour market. As the *Glasgow Herald* expressed it, in language strikingly similar to that employed by Charles Booth in his description of his 'Class A',

> unemployment must not be confounded with the phenomenon of the unemployable. The one has its root in industrial conditions, some of which can be partly controlled. The other is in the main a

moral disorder. The unemployable is humanity's failure. He is to a
large extent the nerveless, pithless product of degeneracy, and as
such demands treatment of a nature which the State could not
prescribe for useful and potentially useful citizens.[26]

But it is precisely because this monocausal explanation ignored the basic
question as to whether or not such 'disorders' could in part be caused
by exogenous socio-economic pressures, that so much of contemporary
comment upon 'the unemployable' shed so little light upon what was in
reality an exceedingly complex problem.

Much the same criticism, however, can be levelled at the historian
who insists upon treating the different forms of unemployment as
mutually exclusive, rather than mutually reinforcing, forces. For while,
for analytical purposes, there is every justification in dividing the
subject into five compartments, it would be a cardinal mistake to over-
look the interrelationships which existed among these categories. Already
the point has been raised of the degree of overlap between those who
were subject to casual unemployment and those who suffered from
seasonal unemployment. But at the same time it is equally clear that
certain grades of regularly employed workers, when their livelihood had
been destroyed by the downswing of the trade cycle, sought temporary
work in, and experienced the erratic rhythms of, the casual market.
Similarly, casual and seasonal workers in their turn were among the first
casualties of a rising volume of cyclical unemployment. In short, it was
quite possible for an individual to suffer simultaneously from the adverse
pressures generated by different forms of unemployment. In Edwardian
Glasgow the awareness of this fact was perhaps best captured, not in the
columns of the local press, but in the moving, and painfully constructed,
letter of G. Lyon, a sailmaker, appealing for relief from the Lord
Provost's Fund during the acute and prolonged crisis of 1908—9. In
Lyon's words,

I am A. Sailmaker to Trade but Sailing Ships being A. thing of the
past also sewing machines taking our place the Trade has left Me and
having the misfortune to want the Leg. I go with A. Pinleg the trade
suited me very well but I cannot get My living at it now upon an
average I only work Three Months in A year the little I saved when
Trade was good is done now I do not now [sic] what to do unless
I get employment that will suit My Case for I am Handicapped owing
to the want of the Leg. I have been a Ratepayer for the last 28 years.
I have A. Wife and A. Daughter at School hoping you will give this

your earnest Consideration an early reply or A Personal interview will much Oblige.[27]

It is against this sombre backcloth that contemporary exchanges within Glasgow about the nature of, and cure for, unemployment have to be set.

I

In the pre-1905 period that debate was largely dominated by those sections of Glasgow's middle classes — town councillors, Poor Law inspectors, and the officials of the Charity Organisation Society among them — who were most closely involved with the practical aspects of poverty. United by the belief that it was possible to highlight the existence of two quite separate routes to unemployment, they were largely content to reply upon an analytical framework which derived its social inspiration from the value-system of the early and mid-Victorian era and which, despite the work of Charles Booth and Seebohm Rowntree, strongly underlined the moral, as well as the economic, dimensions of the problem. According to this local formulation of the central tenets of the Smilesian creed, the 'detritus' of the working class — that 'low type of humanity' as it was styled[28] — was frequently unemployed because of fundamental flaws in its character. Drink, unpunctuality, improvidence, the corrupting influence of the model lodging house, early marriages, and vagrancy were at different times cited as powerful contributors to a pattern of life, of which irregular working formed an integral part.[29] On the other hand quite separate from this 'undeserving' category, were those 'respectable' workmen who were called upon to bear the brunt of mass unemployment with fortitude and often in silence. This last group was thought largely to consist of those who belonged to the skilled sector of the labour market, although it was periodically made plain that it included elements drawn from those of a more humble socio-economic back-ground, washerwomen among them.[30]

The logical corollary of these premises was that such local initiatives as were mounted to aid the unemployed should, as far as possible, treat each of these groupings in quite separate ways. In relation to the 'undeserving', for example, two distinct approaches were recommended. Firstly, there should be an attempt to promote among them the virtues of 'prudence, thrift, industry, and sobriety, and the avoidance of early and improvident marriages', not only because these were desirable social goals *per se*, but also because it would enable individuals to protect themselves and their families 'against the days of idleness' out of their own resources.[31] However, whether or not such an end could be secured if they continued to be exposed to those countervailing deleterious influences which had hitherto shaped their culture and *mores* was open to considerable doubt. By the late 1890s and early 1900s strident voices within the community were arguing that nothing short of radical, coercive measures could hope to effect a lasting improvement in this sphere. Above all, as James Motion pointed out, there was a need for a deterrent farm colony, modelled in part on continental experience, to segregate habitual vagrants, loafers, and 'men of predatory habits and loose morals, who demoralise alike the casual and unskilled labour markets, and the [municipal] relief works', from the rest of society. For such an institution to work properly would require legislative action, bestowing upon the magistracy limited powers of detention over certain well-defined groups. But once that had been conceded, there was little doubt, in its supporters' minds, that the scheme would be 'a great boon to themselves [the farm colonists] and an immense benefit to the city'.[32]

The second line of attack upon the 'undeserving' was of more immediate relevance since it was concerned with defining their relationship to the various 'make work' schemes which were launched, and underwritten, by the Corporation during this decade and a half. To permit them uninterrupted access to such projects was, it was felt, a counsel of despair since such a policy was inimical to all hope of sustained social improvement. In particular it could breed a reliance upon relief works which would increase still further the rigidities of what was already a highly imperfect labour market, by reducing the incentive of the underemployed to seek to improve their economic position. In the words of Mrs M'Callum of the Glasgow Charity Organisation Society,

> will not the recurrence of this [form of] relief tend to confirm the class aptly described as the unemployable in their wretched mode of life, and will it not strangle attempts at providence among men on the fringe of skilled labour who, if they are sober, can meet the recurrent slack seasons, though with difficulty, but who will now see relief given to those whose difficulties are due to betting and drinking?[33]

It was in order to guard against this kind of imposition that the Council insisted that, in relation to its own relief programmes, certain

basic rules should, as far as was practicable, be observed. In the first
place a searching enquiry into the credentials and claims of each
applicant should be undertaken. In some cases, as in 1892–3, this
operation might be largely directed by the Charity Organisation Society;
in others, as in 1904 and 1904–5, the assistance of the Poor Law
inspectorate might be invoked.[34] Nevertheless, irrespective of the
channel through which it was directed, the aim of this exercise should
be to discover not merely whether or not the individual was destitute
through 'want of employment', but also his length of residence within
the city and the nature of his accommodation. The residence question
was in fact crucial to the success of the Corporation's strategy since,
at every major crisis, the unemployed and 'loafers' of the surrounding
towns — in 1895 they were drawn from 'Partick and Govan, from
Airdrie and Coatbridge, various towns in Ayrshire, and even from
Campbelltown' — 'having heard of the efforts being put forth on
behalf of the unemployed in Glasgow are coming here for relief'.[35] A
minimum residential qualification, therefore, was to be insisted upon
to preserve intact the essentially parochial nature of Glasgow's relief
measures, both in the interests of the city's own workless population
and, what was less easily reconcilable with the preceding objective,
in the interests of containing the size of the deficits on these projects
which the Common Good Fund might be expected to meet.
Significantly enough, that limit, fixed in 1892–3 at three months'
unbroken residence in the period immediately prior to the date of
application, had been raised to one year by 1904.[35a]

But, in the context of Glasgow's own 'undeserving' problem, what
was of equal importance was the periodic attempts which were made
to establish clear-cut criteria to determine how work should be allocated
among competing socio-economic groups. In 1892–3 and 1895, for
instance, it was stipulated that the first option for relief employment
should be given to married householders who had fulfilled the necessary
residential requirement.[36] In November 1904 on the other hand a trifle
more flexibility was introduced into these arrangements when it was
decided that the available work should initially be confined to householders or married men with dependants who had lived in the city for
the previous twelve months.[37] Conversely, single men and the inmates
of model lodging houses — long identified in the public mind with the
unemployable and the casual worker — were summarily dismissed from
the public works programme in December 1892, and, 1895 apart, there
is no evidence to suggest that they were treated any more tenderly in
subsequent periods of economic dislocation.[38] It was for essentially the

same reasons— the desire to guard against the undeserving – that the Corporation's Executive Sub-Committee on Relief Employment resolved in February 1904 to refuse work to all individuals who had lost their previous situation in the labour market 'through carelessness or inattention to work'.[39]

Nonetheless, if 'make work' schemes were widely endorsed as the most suitable way of helping the deserving at times of cyclical unemployment, they were themselves surrounded by powerful constraints. There were, for example, pertinent questions concerning the financing of these operations which had to be faced. In one sense the scale of the council's commitment was bound to be circumscribed by the fact that it possessed 'no rating power for that purpose'. There can be little doubt, however, that its difficulties were exacerbated in two crucial respects by the uncompromising attitude of the 1845 Scottish Poor Law Act towards the able-bodied unemployed. Firstly, the relieving of such individuals formed no part of the legal duties of any parish board. As the Board of Supervision, until 1894 the central administrative mechanism of the Scottish system, made plain, 'parochial boards had no power to expend any of their funds in the relief of persons who are not both destitute and (wholly or partially) disabled'.[40] Secondly, as the Executive Committee of the Glasgow Unemployed Relief Fund discovered in 1878–9, it was also *ultra vires* for the parish authority to contribute in any way, out of its rate income, to municipally-sponsored unemployment projects, although it was accepted that such schemes, by helping to keep the participants in reasonable health, thereby held in check the level of expenditure upon the sick poor.[41]

In the last analysis, therefore, the corporation was committed to utilising either the resources of the Common Good Fund, or – as in 1903 and January–April 1904 until it was exhausted – the accumulated surplus of the Lord Provost's Fund, raised in 1895 by private subscription to assist the unemployed, to meet the losses which were always incurred in this kind of exercise.[42] Furthermore, it was precisely because such undertakings could be pronounced, in terms of the philosophy of the market economy, both inefficient and unviable, that their size and scope was constricted still further, for local opinion was reluctant to sanction large and continuing subventions from the Common Good Fund in return for essentially chimerical benefits.

Reinforcing the constraining influence of purely financial considerations was a broader philosophical debate about the function which a local authority might legitimately fulfil in the contentious area of

unemployment relief. In this sphere most middle-class groupings sub-
scribed to three general theses. Firstly it was accepted that the work
itself should be largely unskilled, so that all those who, after investigation, were deemed 'deserving', could participate in it. But by very
definition this doctrine ruled out grandiose plans of holding in reserve
major corporation projects until cyclical unemployment afflicted the
community. Indeed, the very idea of this kind of 'dovetailing' was
thought to be tinged with utopianism. James Bell, the city's Lord
Provost, spoke for many of his contemporaries when he sought to
expose what, in his view, were the fundamental fallacies of this
proposition. Writing in 1895, he observed that,

> It has been advanced by some that local authorities in times of
> undue distress ought to carry out public works. These suggestions
> can be advanced only by those who are not cognisant of the working
> of municipal institutions. We are constantly carrying out all the
> work which we think is necessary for the Corporation, and that as
> speedily as possible, without increasing our rates; but no work,
> beyond stonebreaking or digging, which the Corporation can
> originate or carry out, would be of the slightest use to relieve undue
> distress such as we had last winter. Take the building of a bridge, for
> example. We, first of all, require to get an Act of Parliament; and
> the same preliminary applies to any large work or expenditure of
> money which the Corporation can undertake; and this would require
> nearly a year. In the case of a bridge, the granite would likely come
> from Aberdeen or Cornwall, where there might be no undue distress;
> the iron and steel work from a district probably well employed; and,
> when we had the materials here we would find the building work
> possibly interrupted by frost at the very time when we wished to
> utilise them, for the purposes of giving employment. It is the same
> with other work; and similar objections can be advanced against any
> work in which a local authority can engage.[43]

Secondly, although the writ of Chamberlain's 1886 Local Government
Board Circular did not run in Scotland, one of its central features —
the temporary nature of all 'make work' proposals — was warmly
endorsed by the corporation, with its enthusiastic adoption of those
tasks — stonebreaking, trenching, digging, ditching and levelling — which
most closely conformed to this rubric. Furthermore, in order to ensure
that those who were the beneficiaries of these schemes would seek
employment at their own trades as soon as economic recovery set in,

there was initially a firm commitment by the municipality to the principle of a 'less eligible' wage structure. In 1892–3 and 1895, despite representations from the Trades Council, remuneration for six days' work was fixed at 7s, together with meals.[44] In 1903, January–March 1904, and 1904–5, however, it was argued that this principle was in one significant respect weakened when the lowly figure for the early 1890s was abandoned in favour of a sliding scale. One shilling per day with meals was still to be the reward for the adult male worker, but this was supplemented by daily allowances of 9d for his wife and 3d for each child, subject to an upper global limit for each family which fluctuated from 2s 6d per day in 1904–5 to 2s 9d in 1903 and the opening months of 1904.[45]

The scope of these changes led James Ferguson, Chief Assistant Inspector of the Poor with Glasgow Parish Council, to lament that men on relief work now enjoyed a 'more eligible' existence than underemployed and poorly remunerated foundry and general labourers, 'as no employer when engaging a man, pays him according to the number of his family'.[46] Nevertheless, while there was an element of truth in this accusation, it would be a mistake to apply Ferguson's conclusion even to the unskilled labour market generally. As the corporation was well aware, 'less eligibility' had been modified rather than abandoned.

Finally, there was a profound hostility to the kind of state involvement which Keir Hardie and isolated groups of the Scottish Labour Party and the Social Democratic Federation were advocating in Glasgow during the 1892–3 depression.[47] State intervention, it was felt, would begin by corrupting the individuals most intimately touched by it; for

while not altering the character of the well-doing, [it] would certainly deteriorate weak natures, make the indolent more idle, the careless more indifferent, and the bad-tempered almost unmanageable.

But in the longer term it posed an equally insidious threat to the role of local authorities who ought to attend to the social needs of the unemployed 'in times of exceptional distress, and exceptional distress only'. For the inevitable sequel to central government initiative would be to 'weaken municipal responsibility, which is a responsibility more of a social than of an official character, to be called into operation only to avert a calamity'.[48]

It did not follow, however, from this firm resistance to any threat of government encroachment that contemporaries believed that the whole burden of relief should be devolved upon the shoulders of the local authority. If the state had to be resisted in the name of preserving the social health of the nation, it was widely accepted that charities and voluntary associations could usefully supplement the efforts of local authorities in alleviating the burden of acute distress.

In its most popular form, charitable aid would provide relief in kind, usually through the ubiquitous soup kitchen. In 1892–3 the Glasgow Unemployed Committee, under the aegis of trade unionists and socialists, undertook to feed, and clothe, at its Gallowgate headquarters, a small part of the city's workless population, while the Gospel Army sought the use of the Globe Theatre to give free breakfasts to roughly 2,000 women and children who were the indirect casualties of the rising tide of male unemployment.[49] Again, in 1895, the Gaiety and Scotia theatres, out of money collected from their patrons, joined with the various churches in dispensing soup to the unemployed, while it was the turn of the Salvation Army to establish free breakfast rooms at several points – including Cowcaddens and Bridgeton – within the city.[50]

At a quite different level there was the assistance offered to different categories of unemployed men and women by the local Charity Organisation Society, which, compared with the parent body in London, was heterodox in its attitude towards the able-bodied, since it both dealt with cases 'of a lower social grade' and was compelled 'really [to] take the place of the Poor Law'.[51] In relation to the unemployed it tried to grade, and to offer to them appropriate help in one of the assorted institutions – its industrial shelter, opened in 1894, for homeless single men; its ladies' auxiliary sewing room; its firewood factory; and its labour yard, reserved for stonebreaking, in Alexandra Parade – that it ran for this specific purpose.[52] In addition, through the Poor Children's Clothing Fund which it established in 1893, it was usually able to cope with the inevitable increase in demand for its services which, after a short time-lag, always accompanied the downswing of the trade cycle.[53]

Nevertheless, easily the most ambitious manifestation of charitable endeavour was the Lord Provost's Fund since it sought to provide a focal point for the charitable impulses of the entire city. In the period 1890–1905 only one such appeal was in fact launched – in 1895 – when about £9,600 was received in subscription income and roughly £4,600 expended in relief. By the time that it ceased activity, it

could claim to have provided 330,000 meals of soup and bread, distributed over 1,000 tons of coals — half of which had been privately
donated — to some 13,151 households; allocated grocery tickets to
22,669 applicants; paid off rent arrears in several cases 'to save
necessitous and deserving tenants from ejection; purchased boots and
clothing largely for the children of the unemployed; and in a few
instances arranged 'with the police authorities to afford some delay
in the payment of rates'.[54]

Nonetheless, this framework of reference was not without its
detractors. Working-class spokesmen for the unemployed were usually
critical of what they regarded as the artificial distinction drawn between
the deserving and undeserving, and angrily repudiated the assertion that
drunkenness and unpunctuality were the principal routes to unemployment. George Carson, for example, confronted with the claim that shipyard labourers represented a morally weak residuum of the working
classes, denied that

> the men ... are wasters in any sense of the word; they are honest,
> steady, industrious men so far as I know. I have worked among them
> for years and years, and I have never known them lose time except
> when ill or when suspended, as they sometimes are, and I certainly
> decline to accept a statement of that kind from those who are not in
> a position to understand about these things.[55]

Similarly, A.J. Hunter, Carson's predecessor as Secretary of Glasgow
Trades Council, rejected the idea that self-help offered the best hope
of protecting the bulk of the working classes against unemployment, on
the ground that wages in many occupations were so low as to leave no
margin for providing for the ordinary contingencies of life.[56]

But what was of equal importance, working-class leaders did not
hesitate to present an alternative programme of action. This included,
as early as 1892–3, the demand for 'the right to work' as well as more
specific palliatives — *inter alia*, the eight-hour day, afforestation schemes,
home farm colonies, the standard rate for labouring tasks connected
with municipal 'make work' projects — which were to be widely
endorsed in other areas of Britain by the labour movement during the
course of the 1890s and early 1900s.[57] Nonetheless, among small
but vocal groups of socialists, such measures, valuable as they were
in mitigating distress, merely served to underline the validity of their
belief that unemployment was essentially a product of the inner
contradictions of the capitalist system and that until 'the arrival of

the time when industry will be organised on the basis of supplying the requirements of the community', major upheavals in the economy would recur, with 'everyone' [sic] growing 'more intense and longer in duration than its predecessor'.[58]

Assessed over all, however, the campaign, led by the Scottish Labour Party, the Trades Council, the Independent Labour Party, and the Social Democratic Federation, can at best be described as fitful, marked until late 1904 by the lack of any permanent organisation to protect, and advance the interests of, the unemployed, and what was the inevitable corollary of organisational weaknesses, by any systematic effort to carry its message to the working classes as a whole. In short, labour leaders reacted to, rather than anticipated, each cyclical crisis; they responded to events, rather than endeavoured to shape them. But, particularly in the early and mid 1890s, little more could be expected when the local leadership was divided upon tactics and the demands that it asked society to sanction. Thus, in December 1892 when Keir Hardie was exhorting Glasgow's unemployed to 'demand not bread, but demand work that they might earn bread', Hunter was assuring the corporation that 'he did not think any one wished large [relief] works started'.[59] Again, while Hardie in the early months of 1895 was trying to secure state funds for an extended relief programme, Hunter was compelled to admit that, apart from minor palliatives, the Trades Council had not any ready-made solution to the unemployment problems: 'it is not that [the Trades Council had not considered the question from the perspective of trade unionism] ; they find themselves helpless to do anything'.[60]

Such steps, therefore, as were taken to provide work for the unemployed conformed almost exactly to the blueprint which has already been described. Because of its insistence upon intervening solely at times of acute and widespread unemployment, the corporation would only act after a comprehensive survey, sometimes carried out by the Magistrates' Committee and at other times by a Special Committee on Relief Employment, had established the broad parameters of the problem.[61] Effectively this was to mean that it confined its attention to five distinct periods of crisis — December 1892—March 1893; February—March 1895; January—March 1903; January—April 1904; and November 1904—April 1905 — when an assorted collection of unskilled projects — among them stonebreaking, trenching and digging work at Springburn Park, road repairs, cutting peat, railway navvying at Robroyston, and levelling the surface at Westerhill — was mounted and placed under the general supervision of the council's

Parks and Labour Departments.[62]

Moreover, if, once such action had been approved, the relevant committees and departments moved with commendable alacrity, as was demonstrated by the fact that almost without exception the numbers thus employed 'peaked' relatively early,[63] there is also little room for doubt that the corporation was equally keen to run down, or to terminate, these works as soon as was practicable. Thus, the most modest flickerings of economic recovery were invariably accompanied by a contraction in their scale, although this process, as in 1895, could sometimes be accelerated by the introduction of a system of piecework payment.[64] Nor, to much of contemporary opinion, was a commitment to strictly demarcated projects unreasonable in view of the sizable gap which emerged between the commercial value of the tasks which were executed and the total wages bill. (See Appendix 1.)

For the most part, therefore, the council was content to rely upon a programme which had strong continuities with the past. Certainly, in terms of the type of undertaking which was sanctioned, it was almost indistinguishable from that followed in 1878–9 and 1884–7. Furthermore, even when faced with a deepening depression in 1903–5, there were only the smallest indications in council thinking that *ad hoc* measures of this nature might be an unsatisfactory way of coping with a chronologically extended crisis. For of the two new initiatives then mooted, the Special Committee on the Purchase of an Estate for the purpose of Relief Employment, which took almost a year to reach the verdict, delivered in January 1905, 'that it is advisable that the Corporation should purchase an estate, not far distant from the City, in order that the whole, or some part of the same, could be made available for the purpose' of providing work for the 'deserving' unemployed, achieved nothing, while the Executive Sub-Committee on Relief Employment secured little more than a paper concession when, in November 1904, it was permitted to consult with the corporation's direct works departments about projects, 'the intended time of execution of which could be anticipated'.[65]

II

The task remains of evaluating the strengths and weaknesses of this approach. At the outset it can be claimed that since the field of vision of Glasgow's middle classes was largely restricted to the difficulties of the unemployable on the one hand and the deserving on the other, it was impossible, within such a narrowly conceived framework, to devote much attention to the broad issues of the local casual labour problem

which had already been well defined in the voluminous reports of the
Royal Commission on Labour. Again, seasonal unemployment was rarely
debated, although municipal ownership of the gasworks meant that the
corporation itself was one of the principal employers of labour whose
work rhythms were dictated by a seasonal pattern of demand. Finally,
female unemployment, irrespective of its cause, was left completely
untouched by successive council initiatives, despite the fact that the
detailed work of the Scottish Council of Women's Trades, under the
guiding hand of its secretary, Margaret Irwin, had shown that female
labour was usually poorly remunerated, for the most part unskilled, and
in a few instances, an integral part of the casual labour market.

But in one sense such apathy was to be expected since Glasgow's
lack of reaction simply reflected the continuing indifference of central
and local government to these aspects of the unemployment question.
Indeed, there were few positive steps that the corporation could have
taken to promote decasualisation in any major area of the local economy
during this decade and a half, since its direct contact with the casual
market was at best peripheral. While, for example, the council was well
represented upon the Clyde Port Authority, the hiring of dock labour
was devolved not upon the Authority but upon the major shipping lines
and the master stevedores, both of whom remained adamantly opposed
to any form of decasualisation throughout the entire period under
review.[66] None the less, if its attitude towards its own Labour Bureau,
opened in 1894 and principally used as a source of supply for charwomen, were any guide – the corporation ignored it completely when it
came to meeting its own requirements for unskilled hands[67] –
decasualisation of dock labour could never, at the parochial level, have
come even remotely within the realm of practical politics. Similarly,
there was relatively little that it, acting alone, could have achieved
within the seasonal market, although, when faced in May 1905 with a
demand from the Scottish Society of House and Ship Painters that its
own painting contracts should be carried out in the autumn and winter
months, the Parks Department was prepared to accept that this proposal
should, 'as far as practicable, be kept in view when any painting work
requires to be done'.[68] Lastly, if the main outlines of the problem of
female unemployment were already well established, none of the lobbying
which was to be exerted on their behalf in the City Chambers by the
various women's organisations in the post-1905 years was mounted in this
earlier period, with the result that the case for 'make work' projects for
unemployed female labour was allowed to go by default.

What, however, perturbed contemporaries much more than the

existence of whole areas of the unemployment question which were left almost untouched by the joint endeavours of the municipality and private charity, was the fact that the relief programmes which were ultimately approved seemed to have failed to realise any of their objectives. For, as in 1878–9, in the wake of the failure of the City of Glasgow Bank, and 1884–7, 'make work' schemes were for the most part treated with an air of calculated aloofness by the unemployed craftsmen, for whose benefit they had been primarily initiated. But such a reaction among skilled workmen should at least in part have been anticipated since there were four mutually reinforcing factors at work in local society which made their heavy involvement in this type of undertaking inherently unlikely.

In the first place, provided that the particular crisis was not unduly protracted, a sizable proportion – although not all – of Glasgow's craftsmen could rely upon 'idle pay' from their union to ease some of those adverse social pressures which were the inevitable concomitant of the downswing of the trade cycle. Secondly, whatever form a 'make work' project assumed, it was palpably work which, in the market economy, was the exclusive prerogative of the unskilled. To many skilled men, therefore, the nature of the work itself possessed a stigma which devalued their craft-training and their place within the local hierarchy of labour. Thirdly, there was equally deeply felt resentment at the rates of pay attached to these schemes, particularly in 1892–3 when the Trades Council, dominated by craft unions, tried to secure 2s daily compared with 1s offered by the corporation.[69] On this occasion its efforts were powerfully supported by the workers' Unemployed Committee which attempted to organise – albeit unsuccessfully – a boycott of the entire programme on the grounds that any individual working for less than 2s per day was 'an enemy to his class and a slave – mean, contemptible, and despicable'.[70] The magnitude of the differential, therefore, between the wages offered by the municipality and those which craftsmen were accustomed to receiving acted as yet another deterrent against a substantial commitment of the skilled to all such schemes.

Finally, there was profound hostility at the 'inquisitorial' proceedings of those who were appointed to test the moral and social worth of all applicants for relief. As A.J. Hunter expressed it, 'in connection with relief funds, many of the workmen have at all times had very strong objections to being subject to the investigations of the Charity Organisation Society', although he conceded that in 1895, when the investigative mechanism was largely abandoned, 'it was done with less offence to their feelings than at any other previous time'.[71]

Thus as occurred in other parts of Britain, 'make work' employment in Glasgow tended to become the preserve of the unskilled. In 1892–3, for example, 61.6 per cent of the total number of applicants came from a labouring background, in 1895 73.2 per cent, while the comparable figures for January-April 1904 and November 1904–April 1905 were 80.3 per cent and 63.7 per cent respectively.[72] Indeed, as the data for 1892–3 and 1904–5 illustrate, it was only in periods of prolonged dislocation of the labour market that a skilled element, having exhausted its right to 'idle benefit' and its modest savings, was ever likely to swell on any scale the ranks of those who were engaged on this kind of undertaking.

The only consolation which those who were responsible for the formulation, and administration, of corporation policy derived from this outcome was that it appeared to demonstrate the reality of an 'unemployable' class, which was largely the victim of its own purposeless existence. In 1892–3, for instance, it was argued 'that a very large amount of distress, while it might be real enough, was the result of habits which would produce poverty and suffering in any circumstances',[73] while in 1895 James Motion alleged that those who sought assistance from the Lord Provost's Fund belonged

> entirely [to] the loafing-class; the men really who have never done any work; as anyone who took the trouble to observe the palms of their hands, and also that class who mainly frequent the model-lodgings in the city, where they get a bed from 2½d upwards.[74]

Again, in March 1904, in his report upon the schedules of applicants for corporation employment, James Ferguson

> noted that a large number ... had only been a few weeks or months in their last situations, showing further that we have a Chronic Class of Unemployed, no matter what the state of trade is.[75]

Such comments, however – and this list could be considerably extended – were particularly unhelpful when it came to examining the broader socio-economic background of the unemployed'. For, quite apart from the fact that they overlooked completely those forces which kept the bulk of the skilled from having any contact with relief works, they also tended to treat, with but minor qualifications, the unskilled applicants as a homogeneous class.

Such a tidy, monocausal explanation, however, could not even be easily reconciled with the weight of contemporary evidence; for it was clear that there were solidly economic reasons, totally divorced from the moral plane, which would mean that labourers would always form the largest single grouping among those who applied for relief. Among other things, they were never in receipt of 'idle pay' from a trade union; their wages were too near, and in some cases, below, the poverty line to enable them to save when in full work; and they operated in a chronically glutted sector of the labour market. In Hunter's words, there were 'too many competitors for the work that is to be done'.[76] This judgement, given in 1895, was not to be seriously modified fourteen years later when the Rev J.C. Pringle accepted that 'the short engagements and the long intervals between them indicate a very marked surplus of unskilled labour in Glasgow'.[77]

Furthermore, as has already been pointed out, labourers were usually among the first casualties in the labour market at the onset of a period of bad trade. This was largely borne out in an analysis of 675 circulars which were returned from the last employers of applicants for relief work during January–March 1904. Of this total, no fewer than 411, or slightly in excess of 60 per cent, had lost their job because of 'dull trade', as against 19 through drunkenness, 52 through 'bad timekeeping and inattention', and 83 who left of their own accord. Similarly, in the same period of time, only 815 out of 2,267 applicants had been less than three months in their last situations.[78] Although these data include a broader spectrum than the category of general labourer, there can be little doubt that, after making the maximum allowance for that fact, they modify quite considerably the concept of a thriftless and feckless class of men. Simply put, a sizable proportion of the labouring applicants were unemployed rather than unemployable.

Finally, while it must be accepted that a further substantial element of those who were relieved, could be designated 'unemployable', it by no means followed that all individuals in this position had reached it by pursuing an identical course. Indeed, instead of endorsing the concept of the 'born tired', there was a need to place the 'unemployable' against a backcloth which took into account the over-all pattern of demand for unskilled labour and the total environment into which the unskilled were born.

By 1905, therefore, much of the basic thinking in the extensive field of unemployment remained still to be done. But what at the parochial level could not be disputed was that the scale and *modus operandi* of relief works and the efforts of private philanthropy left largely untouched a mass of destitution whose origins could be traced back to one or more of the various forms that unemployment assumed in the lives of working-class Glaswegians. In that sense the auguries were scarcely promising for the Glasgow Distress Committee, formally instituted in December 1905, under the Unemployed Workmen Act, as it began its task of assisting applicants 'honestly desirous of obtaining work, but . . . temporarily unable to do so from exceptional causes over which they had no control'.[79] For, given these terms of reference and its limited financial powers, there was little to suggest that Glasgow's unemployment problem would be tackled any more incisively in the future than had occurred in the immediate past.[80]

Notes

1. *Glasgow Unemployed Relief Fund 1892–3. Report by the Committee . . . to deal with the Relief of the Unemployed in the City*, p. 1; *Board of Trade Labour Gazette* for 1903–5, 'All Union' Unemployment returns for Glasgow and the West of Scotland.
2. Glasgow City Archives (henceforth cited as GCA), DTC 8/65. James Henry to John Lindsay, Clerk of Police, 26 February 1903. Bad weather in 1903 merely reinforced the pervasive influence of generally dull trading conditions in helping to swell the numbers of those who were without work.
3. *Report of the Chief Inspector of Factories and Workshops for 1894*, PP C-7745, 1895, p. 220.
4. S.D. Chapman (ed.), *The History of Working-class Housing* (1971), pp. 72, 74.
5. *Royal Commission on the Poor Laws, Vol. IX, Minutes of Evidence*, PP Cd. 5068, 1910, p. 1089.
6. This paragraph is based upon my forthcoming article 'The Seasonal Demand for Labour in Glasgow 1890–1914', *Social History* No. 7 (1978).
7. *Glasgow Herald*, 28 February 1907.
8. This paragraph is based upon my general research into Glasgow's casual labour problem.
9. *Royal Commission on Labour, Answers Group B.*, PP C. 6795-VIII, 1892, No. 341. National Union of Dock Labourers, Glasgow Branch.
10. *Annual Report of Glasgow United Trades' Council 1884–5* (1885), p. 7.
11. *Royal Commission on Labour. The Employment of Women*, PP C. 6894-XXIII, 1893, pp. 280–1; *Answers to Schedules, Group C.*, PP C. 6795-IX, 1892–3, No. 418. Operative Bakers of Scotland; *Minutes of Evidence, Group C.*, PP C. 6795-II, 1892–3, qq. 17983–4.
12. *Forward*, 11 September 1909; *Royal Commission on the Poor Law, Appendix XI, Miscellaneous*, PP Cd. 5072, 1911, p. 23.
13. *Annual Report of the Chief Inspector of Factories and Workshops for 1902*, PP Cd. 1610, 1903, p. 126.
14. *Royal Commission on Labour. Minutes of Evidence, Group C, Vol. II*, PP C.6795-II, 1892, q. 17806; for sailmakers, see note 27.
15. *Royal Commission on Labour. Minutes of Evidence, Group A, Vol. II*, PP C.6795-IV, 1892, q. 16226.
16. *Forward*, 16 January 1909.
17. In my article 'The Market for Unskilled Male Labour in Glasgow 1890–1914'

Appendix I: Municipal Employment Relief Schemes in Glasgow, 1890–1905

Duration of Scheme	No. of applicants	No. of orders issued for work	Highest no. employed on one day	Amount spent on wages alone	Total amount spent on relief employment	Value of work performed	Overall deficit on each scheme
8 Dec. 1892–4 March 1893	2,801	2,328	870	£2,115 13s 7½d	£3,103 6s 0d	£1,401 15s 2d*	£1,710 10s 10d
4 Feb.–16 March 1895	3,643	3,643	2,543	£2,184 14s 4d	£4,854 15s 7d	£1,894 14s 11d	£2,960 0s 8d
1902–3[1]	1,836	566	–	£500 8s 10d	£636 2s 9d	£283 4s 9d	£352 18s 0d
25 Jan.–24 April 1904[2]	2,267	1,139	–	£4,366 4s 6d	£6,167 12s 11d	£2,099 0s 11d	£4,168 12s 0d
25 Jan.–24 April 1904[3]	–	–	–	£4,728 7s 9d	£6,155 16s 7d	£2,098 10s 11d	£4,157 5s 8d
23 Nov. 1904–1 April 1905[4]	6,300	2,453	–	£14,768 3s 0d	£20,619 14s 1d	£8,353 19s 9d	£12,266 14s 4d

The data for 1892–3 and 1895 have been assembled from the *Third Report of the Select Committee on Distress from Want of Employment (365), 1895, Glasgow Unemployed Relief Fund 1892–3. Report by the Committee, and Royal Commission on the Poor Laws, Appendix Vol. XIX A* [Cd. 5073], 1910.

[1] Data based on *Royal Commission on the Poor Laws, Appendix Vol. XIX A* [Cd. 5073], 1910, and GCA, Minutes of the Corporation of Glasgow C1.3.32, Special Committee on Relief Employment, 16 November 1904.

[2] Data taken from *Royal Commission on the Poor Laws, Appendix, Vol. XIX A* [Cd. 5073], 1910.

[3] Data taken from GCA, Minutes of the Corporation of Glasgow, C1.3.32. Special Committee on Relief Employment, 16 November 1904.

[4] *Royal Commission on the Poor Laws, Appendix, Vol. XIX A*, 1910.

*This sum includes £23 2s 0d which was realised from the sale of the workers' tools and £400 which was the assessed 'value of plant in stock'.

in I. MacDougall (ed.), *Essays in Scottish Labour History* (in press).

18. *Royal Commission on Labour, Minutes of Evidence, Group A, Vol. III*, PP C.6984-VII, 1893, p. 494.
19. *Glasgow Municipal Commission on Housing* (1902–3), qq. 13425, 13430.
20. Ibid., qq. 13415–6.
21. While the amount of voluntarily lost time in the shipyards could in certain yards be considerable – ibid., q. 13352 – there was much debate over both its incidence and causes. For a defence of the 'steady character' of shipyard labourers, see Carson's evidence, ibid., qq. 12095, 12098, 12100.
22. *Royal Commission on the Poor Laws, Vol. IX, Minutes of Evidence*, PP Cd. 5068, 1910, q. 89615.
23. *Corporation of Glasgow. Return of Unemployed for 1904*, pp. 3, 12, 15.
24. *Third Report of the Select Committee on Distress from Want of Employment*, PP (365), 1895, q. 8115.
25. *Royal Commission on the Poor Laws. Appendix Vol. XIX A*, PP Cd. 5073, 1910, p. 192.
26. *Glasgow Herald*, 16 March 1911.
27. GCA, G3 36(1) Lord Provost's Relief Fund 1907–9, G. Lyon, 50 Kinning Street, Kingston, Glasgow to the Relief Committee, 14 October 1908.
28. *Third Report of the Select Committee on Distress from Want of Employment*, PP (365), 1895, q. 8211.
29. Ibid., qq. 8115–6, 8139, 8172–3, 8211; *Corporation of Glasgow Return of Unemployed for 1904*, passim.
30. *Third Report of the Select Committee on Distress from Want of Employment*, PP (365), 1895, q. 7845; *Glasgow Municipal Commission on Housing* (1902–3), q. 11336.
31. *Third Report of the Select Committee on Distress from Want of Employment*, PP (365), 1895, p. 521.
32. *Royal Commission on the Poor Laws. Appendix Vol. XIX A*, PP Cd. 5073, 1910, p. 42.
33. *Organised Help,* January 1905, p. 41.
34. Even when the Charity Organisation Society in Glasgow was not directly involved in investigating the unemployed, it is clear that its views were powerfully represented by the local Poor Law inspectorate.
35. GCA, Miscellaneous Prints Vol. 26, D-TC 14.1.26; *Glasgow Herald*, 20 February 1895.
35a. GCA, Minutes of the Corporation of Glasgow C1.3.32, 16 November 1904. Special Committee on Relief Employment.
36. GCA, Miscellaneous Prints, Vol. 26, D-TC 14.1.26, Minutes of the Committee on Employment, 29 January 1895.
37. See note 35a.
38. For the exclusion of single men and those who lived in 'model' lodging houses in 1892–3, see GCA, Miscellaneous Prints, Vol. 25, D-TC 14.1.25. *Glasgow Herald*, 14 December 1892; *North British Daily Mail*, 20 December 1892.
39. GCA, Minutes of the Corporation of Glasgow, C1.3.32, Executive Sub-Committee, 19 February 1904.
40. *Report by the Board of Supervision on the Measures taken by the Local Authorities of the Principal Centres of Population in Scotland for the Relief of the Ablebodied Unemployed during the Winter of 1893–4*, PP C-7410, 1894, p. 4.
41. *Report on the Administration of the Glasgow Unemployed Relief Fund of 1878–9* (1879), pp. 30–2.
42. Whenever resort was made to the Common Good Fund, the amount allocated to 'make work' projects was always severely limited.

43. *Third Report of the Select Committee on Distress from Want of Employment*, PP (365), 1895, p. 521.
44. *Glasgow Unemployed Relief Fund 1892–3. Report by the Committee . . . to deal with the Relief of the Unemployed in the City*, p. 2; GCA, Miscellaneous Prints, Vol. 26, D-TC 14.1.26, Minutes of the Magistrates' Committee, 28 January 1895.
45. GCA, Minutes of the Corporation of Glasgow, C1.3.32, Executive Sub-Committee, 8 February 1904; Special Committee, 18 November 1904.
46. *Corporation of Glasgow. Return of Unemployed for 1904*, p. 4.
47. GCA, Miscellaneous Prints, Vol. 25, D-TC 14.1.25, passim.
48. See note 43 for this reference.
49. GCA, Miscellaneous Prints, Vol. 25, D-TC 14.1.25. *Glasgow Herald*, 7, 12, 15 December 1892.
50. Ibid., Miscellaneous Prints, Vol. 26, D-TC 14.1.26. *North British Daily Mail*, 14 February 1895; *Glasgow Herald*, 19 February 1895.
51. *Royal Commission on the Poor Laws. Report by Miss Constance Williams and Mr Thomas Jones on the Effect of Outdoor Relief on Wages and the Conditions of Employment*, Cd. 4690, 1910. p. 273.
52. For a brief discussion of the general activities of the Glasgow Charity Organisation Society, see *Organised Help*, January 1912, pp. 718–21.
53. GCA, Parish of Glasgow Collection of Prints, Vol. XXII, T-Par 1.10. *35th Annual Report of the Glasgow Association for Organising Relief . . . for the year ended 31 May 1909*, p. 15.
54. *Third Report of the Select Committee on Distress from Want of Employment*, PP (365), 1895, pp. 519–20.
55. *Glasgow Municipal Commission on Housing* (1902–3), q. 12095.
56. *Third Report of the Select Committee on Distress from Want of Employment*, PP (365), 1895, q. 8334.
57. GCA, Miscellaneous Prints, Vol. 25, D-TC 14.1.25, passim.
58. Ibid. *Glasgow Herald*, 28 November 1892. The last part of this quotation is taken from a speech of Keir Hardie.
59. Ibid. *Glasgow Herald*, 28 November, 2 December 1892.
60. *Third Report of the Select Committee on Distress from Want of Employment*, PP (365), 1895, q. 8378.
61. GCA, Miscellaneous Prints, Vol. 26, D-TC 14.1.26, Minutes of Town Council, Magistrates' Committee, 11, 21, 28 January 1895. Minutes of the Corporation of Glasgow C1.3.31, 28 December 1903.
62. This list, although not exhaustive, includes all 'make work' projects which were large employers of labour.
63. For the early 'peaking' of numbers, see the statistical data for 1892–3 and 1895, *Third Report of the Select Committee on Distress from Want of Employment*, PP (365), 1895, pp. 516–17.
64. Ibid., qq. 7822, 7839.
65. GCA, Minutes of the Corporation of Glasgow, C1.3.32, Special Committee on Employment, 16 November 1904; Special Committee on the Purchase of Estate to give relief to the Unemployed, 13 January 1905.
66. *Royal Commission on the Poor Laws, Vol. IX, Minutes of Evidence*, PP Cd. 5068, 1910, qq. 89615, 89962, 89871. But for one of the few voices in favour of decasualisation, see p. 1111.
67. It was only after the Municipal Labour Bureau had been taken over, in the post-1905 period, by the Glasgow Distress Committee that the Corporation reversed this policy.
68. GCA, Minutes of the Corporation of Glasgow, C1.3.33, Parks Committee, 4 May 1905.

69. GCA, Miscellaneous Prints, Vol. 25, D-TC 14.1.25. *North British Daily Mail*, 10 December 1892.
70. Ibid., *North British Daily Mail*, 9 December 1892.
71. *Third Report of the Select Committee on Distress from Want of Employment*, PP (365), 1895, q. 8316.
72. *Royal Commission on the Poor Laws, Appendix Vol. XIX A*, PP Cd. 5073, 1910, p. 30. The figure for 1895 has been calculated from the data contained in the source quoted in note 71, pp. 518–19.
73. *Glasgow Unemployed Relief Fund 1892–3, Report by the Committee . . . to deal with the Relief of the Unemployed in the City*, p. 2.
74. *Third Report of the Select Committee on Distress from Want of Employment*, PP (365), 1895, q. 8115.
75. *Corporation of Glasgow. Return of Unemployed for 1904*, p. 4.
76. *Third Report of the Select Committee on Distress from Want of Employment*, PP (365), 1895, qq. 8281–2.
77. *Royal Commission on the Poor Laws, Appendix Vol. XIX A*, PP Cd. 5073, 1910, p. 63.
78. *Corporation of Glasgow. Return of Unemployed for 1904*, pp. 8, 11.
79. *Unemployed Workmen Act*, 1905.
80. I wish to thank Bette Duncan of the University of Strathclyde for assitance in researching into the general question of unemployment in Glasgow. I am grateful to Mr R. Dell and the staff of the Strathclyde Regional Archives Office and the staff of the Glasgow Room of the Mitchell Library for their guidance and help. Finally, I am indebted to my colleague, Dr W.H. Fraser, for his critical evaluation of this article.

FAMILY ALLOWANCES AND LESS ELIGIBILITY

John Macnicol

'Remarkable by reason of the multiplicity of sources from which it draws its inspiration and the diversity of desirable ends which it is designed to achieve.'[1] This rather sceptical verdict by a contemporary classical economist was nevertheless an astute one: throughout its history in the inter-war years the movement for family allowances in Britain attracted support (and opposition) from a wide range of opinion, often for very confused and contradictory reasons. This makes family allowances a particularly interesting case-study for the social policy historian: the fact that they could be seen by ILP intellectuals as part of an exclusively socialist approach to the family, by right-wing Conservatives as an imperialistic pro-natalist measure aimed at ensuring the 'continuance of the white races', and by the Treasury as most definitely neither makes family allowances a good example of welfare serving different masters.

This complexity hardly lends itself to a short summary, however. Every argument for family allowances took on a slightly different nuance according to who was voicing it, and at what time: a glance through the pages of the *Eugenics Review*, for example, soon shows how complicated was the attitude of eugenists and population experts in the 1930s.

Nevertheless, it is fair to say that the campaign for family allowances in Britain rested its case on two pillars of support, economic and demographic. The latter was far too involved to warrant anything more than a brief mention here: it had its roots in the fears over Britain's declining birth-rate that came to a head in the early 1930s, drew its support from eugenists, demographers, social scientists and some rather racialist-minded politicians, and introduced into discussions on family allowances many of the myths and misconceptions that still abound.[2] The former was undoubtedly the more important half of the case for family allowances, Beveridge for example insisting that his Report's recommendation was 'almost entirely' on economic grounds as opposed to demographic.[3]

What exactly were these economic grounds? From the evidence of secondary sources it would appear that the 1945 Family Allowances Act was primarily an anti-child poverty measure. In presenting the economic case for family endowment Eleanor Rathbone and her supporters drew much inspiration from the poverty surveys of the inter-war years, all of which showed large families to be a major cause of poverty. Only a few examples need be quoted. In York in 1936 Rowntree found that nearly half the persons in primary poverty were children under 14 years of age, and of these 61 per cent were in families where there were more than three children.[4] The Pilgrim Trust found in Liverpool that of the 97 families studied who had two or more children under 14 years of age, 83 were in poverty.[5] In Southampton 34 per cent of the working class families with dependent children were in imminent danger of falling into poverty through the head of the household's having insufficient income to maintain his wife and children at the poverty line without assistance from supplementary earners.[6] The Bristol survey discovered that 44.3 per cent of all persons in poverty were children and concluded that

> if any form of remedy could be devised to raise to a higher level those families which contain three or more children and fall below the (poverty) line . . . seventy-six per cent of child poverty would be abolished.[7]

In addition, the 1930s witnessed a large number of investigations made by doctors, medical officers and nutritionists into the health of infants, school children and pregnant or nursing mothers in the Depressed Areas — all of which reinforced the findings of the poverty surveys and made out a strong case for some form of economic support for large families.

By the time Beveridge came to write his Report it would appear that this evidence (further confirmed by the experiences of wartime evacuation) had become so overwhelming as to arouse a response from those within Government. The Report certainly gives this impression: repeatedly Beveridge acknowledged the influence of the 'impartial scientific authorities' who had 'made social surveys of the conditions of life in a number of principal towns in Britain' before the war, and who had 'determined the proportions of the people in each town whose means were below the standard assumed to be necessary for subsistence'. These surveys had shown that between one-quarter and one-sixth of 'Want' was caused by a failure to relate income during earning to family size. Family allowances were the remedy for this, and were also an essential part of the Report's innovatory 'minimum substistence principle' — which again drew heavily on the findings of the poverty surveys.[8]

In fact, this picture of a 'rational' response by the Government to the evidence of child poverty is wholly misleading. Government interest in family allowances was first aroused in 1939–40 and centred on a Treasury plan to introduce a temporary wartime scheme as a means of controlling wages and thereby reducing the risk of runaway inflation. By about the middle of 1940 the need for this had passed, and thereafter the Treasury fought a rearguard action to have family allowances either postponed until after the war (by which time, they argued, public pressure for their introduction would have abated considerably) or introduced at as limited a scope and low a cost as possible (for example, financed out of contributions).[9] Very few civil servants shared Eleanor Rathbone's belief that family allowances would improve the economic status of mothers and children; if any hardship did exist, they maintained it should be met in some way other than by an expensive and potentially wasteful scheme of universal cash payments. Of course, just as the proponents of family allowances outside Government pledged their support for many different reasons, so is it impossible to speak of one single 'Government view': the Board of Education based their opposition on a preference for services in kind;[10] the Ministry of Labour, ever watchful of trade union feelings, feared that family allowances would affect wage negotiations;[11] the Assistance Board only wanted a limited scheme that would concentrate on families with more than three children.[12]

During the Second World War, as Hilary Land has shown,[13] family allowances won a grudging acceptance by the Government for a variety of reasons that had little to do with family poverty and a lot to do with the over-all management of the economy. One of these was the need to ensure that in any postwar reorganised system of social security, rates of unemployment benefit and assistance should always be appreciably lower than low wage levels in order to produce the mobility of labour and work-incentives essential to an economy geared to full employment. This was a lesson learned from the mass unemployment of the inter-war years when, with dependents' allowances added to unemployment pay and none to wages, the unemployed man with a large family frequently found himself better off whilst idle. By the late 1930s this situation was arousing considerable concern within those Government Departments responsible for unemployment insurance and assistance.

In as much as the root of the problem was essentially one of low wages, family allowances were a means of making the minimum necessary adjustment to wage levels without really tackling the question of low pay; 5s per week for the second and subsequent children[14] was just enough to ensure that in almost every case an unemployed man with a large family would be economically 'less eligible' whilst out of work than when employed. It is the emergence of this function of family allowances as a preserver of 'less eligibility' that is the subject of this paper.

In the early 1920s, with nearly two million unemployed, the Government were faced with a serious problem: how could the insurance scheme be applied to this large army of able-bodied men, who had to be kept alive and reasonably content and who would not tolerate being thrown on to the Poor Law? The 1911 system of unemployment insurance had deliberately avoided all pretence at subsistence. Benefits were only 7s per week for the adult man (equivalent to about one-third of Rowntree's 1899 poverty line) and were merely intended as a 'tiding over' sum to encourage thrift; only certain trades were covered; and the strict actuarial basis of the scheme avoided any consideration of need. In the 1920s, however, this reassuring concept of the 'deserving' and thrifty skilled worker broke down completely in the face of mass unemployment. Out of the confused jumble of *ad hoc* solutions, last-minute compromises and numerous 'temporary' extensions of insurance that constituted Government unemployment policy in these years, there clearly emerged two principles that were vitally important to the history of family allowances.[15]

The first was the recognition of family needs via the payment of dependents' allowances to the unemployed. This has been seen by some observers as a dramatic precedent, the first example of family endowment in Government policy and a sudden departure from the strictly actuarial basis of insurance. In fact, by the time these allowances were introduced, in November 1921, there had already been three family endowment precedents — child tax allowances in 1909, service pay separation allowances in the First World War, and out-of-work donation in November 1918. Given the policy-making chaos of these years, it is hardly surprising that dependants' allowances were intended to be no more than a temporary expedient and that their implications were little discussed. To meet any exceptional hardship that might arise over the winter of 1921–2 (benefits having been reduced in July 1921 from 20s to 15s per week for a man and from 16s to 12s per week for a woman), dependants' benefits of 5s for a wife and 1s for each child were introduced through a separate self-supporting fund. In 1922 they were made a permanent feature of the main insurance scheme.[16]

The second and much more interesting principle that emerged in the early 1920s was the realisation within the Government that some sort of relief agency was needed, capable of supporting the able-bodied unemployed who had exhausted their right to insurance benefit without throwing them on to the hated Poor Law. On the one hand these men could not be dealt with by endless extensions of benefit rights, because this would in the long run destroy the whole actuarial basis of the insurance scheme and make it into a quasi-relief agency; yet on the other hand it was politically very dangerous to force them (particularly the ex-servicemen) to undergo the stigma of poor relief.[17] Within the Ministry of Labour, civil servants seem to have grasped this point as early as 1923, for around the time of the 'all-in insurance' vogue[18] they began to discuss the setting up of just such an intermediate agency. The unemployed would be classified into three groups: those entitled to insurance benefit would come under a strictly actuarial scheme subject to firm rules; those able-bodied who had exhausted their right to benefit would be paid uncovenanted benefit out of a special 'distress fund' supervised by the Treasury and the Ministry of Labour and subject to a 'genuinely seeking work' clause; and at the bottom of this three-tier system would be the Poor Law.[19]

This, however, would create a problem. In any such reorganisation the whole relationship between wages, benefit rates and public assistance would have to be carefully thought out. Each category of worker would have to be assigned a clear economic and moral status based on the level of his income and the amount of stigma attached. The aim should thus be that

> a person in receipt of insurance benefit should be less well off than a person in receipt of wages, and that a person disentitled to benefit should be less well off than a person receiving benefit. Whereas the old poor law held that the condition of the man relieved must of necessity be less eligible than that of the man maintaining himself, a second intermediate grade, that of the insured man, should ultimately be introduced.[20]

In the meetings of the 'all-in insurance' Anderson Committee this proposal was considered at length by senior civil servants. Sir Horace Wilson repeatedly warned that the potentially dangerous question of wages, benefit and assistance would have to be clarified; if the principle of insurance as a stigma-free payment was to be preserved, then the unemployed man in receipt of relief *must* be made to feel worse off than his insured counterpart. In some areas (particularly those with high unemployment) the unemployed were receiving both benefit and relief simultaneously, resulting in payments which frequently equalled or exceeded what they could expect in full-time wages.[21] When dependents' benefits had been introduced in 1921 the Government had attempted to subject them to an upper income limit of 9s, but this had had to be dropped in the face of Parliamentary opposition. If these child allowances were raised above 1s 6d each, Wilson warned, 'the possible interaction of benefit and wages in low-paid employment would have to be taken into consideration' and the scale of benefits for a man and wife would have to be lowered.[22]

The evidence left by the 1923 Anderson Committee shows the remarkable prediction by Ministry of Labour officials of the problems that were to arise in the 1930s and were to point the way to family allowances in wages.* The 1934 Unemployment Act established a three-decker system virtually identical to the one they had discussed over ten years earlier: at the top, the Unemployment Insurance Statutory Committee controlled a strictly actuarial insurance scheme; in the middle was the Unemployment Assistance Board granting means-tested relief on uniform scales ostensibly based on need; and at the bottom the Public Assistance Committees dealt with categories like the sick, the old, the widows and orphans. From 1934 onwards it became more and more difficult to operate this system without touching on wages, since the real value of benefits had steadily risen.

In the 1930s the whole question of the relationship between wages, benefits and assistance became even further complicated by the inter-vention of a new factor — the science of nutrition. This had developed very rapidly since the turn of the century, and by the early 1930s experiments were beginning to uncover a vast range of human functions that could be influenced by diet.[23] Height, weight, physical endurance, intellectual performance, resistance to disease, maternal mortality, life expectancy, infant mortality — all could be profoundly affected by nutrition, and medical scientists began to grasp the prime importance of proper feeding as a method of preventive medicine; thus Dr Edward Mellanby, Secretary of the Medical Research Council, could confidently assert that

> many of the commoner physical ailments and defects could be
> reduced or even eliminated by proper feeding. Indeed, it is
> probably no exaggeration to say that proper feeding of the

---

*It also demonstrates the way that civil servants seem to have come to terms with mass unemployment much earlier than the politicians.

population of this country would be as revolutionary in its effect on public health and physique as was the introduction of cleanliness and drainage in the last century.[24]

Against a background of nearly three million unemployed many nutritionists found themselves straying on to very politically sensitive topics, as their research into minimum dietary needs was translated into cash terms and compared with the Government's assessment of what an unemployed man and his family should get. From this controversy, which rapidly became marked by great bitterness and acrimony, there emerged what can loosely be called a 'poverty lobby' composed mostly of individual doctors, social scientists and academics acting in an unco-ordinated way but also spearheaded by several pressure groups.

One of these was the Children's Minimum Council,[25] and it was through this body that the movement for family allowances became involved in the debate. Eleanor Rathbone and her Family Endowment Society always tried to campaign for the principle of 'family endowment' to be accepted in as many areas of Government policy as possible (for example, rent rebates proportional to family size),[26] and beyond that also took up the general cause of the welfare of mothers and children. Thus it was natural for her to form this offshoot; avowedly non-political, the Children's Minimum Council had the support of many different organisations (such as the Fabian Society, Save the Children Fund, Workers' Educational Association, Catholic Social Guild) and could thus claim several million supporters; its leadership included several Members of Parliament (Robert Boothby, Harold Macmillan, R.D. Denman, Duncan Sandys, Sir Edward Grigg, etc.) and some nutritionists (Sir John Boyd Orr, Sir F. Gowland Hopkins, Robert McCarrison, Dame Janet Campbell).

At the centre of the Council's programme was the demand that the Ministry of Health should review all the recent nutritional research, state publicly what was its estimate of minimum needs, and then translate this into cash terms. From this would be calculated unemployment allowances, and any wage-earning household that fell below this minimum would have milk and meals provided free for its children. In addition, the Council campaigned for higher child allowances for the unemployed, rent rebates proportional to family size, free milk for expectant or nursing mothers, free milk for children in state-aided schools, and an end to the situation where in the midst of widespread poverty the food-producing industries indulged in a massive programme of food destruction in order to keep up prices.[27]

Throughout the 1930s the CMC bombarded the Ministry of Health with pamphlets, letters, deputations, invitations to conferences, suggestions — all of which met with a hostile response.[28] In the face of all the evidence put forward by nutritionists and poverty investigators the Ministry repeatedly denied that child malnutrition existed anywhere in Britain.[29] Their own school medical inspection figures proved otherwise, they maintained; and when challenged over the accuracy of these figures (many doctors being strongly critical of school medical inspection methods[30]) the Ministry retreated to the assertion that no agreed definition of malnutrition yet existed; finally, their last line of defence was to maintain that poverty *per se* was not their problem, but that of the Unemployment Assistance Board. Both the Ministry of Health and the Board of Education firmly maintained that the school medical service was primarily 'educational', and that therefore child malnutrition was only their concern in so far as it prevented the child from receiving state education.[31]

The controversy over malnutrition in the 1930s was complicated, but throughout, the Ministry of Health was clearly terrified of making any pronouncement that might support its critics' claims that unemployment benefit and assistance were too low, for if these were raised they would of course begin to overlap on to low wage rates — thus demonstrating that many industries paid below-subsistence wages, and opening the way to demands for the sort of Government intervention in industry that simply could not be contemplated.

These far-reaching implications dominated all the Ministry of Health's investigations into malnutrition in the 1930s. For example, when they set up their own Advisory Committee on Nutrition in 1931 under Professor Major Greenwood they specifically warned it that 'there can be no discussion of the translation of diets into money values' on the intriguing basis that 'these are administrative and not scientific questions'.[32] When this Committee arranged a meeting with the British Medical Association's equivalent advisory body they were again expressly forbidden to discuss cash levels as this would 'involve the Ministry in a far-reaching economic issue, which is most important to avoid — an issue which might easily affect wages, cost of food, doles, etc.'[33] The Advisory Committee's publication, the 'Memorandum on the Criticism and Improvement of Diets', thus confined itself to very vague general principles rather than specific cash levels because the latter would have 'wide and possibly embarrassing repercussions', as one of its members admitted in private.[34] Even then, another of the Committee members,

Professor E.P. Cathcart, feared the Memorandum's economic implications since the suggested diet was 'something much better than the average working man can afford' and 'if it is embodied in an official document it may be seized upon by transitional beneficiaries and others as a yardstick to measure what their allowances should be'.[35]

Exactly the same fears dominated the Unemployment Assistance Board and the Unemployment Insurance Statutory Committee. Both came under heavy criticism from the 'poverty lobby' and by the end of the 1930s both were beginning to see family allowances as a possible way out of this embarrassing position. A detailed account of what went on within the UAB and UISC thus provides a revealing insight into how family allowances came to be seen as an essential agency for preserving 'less eligibility'.

When the Unemployment Assistance Board was established in 1934 the Government announced that its scales would be based on need. Implicit in this was the commitment not only to base these scales upon a scientific estimate of minimum physical subsistence but also to ensure that applicants would be kept healthy and fit enough to return to employment whenever the country's economic position improved. Thus when introducing the 1934 Bill in the Commons the Minister of Labour, Sir Henry Betterton, assured MPs that 'we have to provide that there shall be an opportunity for men to keep fit for employment'[36] and said 'you cannot promote the welfare of a man unless you take into account his physical requirements'.[37]

During the passage of the Bill, however, the Government remained studiously vague over exactly how these needs would be calculated. To a deputation from the Children's Minimum Council Betterton insisted that the Board would calculate need in accordance with recent nutritional research,[38] but in Parliament he was less definite. At one point Eleanor Rathbone tried to introduce an amendment to the Bill that would fix the Board's scales according to 'a basis which is fully worked out and clearly laid down by Parliament' and repeatedly asked Betterton to define the meaning of 'need'. In reply the Minister of Labour assured her that the amendment was unnecessary; the Board *was* committed to maintaining the unemployed at a healthy physical subsistence level and the spirit of her amendment was implicit in the Board's regulations.[39] The reply seems to have satisfied most MPs for throughout the many debates on the 1934 Bill there was little mention of this point. Some speakers realised that the assistance scales would have to be lower than insurance benefit (which the Government admitted to be below subsistence, since it was still based on the 1911 concept of a small 'tiding-over' sum), but most critics concentrated their attack on the proposed household means test and on the Board's apparent immunity from Parliamentary control.

Eleanor Rathbone, however, was far from satisfied. Through the Children's Minimum Council she began an intensive campaign aimed at influencing the Board's members while they were discussing their proposed scale rates. In July the CMC submitted a memorandum asking the Board to state publicly the scientific basis upon which its scales would be calculated;[40] in September Marjorie Green (the Council's secretary and a prominent member of the Family Endowment Society) submitted their booklet on 'Evidence of Malnutrition';[41] a month later came a pamphlet criticising in detail the conclusions in the latest annual report by the Chief Medical Officer, Sir George Newman, which had maintained that unemployment was having no adverse effect on the nation's health;[42] in December there was a deputation to the Ministry of Labour to put the case for increased scales;[43] and all the time the Council pestered the Board with letters seeking clarification on minor points.

All this lobbying elicited virtually no response from the Board's members, save for a feeling of mild irritation. In their private discussions they began to grope towards the only definition of 'scientific minimum subsistence' that was open to them; science would have to take second place to three all-important criteria — Treasury limitations, unemployment benefit levels, and, most of all, low wage rates. At the fourth meeting of the Board, on 22, 24 and 25 July 1934, Wilfred Eady (the Board's secretary and an official of the Ministry of Labour) quickly warned of the wages problem: although they could supplement insurance benefit in exceptional cases they must not touch on wages since 'it would obviously have been a very dangerous principle if the Board had accepted any responsibility for the subsidy of low wages to wholly employed persons'. Sir Ernest Strohmenger followed by maintaining that even if under-nourishment existed in Britain, particularly amongst children, there was little evidence that it was confined to the households of the unemployed:

in other words, under-nourishment might well prove to be a matter not so much of inadequate allowances as of bad use of income. It was very important that the Board should have this clearly in mind because they could not accept responsibility for general malnutrition.[44]

Thereafter, discussion centred on the question of exactly how far below wage rates the Board's scales should be. One suggestion, for example, was that they should be anchored just below the levels of unskilled wages recognised by local Trades Councils. All members 'recognised that where there was a large family the scale came very near to, if it did not exceed, the earnings of low paid workers' and that therefore the problem was essentially one of keeping these cases of overlap to a minimum by arriving at the most appropriate scale levels. As Sir Ernest Strohmenger warned, to provide large children's allowances 'on the lines suggested by Miss Rathbone leads to the dilemma of either cutting across wage levels or of establishing a very low scale for childless couples'. Eventually the Board chose the latter course and cut the allowance for a married couple from 24s to 22s.[45]

This, therefore, was how the Unemployment Assistance Board calculated 'scientific minimum subsistence': 'the provision of allowances to meet need must be conditioned by wages'.[46] Professor Hallsworth warned his fellow members of the dangers of touching on wage levels; the Board's scales

> would be taken as representing the official standard of minimum subsistence over the whole country. The Board would be operating largely in areas whose wages are subject to world conditions. It would be a grave matter if the scale prevented any adaptation of the wage level which economic circumstances might require.

In other words, fixing the scales too high might make it impossible for industry to impose wage cuts in the future if these became necessary. Eady firmly told the other members that there was

> no scientific standard for the calculation of all the needs to be covered by the Board; the matter was one of social convention and expediency. The Office had therefore proceeded on the principle of less eligibility.[47]

Low wages had to be accepted as an unavoidable fact of industrial life; to make the unemployed better off than the employed 'would be resented not only by employers but, more strongly, by other workpeople'.[48]

Given this method of assessing need it was hardly surprising that the Board refused to take up the challenges of the Children's Minimum Council. When answering its critics it claimed on the one hand that it *had* translated into cash terms the nutritional findings of the British

Medical Association, the Ministry of Health Advisory Committee, the
Merseyside Survey and the New Survey of London; but on the other
hand this was carefully qualified by the assertion that there was as yet
'no absolute criterion or scientific basis of need'.[49]

When the Board eventually published its scales and put them into
operation they were criticised repeatedly by groups such as the Council
as being a betrayal of Betterton's original promises in Parliament. In
1936, for example, the Council pointed out that using the BMA
nutritional standard, the Merseyside estimate of expenditure on clothing,
light and fuel, and the Board's own basic rent scale, the following comparison could be made:[50]

	Minimum needs	Standard unemployment benefit	UAB scale
Man, wife and one child	29s ½d	29s 0d	28s 0d
Man, wife and 3 children	40s 0d	35s 0d	34s 6d
Man, wife and 5 children	52s 3d	41s 0d	40s 6d

To empirical criticism such as this the Board either refused to reply, or
else invented the most convenient excuse. For example, in discussion
with the Children's Minimum Council they defended their policy of
reducing allowances for children in households of more than five
members (by the sum of 1s each) by maintaining that with such an
increase in numbers there was not an equivalent increase in costs:
clothes could be passed on to younger children, for instance.[51] But in
private they admitted that

> the scaling down of children's allowances where there are three or
> more children is desirable because the graduated scale for children
> originally proposed, if allowed to operate fully, would quickly
> produce for the family of normal size allowances in excess of the
> wage rate, and thus necessitate the application of the 'stop' clause
> ... too frequent application of this clause is likely to create dis-
> satisfaction.[52]

The Board's position was hopeless. Having decided to follow the
principle of 'less eligibility' all it could do in the face of such criticism
was retreat along prepared lines, and its members were instructed as to
what these should be. Critics should first be told that no scientific
calculation of minimum needs was possible; if they persisted in their

attacks, then they should be told that if malnutrition did exist it was not confined to the households of the unemployed; the final defence against criticism such as Rowntree's contention that a family of five needed 53s a week for the maintenance of health and efficiency was for the Board to wash its hands of all responsibility: 'the best line of reply', members were told on this point,

> is probably that if this were true, the Unemployment Assistance Board is a relatively small member of a good company and that in order to bring this doctrine about the general wage structure of the country would have to be revolutionised.[53]

It was precisely such a wage revolution that Eleanor Rathbone and her followers believed they were campaigning for, and having had no success in getting the Board to raise its scales during 1934 and 1935 she changed her line of attack: from 1935 onwards the Family Endowment Society and the Children's Minimum Council, realising the Board's quandary, began to campaign for the whole problem to be tackled at the wages end, by family allowances.

This new approach found a more favourable reception from the Board's members, for now the problem of overlap with wages was beginning to exacerbate a situation about which they felt growing unease. As the economy began to pick up after 1934, the problem of the long-term unemployed assumed increasing importance. Would these men be able and willing to return to work once the economy had completely recovered? Would they refuse to enter jobs with wages only slightly higher than the amount they had been receiving from the Board? Unemployment began to fall steadily from 1936 onwards, and the following year the Board calculated that nearly 20 per cent of its male applicants under 30 years of age had settled down to life on the dole.[54] 'What cumulative consequences are likely to pile up for the nation in a few years time,' Violet Markham warned, 'if the dole habit spreads and grows and the theory of money for nothing becomes an established practice amongst the younger generation?'[55]

What the Board feared was not so much the numerical incidence of these overlap cases as their disproportionate effect on the work ethic of future generations. After all, in 1937 only about 6 per cent of the Board's applicants received allowances within 4s of their normal wages;[56] but, they argued, since these cases occurred chiefly in households with a large number of children perhaps an increasing number of young married unemployed would regard large families as a way of maximising their income and also spread the 'dole habit' to their children.

Furthermore, there was another serious long-term problem. By industrial standards, many of the Board's applicants were relatively old: in 1936 45 per cent of those between the ages of 18 and 64 were over 45 years old, as compared with only 27 per cent of claimants to insurance benefit, and thus it would be extremely difficult for these men to be reabsorbed into industrial life once prosperity returned.[57] This was caused by the changing age-distribution of the British population: in 1901 out of every 1,000 people, 149 were aged between 45 and 65; but by 1935 this proportion had risen to 223. The Board's Annual Report for 1936 contained a passage on this very theme, reflecting the 'population panic' of the 1930s, and warning that these older men would need a long period of retraining and acclimatisation before they became efficient workers.[58] In this situation, any reluctance on the part of the younger, fitter men to return to work would be disastrous.

Thus after 1935 the Board's annual reports showed an increasing apprehension about this problem, accompanied by a realisation that it could only be tackled at the wages end. After only a year of operation they were convinced that men with large families showed 'little disposition to take work or hold it when it is given to them'. The whole problem of the relationship between wages and assistance raised 'wider issues' which the Board felt 'should be examined on the widest basis in the near future'.[59] In 1938 there came an even stronger statement about the difficulties raised by cases of overlap, difficulties which had 'far-reaching implications and obviously raise questions of very serious social consequences which go beyond the problems which the Board alone are in a position to solve'.[60]

In private, the members of the Board were taking a growing interest in family allowances as the only way out of this difficulty, short of a drastic state intervention in industry. In May 1938 the Children's Minimum Council sent them a memorandum on this very point; family allowances were the only way to solve the overlap problem without having to resort to 'the negative and inhuman device of keeping down unemployment pay'.[61] This time their arguments fell on more receptive ears. In reply Violet Markham admitted that the memorandum stated 'very clearly a problem with which we are all familiar',[62] and such evidence as can be gleaned from her private papers suggests that her mind was working along these lines. For her the problem of the unemployed was part of the general problem of the low-wage group and she felt particular concern over 'the employed man with a large family and a low wage who is obliged to struggle on without any assistance from the State'.[63] In the face of this, she told Paul Cadbury,

> many of us who are concerned with unemployment are feeling more and more that whatever differences of opinion there may be in the method of application, the principle of family allowances is the only way out of the morass in which we find ourselves.[64]

Officially, the Board had no power to recommend anything as drastic as family allowances, being supposedly an independent body with limited terms of reference;[65] in fact, the Board was closely controlled by the Ministry of Labour and the Treasury, and thus it is likely that when it opened a file on family allowances in June 1938[66] and began gathering information it was preparing the ground for possible future schemes based on the Continental employer-financed 'equalisation fund' method. In September 1938 the Board began writing to firms in Britain which already ran their own family allowance schemes, asking for information. Exactly what was being planned remains a mystery.

This gradual acceptance of the need for family allowances by the UAB was exactly mirrored in the experiences of the Unemployment Insurance Statutory Committee. The prime task of this body was to ensure the solvency of the Insurance Fund. By June 1934 the Fund's debt stood at £105,780,000 (incurred since 1921), and the Unemployment Act of that year stipulated that this should be paid off at the rate of £5 million per annum — which would extinguish the debt by 1971.[67] The Committee were required to report on the condition of the Fund not later than February each year — or any other time, if necessary — and, having reviewed the financial situation, could recommend any change in the levels of benefits and contributions and in the way the debt should be paid off. In coming to a decision the Committee sought advice on the likely level of future unemployment from the Government's Economic Information Committee of the Economic Advisory Council (represented by H.D. Henderson), and then received deputations from interested outside organisations like the National Confederation of Employers' Organisations, the TUC and — inevitably — the Children's Minimum Council.

Ostensibly the Committee was an impartial body independent of direct Government control, its actions being dictated solely by the state of the Fund. In practice, however, its independence was almost as much a myth as the UAB's, and, as with the Board, there was the usual 'uncanny coincidence' between what the Government wanted and what the Committee finally recommended.[68] Like the UAB, the Unemployment Insurance Statutory Committee was designed to shield the Minister of Labour from the embarrassing task of resisting Parliamentary and public pressure for higher benefit rates, and in addition was as much at the mercy of the Treasury as were normal Government departments: the reduction in 'waiting time' from six days to three, for example, introduced in 1937, was designed to cut the number of applicants who might apply for unemployment assistance during this period of no income (which could be up to a fortnight, since benefit was paid at the end of the week) and thus widen the scope of insurance (33 per cent Treasury-financed) over that of assistance (100 per cent Treasury-financed).[69]

However, having Beveridge as its Chairman undoubtedly prevented the Committee from falling completely under Treasury and Ministry of Labour influence,[70] since he was very well versed in the tactical nuances of intra-Government politics. In addition, direct pressure from Government departments was less of a problem for the Committee than the indirect effect its actions had on other areas of social policy. It was here that problems arose. When it was first established, the Committee's main worry seemed likely to be the repayment of the debt; but owing to a decrease in unemployment quite the reverse happened, and the problem was what to do with the growing surplus each year.

Essentially, the Committee's task was to steer a path through a very tricky middle ground. On the one hand, they had to keep insurance benefits above assistance scales; apart from being in line with the Treasury's policy of avoiding supplementation by assistance there was the political necessity of ensuring that applicants to a contributory scheme should always be better off than those receiving means-tested, tax-financed, discretionary payments. Beveridge, a true 'insurance man' characteristically saw this as a cardinal principle, 'not because he thought the applicant for assistance was a less deserving case but because the recipient of benefit had contributed for it' and the rest of the Committee agreed.[71]

However, this posed great problems. The Government still adhered to the 1911 principle that insurance benefit should be a supplement to savings and should thus not represent full maintenance. Any criticism of benefit levels met with this response; the whole principle of insurance was actuarial, not needs-related. Yet at the same time benefits had to be kept above the UAB's scales — which the Government insisted *were* needs-related. This contradiction was further exacerbated every time the UAB raised its scales, for on these occasions the Committee had to do likewise, all the time maintaining the fiction that such increases were solely due to the improved condition of the Fund.

On the other hand, benefit levels had to be kept below wages. The three-tier structure of 'less eligibility' anticipated in 1923 by the members of the Anderson Committee had to be preserved. Again Beveridge justified this in 'insurance' terms: 'unemployment benefit was intended to be an insurance against loss of wages, and in other forms of insurance it was never the practice to over-insure', he reminded his Committee over and over again.[72] However this vital principle that 'the indemnity should never be allowed to exceed the loss' proved increasingly difficult to uphold. As the Fund annually displayed a continuing surplus, and as the UAB periodically raised their scales, it became impossible for the Committee to avoid trespassing on to wage levels. The fact that this occurred exclusively in families with a large number of children pointed to the obvious solution – the adjustment of wages to family size.

The first Report of the Committee, for the year 1934, was very cautious. A surplus of £12,417,185 had been achieved, but Beveridge felt it was too early to make any changes. He merely outlined the five possible ways this surplus could be disposed of: a reduction in contributions (favoured by the National Confederation of Employers' Organisations); an increase in the child allowances which then stood at 2s (favoured by the TUC and the Children's Minimum Council); an increase in the adult man's benefit rate; an extension of the period of entitlement to benefit; and a reduction in the Fund's outstanding debt.[73] These were generally the options throughout the 1930s and deciding between them was by no means easy.

Beveridge was a staunch supporter of Eleanor Rathbone,[74] and another member of the Committee was Mary Stocks who, with Eva Hubback, was Eleanor Rathbone's closest friend and ally in the campaign for family allowances. Raising the child allowances in the insurance scheme was thus a popular cause within the Committee, and both the TUC and the Children's Minimum Council were pressing strongly for such an increase. However, Beveridge clearly foresaw the dangers and thus when in July 1935 the Committee issued a special mid-year Report recommending a rise of 1s in the child allowances, they added a proviso that there should be an upper limit in total benefit of 41s per week, equivalent to the rate for a man, wife and five children, This, the Committee realised, was vital. Without it, cases of overlap would become much more common: an unskilled labourer with a wife and six children, normally earning 40s per week, would be 4s better off when unemployed. A wage-stop might be a better idea, the Report suggested, but since contributions took no account of wages then neither should benefit. Families of more than five children would have to receive supplementation from the UAB — but only if they underwent the Board's means test and proved they had no resources.[75]

This upper limit was rejected by Ernest Brown, the Minister of Labour, on the grounds that such a recommendation was outside the terms of reference of the Committee,[76] and thereafter the problem of overlap began to loom larger and larger. In their end-of-1935 Report the Committee called for a thorough investigation of 'the relations between wages, benefit, unemployment assistance and other forms of assistance' and in their first hint at family allowances they warned that 'the growing direct provision for families, under unemployment insurance and assistance, is beginning to raise acutely the general problem of dependency under a wage system which makes no similar provision'.[77]

In private discussion, the Committee members were beginning to grasp the magnitude of their problems. By the end of 1935 the Fund was making an embarrassingly healthy profit of £290,000 per week, and every indication was that it would become harder and harder to resist pressure to increase benefits — eventually they would rival wages really seriously. The easiest way out would be to leave benefit rates alone and concentrate on extending the scope of insurance as against assistance. Naturally both the Treasury and the Ministry of Labour saw this as the best course, but both departments realised that it would not be possible to spend rather more than £17 million in this way over the next seven and a half years. Similarly, it would be politically very unpopular to devote the growing surplus or a reduction in the debt repayment period; such an action would benefit the workers of the 1970s as against those of the 1930s.[78]

Throughout 1936 and 1937 the Committee tried to find a way out of this problem, with no success. When asked its opinion the TUC emphasised strongly that 'in so far as wages are so low that the rate of benefit is above them the question is not whether benefit is too high but whether wages are not too low' and pressed for child allowances of 5s a week; but beyond that they could think of no solution to the overlap problem.[79] Similarly a long meeting with three members of the Unemployment Assistance Board in November 1936 solved none of the Committee's difficulties.[80]

As in the case of the Board at this time, there now began to creep into the Committee's discussions fears about the possible long-term effect of this situation on work-incentives.[81] During 1937 an investigation was made; applicants for benefit were asked to state their weekly wage when last in employment. The results showed that average benefit rates for men, including dependents' allowances, were only two-fifths of median wage rates — 24s 6d per week as against 55s 6d. However, there was considerable inequality in wage rates, ranging from less than 14s to over 100s per week (in the case of men) and less than 12s to over 60s per week (women).

As with the Board, the problem of overlap was numerically small: only 2.3 per cent of men and 5.2 per cent of women were as well or better off when on benefit than in their last employment. But, again like the Board, it was a problem the Committee felt would have dangerous long-term repercussions. Of the men on 41s benefit, 10 per cent were as well or better off than when in employment, but of those on 50s benefit the proportion was over one-third. The Committee were being pressed on all sides to raise child allowances by 1s per week, but to do this would increase the incidence of overlap by a third; and in the case of large families by even more: at the 41s rate of benefit it would rise from 10 per cent to 25 per cent.

To Beveridge this was complete anathema. Again and again he repeated his dislike of 'over-insurance', and in the 1937 Report finally suggested that there were only two possible remedies, a 'wage-stop' or else family allowances in wages. The former had been rejected by the Minister of Labour in 1935. A recommendation of the latter went way outside the Committee's terms of reference, but nevertheless recommend them they did on the grounds that 'if the wage system made allowance for dependency, the main objection to further increases in rates of benefit would be removed'.[83] The issue could no longer be dodged; with a continuing surplus in the Fund benefits would have to be raised sooner or later, and the whole question of family dependency considered *in toto*.

In the event, the Committee did manage to avoid the problem for another year. Despite pressure from the TUC for further increases the 1938 Report simply recommended that the annual surplus be used to reduce the outstanding debt by £6 million per annum instead of £5 million.[84] The following year the Committee relented and raised child allowances to 4s per week for the first two children and 3s for every other.[85] By then, however, the outbreak of war had changed everything.

By the late 1930s, therefore, both Government bodies dealing with

the able-bodied unemployed had come round to a virtual recommendation of family allowances. Despite public pronouncements to the
contrary, both worked on the principle of 'less eligibility', and it was
the impossibility of sticking to this principle when dealing with large
families that led them to realise that the problem could only be solved
at the wages end.

This, however, raised acutely controversial issues and brought to a
head the two conflicting attitudes that have always dogged the history
of family allowances. All agreed the problem was essentially one of
low wages, but the two solutions proposed were very different.

To those on the political left, this call for family allowances by the
two Government-supervised bodies merely obscured the real issue,
which was that many industries were paying grossly sub-standard wages.
Both the UAB and UISC, they maintained, had followed a policy of
'less eligibility' for fear of provoking a confrontation with industry. If
rates of benefit and assistance were raised to nutritionally-defensible
levels then the resultant enormous number of cases where it was more
profitable to be unemployed than in work would simply demonstrate
how many wage-rates were below minimum human needs.[86]

This very point was investigated by the economist Juergen Kuczynski.
Using official Ministry of Labour figures for 1935 Kuczynski compared
wage levels with Rowntree's 1937 'human needs' standard of 53s per
week for a man, wife and three children, emphasising that in arriving at
this figure Rowntree had pared down minimum needs to the most
Spartan level and had allowed for no luxuries. The result showed, for
example, that about two-thirds of the weavers in the cotton industry
needed a rise in weekly full-time earnings of 33 per cent or more in
order to come up to Rowntree's minimum.[87] The proportion of workers
in various industries who earned wages below this level was: coal mining,
80 per cent; railways, 25 per cent; building, 50 per cent; textiles, 40
per cent of men and 50 per cent of women; clothing, 12 per cent of
men and 35 per cent of women. In all, 4 million adult male workers and
2 million adult female workers earned less than the Rowntree minimum:
which, including their dependents, made a total of 10 million people.[88]
Yet, maintained Kuczynski, although in the period 1931 to 1938
unemployment benefit in real terms had fallen and real wages risen by
only 5 per cent, industrial production per employed worker had risen
by fully 20 per cent.[89] Viewed in this light, the call for family allowances
was a means of perpetuating this situation. Family allowances would
alter the wages of the married man just enough to shore up the principle
of 'less eligibility', and the real issue of wages *vis-à-vis* profits would be

neatly avoided.

On the other hand, supporters of family allowances argued that over-all wage rates were a separate issue. Across-the-board wage increases based on the three-child family would be both wasteful (in the case of families with less than three children) and insufficient (for the really needy families with more than three). The three-child family, as Eleanor Rathbone pointed out over and over again, was a 'statistical fallacy'. This was the nub of her argument as early as 1924 in her classic *The Disinherited Family*: the family-of-five minimum wage would make provision for 3 million non-existent wives and over 16 million non-existent children, while still leaving 1¼ million children unprovided for.[90] By the end of the 1930s this argument had attracted the support of many politically middle-of-the-road social investigators and politicians. The Pilgrim Trust, for example, discussed the connection between large families and poverty, found that about two in five persons dependent solely upon unemployment assistance were being forced to live 'at a level that cannot be defended except on grounds of maintaining the wage incentive' and concluded that family-adjusted wages were a likely answer.[91]

Especially interesting in the light of the Beveridge Report five years later was the 1937 Report by Political and Economic Planning into the social services in general. These services, it pointed out, had 'grown up in a very piecemeal way, without much regard either for consistency of principle or for the effect of one service on another' and badly needed a complete reorganisation by some sort of statutory commission; but it warned that 'the failure of the wage-system to take any account of the disparities in family responsibilities is one of the greatest obstacles to further extensions of social provision'.[92] Those who followed this line of thinking maintained that the issues raised by family allowances were entirely separate from those relating to low wages. But the fact that this section of opinion included a fair number of employers inevitably aroused trade union fears that such arguments were too innocent by half, and that the introduction of family allowances would ultimately weaken their wage-bargaining power. The outbreak of war in September 1939 radically altered this situation and pushed family allowances to the forefront of Government economic policy.

This sudden change was brought about not by any pressure-group activity but by a Treasury plan of 1939–40 to introduce family allowances as a means of controlling wages and minimising the risk of runaway wartime inflation. The Treasury had in fact opened a file on family allowances in 1938[93] (the same year as the Unemployment

Assistance Board) in response to growing Parliamentary pressure and the need to keep the Chancellor well briefed on the subject, but their attitude was one of cautious hostility. Like the Board they showed some interest in the possibility of encouraging employer-financed schemes, perhaps supplemented by a very limited State contributory system, but no more. However, as war loomed larger, economists both inside and outside the Government began pressing strongly for a carefully worked-out economic strategy in the event of war, covering price controls, wage regulation, taxation levels, industry's adjustment to war needs, the financing of the war effort, and so on.

In June 1939 such a committee was set up under Lord Stamp and including H.D. Henderson (a supporter of family allowances).[94] Through-out the winter of 1939–40 the 'Stamp Survey' worked hard to get agreement between TUC, employers and other Government Departments on the problem of how to introduce a wages policy that would compensate for the great increase in the cost of living since the start of the war, yet would not set up an inflationary spiral.[95] One answer was to grant wage increases for the poorest on the basis of family needs; and thus throughout the 'phoney war' period of September 1939 to May 1940 various family allowance schemes were discussed in great depth.[96] By the middle of 1940, however, the Treasury had turned hostile once again: the TUC were still firmly opposed, as were other Government departments; price rises were flattening off; and the Treasury had realised that once introduced, an apparently temporary scheme would soon become permanent.*

The full story of how family allowances came about during the Second World War is extremely detailed and cannot be gone into here.[97] The Treasury's initial interest, however, was not really concerned with the question of preserving 'less eligibility'. Instead, it centred on that other highly controversial aspect of family allowances — their use as a wage-depressant; for the Treasury the basic question was, as Sir Edward Hale put it, 'whether the grant of family allowances in any form will in practice make it possible to avoid increases in wages which would cost more than the family allowances'.[98] However, from the complex policy decisions and pressure-group activity of the war years two phases of development can be picked out to round off the theme

---

*Ironically, it was just at this time that J.M. Keynes entered the Treasury as an adviser. Keynes had popularised the idea of family allowances as part of his scheme of wartime finance in *How to Pay for the War* (1940), and of course had much influence on Stamp and Henderson. But in the early months of the war he was ill, and only gradually took part in Treasury policy discussions from June 1940 onwards.

of this paper.

In the formulation of the Beveridge Report, 'less eligibility' cropped up once again. From his experiences as Chairman of the Unemployment Insurance Statutory Committee and his faith in the insurance principle Beveridge was obviously determined from the outset to avoid any repetition of the events of the 1930s. Thus in his Report he quite openly declared that the second reason for his advocacy of family allowances was that 'it is dangerous to allow benefit during unemployment or disability to equal or exceed earnings during work', justifying this on the gounds that a large gap between benefit and wages would encourage the mobility of labour that was essential to maintain full employment after the war — full employment being the most important of the three assumptions upon which his plan rested.[99]

In their private discussions the Committee members were well aware that in fixing rates of benefit they would have to take into account more than just science. Beveridge made it clear to them that apart from finance the two main obstacles in the way of providing adequate benefits would be, firstly, the effect on voluntary insurance, and secondly, the effect on work incentives.[100] Thus the special sub-committee set up to calculate minimum subsistence (Seebohm Rowntree, A.L. Bowley, R.F. George and H.E. Magee) were early on warned by the main Committee's Secretary, D.N. Chester, that benefit rates should not be fixed so high as to reduce incentives to insure voluntarily or to conflict with wages; however, if on the other hand they arrived at a figure that could be attacked as being too low, 'it would raise the much wider question of minimum wages and the raising of the standard of living of the working classes'.[101] Reading through the detailed calculations of this sub-committee one can detect the underlying influence of these decidedly unscientific considerations, Rowntree, for example, on one occasion stating that

> in arriving at the amount of benefit to be paid to unemployed persons it would in our opinion be unjustifiable to allow for a dietary more costly than can be afforded by a large proportion of working-class families when the chief wage-earner is in work.[102]

The way out of this difficulty was through the lesson learned from the 1930s:

> a system of universal family allowances would allow benefits for adults to be increased considerably above subsistence level without

> seriously conflicting with the lowest wages . . . if there is no universal
> system of family allowances even the payment of benefits on sub-
> sistence level would be above the lowest level of wages.[103]

Family allowances were thus an essential cornerstone of any postwar
reorganised social security scheme.[104]

Ostensibly, Beveridge arrived at the figure of 8s per week for every
child after the first by calculating the cost of maintaining a child (9s per
week) and deducting 1s in respect of increased services in kind. However,
this was nowhere near a realistic figure: on the Boyd Orr standard, for
example, the sum would have had to be about 14s.[105] The suspicion
must remain that although Beveridge *did* genuinely see family allowances
as combating family poverty and encouraging parenthood nevertheless it
was their 'less eligibility' function that appealed to him most, and it was
on these grounds that the figure of 8s per week was chosen. For instance,
when weighing up possible reductions in the cost of his plan in August
1942 (in response to Treasury pressure) he emphatically stated that the
'main objection' to a possible reduction in family allowances to 6s was
that this 'would lower the gap between earnings and benefit'.[106]

The second wartime stage relevant to the theme of this paper was the
period from the Report's publication in December 1942 to the passage
of the Act in 1945. During this time the administrative details of family
allowances (e.g. what to do with orphans) were worked out at great
length by a Central Staff of senior civil servants acting in place of the
delayed Ministry of Social Security.[107] By 1945, of course, the
Government had abandoned any pretence at providing subsistence-
based benefits, arguing that in any universal insurance scheme flat-rate
contributions would have to be fixed at a level which the lowest-paid
could afford, and this necessarily pegged benefits at a low rate. Family
allowances were cut to 5s, the justification being based on some rather
woolly phrases about not wishing to weaken parental responsibility
plus the greatly extended scope of services in kind.[108] In fact, a figure
of 5s had been recommended as early as December 1942 by the senior
civil servants of the Phillips Committee (set up to judge Beveridge's
proposals) on the basis that 5s

> had the virtue of *not* pretending to be a subsistence rate. If an
> attempt at a subsistence rate were made (especially in a non-
> contributory scheme) it would be very unstable and there would
> be pressure for its increase if the cost of living rose or if medical
> experts revised their views on the minimum adequate diet. It was

therefore advisable to start low.[109]

With benefits lowered below the Beveridge levels (as the 1944 Social Insurance White Paper outlined) then obviously family allowances could be pared down too.

During all the detailed negotiations of 1942—5 civil servants seem to have accepted only two arguments in favour of family allowances: firstly, the 'less eligibility' work-incentive one; and secondly, the necessity of giving way to public opinion which, in the aftermath of the Government's lukewarm reaction to the Report, was pressing strongly for the Beveridge proposals to be implemented without delay. Beyond these, arguments about family poverty or encouraging parenthood seem to have made little impression: for example, civil servants were clearly puzzled at the strength of feeling within the Family Endowment Society over the point that paying the allowance to the mother would raise the status of wives; they thought it 'curious to rely on the payment of a few shillings each week to achieve this desirable end'.[110]

The 1945 Family Allowance Act was seen by Eleanor Rathbone as 'the triumph of a great principle' and she intended to continue campaigning for similar measures.[111] Undoubtedly it did give *some* financial relief to large families and established an important precedent. But if fighting family poverty had been the Act's main function then family allowances would not have been allowed to slip behind increases in the cost of living in the 1950s and early 1960s and become a notoriously neglected area of social policy. The fact that this happened in years of full employment, when preserving 'less eligibility' became a relatively minor problem, reinforces the theme of this paper. By the end of the 1930s there were two alternative solutions to the problem of the benefit/wages overlap: either there would have to be a drastic Government intervention into large areas of industry in order to guarantee some form of nutritionally-defensible minimum wage; or else there would have to be introduced a system of family allowances capable of pushing married men's wages just high enough to keep them above benefit and assistance levels. The root of the problem was low pay, but the two solutions were very different and represented the great dilemma that has always been posed by family allowances. At £57 million the cost of the 1945 scheme seemed very high at the time, but it was considerably cheaper and far less radical than the alternative.

Notes

1. Alexander Gray, *Family Endowment, a Critical Analysis* (1927), p. 9.
2. Such as the notion that parents are being 'bribed' to produce children. Walley has argued that the unpopularity of family allowances in Britain since 1945 has been due to these population myths. Sir John Walley, *Social Security, Another British Failure?* (1972), pp. 183–7.
3. W.H. Beveridge, 'Children's Allowances and the Race', in *The Pillars of Security* (1943), p. 14.
4. B. Seebohm Rowntree, *Poverty and Progress* (1941), pp. 115, 117.
5. Pilgrim Trust, *Men Without Work* (1938), p. 111.
6. P. Ford, *Work and Wealth in a Modern Port* (1934), p. 200.
7. H. Tout, *The Standard of Living in Bristol* (1938), pp. 39–40.
8. *Beveridge Report, Cmd. 6404, 1942*, pp. 7, 76–90, 154–8, 165–6. Janet Beveridge also acknowledges the influence of the poverty surveys: Janet Beveridge, *Beveridge and His Plan* (1954), pp. 107–8.
9. For example, the memorandum 'Family Allowances' by E. Hale (Treasury), 19/8/41. PRO T 161/1073 (S.43697/02/1).
10. 'I feel sure', minuted the young President of the Board of Education, R.A. Butler, in 1941, 'that if we are out to improve the conditions of childhood the most effective way of doing so would be to provide *free* meals, *free* milk and *free* boots and clothing for all children who satisfy an income test.' R.A. Butler to Kingsley Wood, 21/10/41. PRO T 161/1073 (S.43697/02/1).
11. Ministry of Labour memorandum, 19/2/40. PRO T 161/1116 (S.43697/1).
12. Sir George Reid (Assistance Board) to E. Hale (Treasury), 12/8/41 and 1/5/42. PRO T 161/1073 (S.43697/12/1–2).
13. Hilary Land, 'The Introduction of Family Allowances', in Hall, Land, Parker, Webb, *Change, Choice and Conflict in Social Policy* (1975), pp. 158–230.
14. Introduced by the 1945 Family Allowances Act. Payment commenced in August 1946.
15. Between 1920 and 1934 there were forty different Unemployment Insurance Acts. A good account of this period is given in Bentley Gilbert, *British Social Policy, 1914–1939*, pp. 51–97.
16. Politically, dependents' allowances were attractive because they prevented hundreds of thousands of families from having to fall back on the Poor Law. This would be popular with the unemployed themselves and with ratepayers in high-unemployment areas. Macnamara stated that these were the 'main considerations' that led the Government to continue allowances beyond the original six-month period and until June 1923. Hansard, Vol. 152, 29/3/22, Col. 1369.
17. Note of a discussion at the Ministry of Health, 29/11/23. PRO PIN 1/1.
18. An interesting account of the 'all-in insurance' activity is given in Walley, op. cit., pp. 40–1, 47–8, 57–62.
19. Minutes of meeting of the Anderson Committee for 5/1/24. PRO PIN 1/2.
20. Note of a discussion at the Ministry of Health, 29/11/23. PRO PIN 1/1.
21. Ministry of Labour Memorandum (no date, probably December 1923). PRO PIN 1/2.
22. Memorandum by H.J. Wilson and Sir Arthur Robinson, 14/1/23. PRO PIN 1/1.
23. One estimate was that in 1933 about 5,000 papers describing the results of original work appeared in the world's literature. F.C. Kelly, 'Fifty years of Progress in Nutritional Science', in *The Medical Officer*, 15/2/35.
24. Memorandum by Dr E. Mellanby, 19/3/34. PRO ED 24/1374.
25. Originally called the Children's Minimum Committee.
26. Eleanor Rathbone, *The Use and Abuse of Housing Subsidies* (1931).

27. The CMC was formed to lobby the Minister of Labour and Minister of Health while the details of the 1934 Unemployment Act were still being worked out. Much information on the Council can be found in: PRO MH 55/688 (93216/1/17A and B); PRO AST 7/32; PRO PREM 1/165; Eleanor Rathbone Papers XIV 2. 7.

28. For example, a representative of the Ministry attended the Council's first public meeting on 15 February 1934 and contemptuously reported back that 'a number of disappointed spinsters representing "many millions of mothers" advocated all the old demands for free milk, etc, for nursing mothers, etc'. Lord Balniel to A.N. Rucker, 15/2/34. PRO MH 55/275.

29. Sir George Newman, *The Building of a Nation's Health* (1939), p. 335.

30. For example, R. Huws Jones, 'Physical Indices and Clinical Assessments of the Nutrition of Schoolchildren', *Journal of the Royal Statistical Society*, Vol. 100, 1938, pp. 1–52.

31. Memorandum of Milk in Schools, 13/12/33. PRO ED 24/1367.

32. Hilton Young (Minister of Health) to Edward Mellanby, 11/1/34. PRO MH 55/56 (93414/5/3).

33. Memorandum by Sir George Newman, 17/1/34; ibid.

34. J.C. Carnwarth to Sir George Newman, 4/4/33. PRO MH 56/40 (93414/1/6).

35. J.C. Carnwarth to Sir George Newman, 1/12/31. PRO MH 56/51 (93414/3/2A). The Chairman of the Committee, Professor Major Greenwood, soon became very unhappy about these constrictions and pointed out to his members that 'having laid down certain principles they can hardly refrain from expressing an opinion upon the application of those principles without laying themselves open to another charge ... of behaving like the "scientists" of the comic papers, i.e. of only being interested in a subject so long as it *is* of no practical importance'. Memorandum by Greenwood, 15/7/33. PRO MH 56/48 (93414/3/1B5).

36. Hansard, Vol. 283, 30/11/33, Col. 1089.

37. Hansard, Vol. 286, 26/2/34, Col. 786. A similar assurance was given in the Board's first Annual Report, Report of the Unemployment Assistance Board for 1935, Cmd. 5177, p. 6.

38. Children's Minimum Council Memorandum: 'Observations on the Draft Unemployment Assistance Regulations', 21/7/36. Eleanor Rathbone, reported in Hansard, Vol. 289, 9/5/34, Cols. 1218–19.

39. Hansard, Vol. 286, 26/2/34, Cols. 771, 785–8.

40. UAB Memorandum No. 14, 30/8/34. Violet Markham Papers, Box 29.

41. Marjorie Green to Thomas Jones, 17/9/34. PRO AST 7/32.

42. Green to Jones, 11/10/34, ibid.

43. *The Times*, 17/12/34.

44. Minutes of the 4th meeting of the UAB; 23, 24, 25/7/34. Violet Markham Papers, Box 27.

45. Minutes of the 5th meeting of the UAB, 31/7/34. Violet Markham Papers, Box 27.

46. Statement by Professor H.M. Hallsworth. Minutes of the 6th meeting of the UAB, 13/9/34. Violet Markham Papers, Box 27.

47. Minutes of the 6th meeting of the UAB.

48. UAB Memorandum No. 13: 'Suggested Amendments of Basic Scale'. Markham Papers, Box 29.

49. Annual Report of the UAB for 1935, Cmd. 5177, p. 33.

50. 'A Children's Minimum', *British Medical Journal*, 4/1/36.

51. Ibid.

52. UAB Memorandum No. 13, 13/8/34. Violet Markham Papers, Box 29. In 1936, however, this 'scaling down' policy was abandoned.

53. UAB Memorandum: 'Note on the Basis of the Board's Scale', May 1937. PRO AST 7/337.
54. UAB Memorandum: 'Some Observations by Miss Markham on the Long-Term Policy and Problems of the Board Arising Out of the Annual Report', 1937. Violet Markham Papers, Box 51.
55. Ibid.
56. Annual Report of the UAB for 1937, Cmd. 5752, p. 6. Only 1.3 per cent of male and 3.5 per cent of female applicants received allowances equal to or above their normal wages; op. cit., pp. 81–2.
57. Annual Report of the UAB for 1936, Cmd. 5526, p. 5.
58. Ibid.
59. Annual Report of the UAB for 1935, Cmd. 5177, p. 12.
60. Annual Report of the UAB for 1937, Cmd. 5752, pp. 5–6.
61. Memorandum by the Family Endowment Society to the Unemployment Insurance Statutory Committee, sent by Marjorie Green (CMC) to Violet Markham, 6/5/38. Violet Markham Papers, Box 43.
62. Markham to Green, 12/5/38; ibid.
63. Violet Markham to Elsie Jones, 12/10/38; ibid.
64. Violet Markham to Paul Cadbury, 11/7/39. PRO AST 7/390. The Cadbury family had introduced their own family allowance scheme in their Bournville factory.
65. 'The Board are obviously very interested in the question because of its reactions on their own work; but they have no legal power to take any practical action in regard to it.' Lord Rushcliffe to W. Elphinston (Church Assembly), 31/10/38; ibid.
66. PRO AST 7/390 – *Family Allowances, June 1938–December 1943.*
67. W.H. Beveridge, *The Unemployment Insurance Statutory Committee* (1937), pp. 24–5.
68. J.C. Kincaid, *Poverty and Equality in Britain* (1973), p. 47.
69. Bentley Gilbert, *British Social Policy, 1914–1939* (1970), p. 180.
70. Beveridge himself always strenuously denied that the UISC was a mere rubber-stamp for the Ministry of Labour. Beveridge, op. cit., pp. 34–5.
71. Minutes of the UISC for 7/2/35. Beveridge Papers, VIII 4.
72. Minutes of the UISC for 20/11/36 and for 13, 14/1/38. Beveridge Papers, VIII 4.
73. Report of the UISC for 1934, pp. 3, 15–16.
74. Since 1924, when he had reviewed the *The Disinherited Family* for a journal, the *Weekly Westminster.* Eleanor Rathbone considered him 'my prize convert'. (Eleanor Rathbone Papers, item XIV 3 82.)
75. Report of the UISC for July 1935, pp. 17–18.
76. Statement in Hansard, Vol. 305, 24/10/35, Col. 471. Beveridge, op. cit., p. 41. The real reason may have been Treasury opposition to any change that might raise the cost of assistance.
77. Report of the UISC for 1935, pp. 28–9.
78. Note of a discussion on the Unemployment Insurance Fund by the Ministry of Labour, 25/11/36. PRO PIN 6/216.
79. Statement by J.L. Smyth (TUC). Minutes of the UISC for 9/1/36. Beveridge Papers, VIII 4.
80. Minutes of the UISC for 20/11/36.
81. As Mary Stocks put it, 'a man might find that he could do his duty to his family better by losing his job'. Minutes of the UISC for 14 and 15/1/37.
82. Report of the UISC for 1937, pp. 20–1, 25.
83. Report of the UISC for 1937, p. 25.
84. Report of the UISC for 1938, pp. 3, 8.

85. Report of the UISC for 1939, p. 12.
86. For example, the speech by Aneurin Bevan in the House of Commons debate over the UISC's Report for 1937. Hansard, Vol. 333, 25/3/38, Cols. 1537–8. (Incidentally, although this debate concerned the fate of 14 million insured workers at one point a count had to be taken to see if the requisite quorum of 40 members was present.)
87. Juergen Kuczynski, *Hunger and Work* (1938), p. 26.
88. Ibid., pp. 107, 108–9.
89. Ibid., p. 129.
90. Op. cit., p. 20.
91. Op. cit., pp. 113, 209.
92. PEP, *Report on the British Social Services*, (1937), pp. 12, 31.
93. PRO T 161/1116 (S 43697/1) *Family Allowances, 1938–40.*
94. D.N. Chester, *Lessons of the British War Economy* (1951), pp. 3–4, 37–8. W.K. Hancock and M.M. Gowing, *British War Economy* (1949), p. 47. PRO T 160 (885/F 17545).
95. Other papers relating to the Stamp Survey's comprehensive investigation of family allowances can be found in: PRO T 161/1116 (S 43697/1–2); PRO CAB 89/22, 23 and 24.
96. For example, a contributory scheme based on 8d per week each from employers, employees and the Government would yield an allowance of between 3s and 4s per week for each dependent child. Memorandum by Lord Stamp on 'Wages and the Cost of Living', 30/11/39. PRO T 161/1116 (S43697/1).
97. Hilary Land, op. cit.
98. Memorandum by E. Hale, 29/4/40, PRO T 161/1116 (S 43697/1).
99. Beveridge Report, p. 154.
100. Memorandum by Beveridge on 'Scale of Social Insurance Benefits and the Problem of Poverty', 16/1/42, Beveridge Papers, VIII 28.
101. Memorandum on 'Fixing Rates of Benefit' by D.N. Chester, 5/1/42, Beveridge Papers VIII 27.
102. Memorandum by Seebohm Rowntree (undated, early 1942) on 'Calculation of the Poverty Line – Food Requirements', Beveridge Papers, VIII 28.
103. D.N. Chester, op. cit.
104. Memorandum by Beveridge on 'Basic Problems of Social Security with Heads of a Scheme', 11/12/41, PRO CAB 87/76. Memorandum by Beveridge on 'Benefit Rates and Subsistence Needs', 29/5/42, Beveridge Papers VIII 28.
105. Speech by Hugh Lawson in Hansard, Vol. 408, 8/3/45, Col. 2339.
106. Memorandum by Beveridge on 'Revision of SIC(42)1000 to 24/8/42', Beveridge Papers, VIII 27. 'Another possible saving of about £23 millions indicated in my Report would be to reduce the family allowance by providing for the second child, when the father is earning, not 8s but 4s. If the sole object of family allowances were the abolition of want, then such a saving might be worth consideration. But in my view it would be wrong for two other reasons: as narrowing the gap between earning and benefit and . . . in order to improve both the quality and quantity of the population'. Beveridge, *The Pillars of Security* (1943), p. 125.
107. PRO PIN 8/1–84.
108. Statement by Sir William Jowitt, Hansard, Vol. 408, 8/3/45, Col. 2262, and ibid., Vol. 410, 10/5/45, Col. 2031.
109. Minutes of the 5th meeting of the Phillips Committee, 29/12/42, PRO PIN 8/115. Of course, a figure of 5s had been mentioned by family allowances campaigners ever since the early 1920s. The Government's 1942 White Paper, which simply 'did the arithmetic' of possible family allowance

schemes, also used 5s 'for illustration because this is the rate which has been proposed by advocates of family allowances'. Family Allowances, Memorandum by the Chancellor of the Exchequer, Cmd. 6354, p. 3. What was significant about the Phillips Committee decision was that it specifically altered the Beveridge figure.
110. Memorandum on deputation from Family Endowment Society, 10/10/44, PRO PIN 8/68.
111. Speech for a family allowances reception (after the passage of the Act), 13/11/45, Eleanor Rathbone Papers, XIV 3 82.

NOTES ON CONTRIBUTORS

Pat Thane Senior Lecturer in Social History, Goldsmiths College, University of London

Norman McCord Professor of History, University of Newcastle upon Tyne

M.A. Crowther Fellow of New Hall, Cambridge

P.A. Ryan Lecturer in History, Polytechnic of Central London

J.R. Hay Lecturer in Social Science, Deakin University, Victoria, Australia

John Brown Lecturer in History, University of Edinburgh

J.H. Treble Senior Lecturer in History, Strathclyde University

John Macnicol Associate Lecturer in History, Brunel University

INDEX

Acts of Parliament: Audit (Local
Authorities) Act 1927, 78–9;
Board of Guardians (Default)
Act 1927, 78–9; Education
(Administrative Provisions) Act
1907, 18; Education (Provision
of Meals) Act 1906, 18, 128,
133, 135; Family Allowances Act
1945, 173, 197; Local
Authorities (Emergency Provisions)
Acts 1923, 75; 1927, 78; Local
Government Act 1894, 63; Local
Government Act 1929, 37, 50;
London Authority (Financial
Provisions) Act 1921, 74; Mental
Deficiency Act 1913, 42, 49;
National Insurance Act 1911, 15,
71, 87, 104, 119–21, 127, 135–
41, 143; Old Age Pensions Act
1908, 84–104 *passim*, 130;
Representation of the People Act
1918, 76; Scottish Poor Law Act
1845, 157; Shop Clubs Act 1920,
120–1; Unemployment Act
1934, 178, 181, 187; Unemploy-
ment Insurance Act 1927, 14,
114; Unemployed Workmen Act
1905, 62, 65, 168; Workmen's
Compensation Act 1897, 119
aged poor, 37, 41, 43, 44–5, 47, 51,
53, 84–104 *passim*; Local
Government Board Circular
Concerning, 1900, 63; *See also*
Old Age Pensions, Poor Law
Ancient Order of Foresters, 93–4
Anderson Committee, 177, 178,
189
approved societies, 136, 138, 139,
140; *See also* National Health
Insurance
Askwith, G.R., 109
Asquith, Herbert H., 15, 18, 99, 101,
104
Association of British Chambers of
Commerce, 115, 119, 120
asylums, county, 38, 39, 49–50
Australia, Old Age Pensions in, 19,
96

Balfour, Arthur J., 97, 98
Bakke, E.W., 141
Barnett, Samuel, 64, 126
Basford, Poor Law in, 40
Bath, Poor Law in, 46–7
Bedwellty, Poor Law in, 77, 78
Bell, James Lord Provost of Glasgow,

158
benefit clubs, 115, 118, 119, 120–1;
see also friendly societies, savings
clubs, Shipbuilders & Engineering
Foreman's Mutual Benefit Society,
Shop Clubs Act
Bermondsey, Poor Law in, 67
Betterton, Sir Henry, 181, 184
Beveridge, William, 100–1, 130, 173,
174, 188, 189, 191, 195, 196,
197
Biggart, Thomas, 119
birth rate, decline of, 173
Bishop Auckland, Poor Law in, 23
Bismarck, Otto von, 88, 102
Blackley, W.L., 84–96 *passim*
Blanesburgh Committee, 14, 140–1
Boer War, 18, 98
Boiler Makers and Steel Shipbuilders
Trade Union, 12, 151
Booth, Charles, 16, 17, 45, 95–6,
100, 129
Boothby, Sir Robert, 179
Bosanquet, Bernard, 134
Bow, East London, 57
Bow and Bromley, Parliamentary
Constituency of, 57, 96; Social
Democratic Federation in, 58, 61
Bowley, A.L., 133, 195
Boyle, Sir Courtenay, 12
Brassey, Thomas, Lord, 120
Bristol, poverty in, 174
British Medical Association, 135,
180, 184
Brown, Ernest, 190
Browne, Benjamin, 24, 114
Budget, of 1909, 114
building cycle, 147–8
building societies, 23; Association of
Building Societies, 23
Burns, John, 51
Buxton, Sidney, 62, 65

Cabinet Committee on Old Age
Pensions 1907–8, 97–8, 99–100,
103
Campbell, Dame Janet, 179
Campbell, Bannerman, H., 99
Canning Town, pauperism in, 67
Cardiff, Poor Law in, 45, 49
Carson, George, Secretary of Glasgow
Trades Council, 161
casework, 127, 134, 136, 142–3
casual labour, 57, 59, 85, 89, 92, 96,
97, 98, 103; in Poplar, 57, 59;
unemployment among casual

204